* *

AIDING IRELAND

**GLUCKSMAN
IRISH DIASPORA**

IN THE GLUCKSMAN IRISH DIASPORA SERIES

Kevin Kenny, General Editor

Nicholas Wolf, Associate Editor

* *

Aiding Ireland

The Great Famine and the Rise of Transnational Philanthropy

Anelise Hanson Shrout

* * *

NEW YORK UNIVERSITY

New York

* *

NEW YORK UNIVERSITY PRESS
New York
www.nyupress.org

© 2024 by New York University
All rights reserved

Library of Congress Cataloging-in-Publication Data
Names: Shrout, Anelise Hanson, author.
Title: Aiding Ireland : the great famine and the rise of transnational philanthropy /
Anelise Hanson Shrout.
Description: New York, NY : New York University Press, [2024] |
Series: Glucksman Irish diaspora series |
Includes bibliographical references and index.
Identifiers: LCCN 2023003745 | ISBN 9781479824595 (hardback) |
ISBN 9781479824601 (ebook) | ISBN 9781479824618 (ebook other)
Subjects: LCSH: Ireland—History—Famine, 1845–1852. | Ireland—Foreign relations. |
Food relief—Political aspects—Ireland—History—19th century. |
International relief—Ireland—History—19th century.
Classification: LCC HC260.5.Z9 F375 2024 | DDC 363.8/830941509034—dc23/eng/20230201
LC record available at https://lccn.loc.gov/2023003745

This book is printed on acid-free paper, and its binding materials are chosen for strength and durability. We strive to use environmentally responsible suppliers and materials to the greatest extent possible in publishing our books.

Manufactured in the United States of America

10 9 8 7 6 5 4 3 2 1

Also available as an ebook.

To John Joseph Lee

CONTENTS

Introduction

Local Event with Global Impact

In the spring of 1847, on a plantation near Lowndesboro, Alabama, a group of enslaved people collected fifty dollars for victims of famine in Ireland. A "wealthy planter" named Morgan Smith arranged a meeting of the enslaved people who labored on his plantation. He told them "of the terrible distress prevailing in Ireland, and asked them if they would do anything to aid those who were perishing for want of food." He did not initially suggest a donation of money. Instead, "he asked them what they would do, whether they would give up one meal a day?"[1]

Lowndesboro, situated in Lowndes County, was in the heart of cotton country and at the center of the United States' slave economy. The enslaved people who lived and labored there—like enslaved people across the South—were subject to persistent racialized violence.[2] Even by the standards of his own time, Smith was particularly brutal. He regularly—and with apparent impunity—raped, beat, tortured, and killed enslaved women and men.[3] This violence made the response to Smith all the more surprising. After deliberating, the enslaved men and women agreed that they would act to aid Ireland. However, they emphatically rejected Smith's proposal that they give up food; according to one newspaper account of the meeting, "They said, no!" In lieu of food, they chose to take up a collection among themselves. That collection produced fifty dollars.[4]

This was an extraordinary sum, equivalent to more than one thousand dollars in 2023.[5] It was also an extraordinary act. The Lowndesboro donors did not simply capitulate to the demands of the person who enslaved them; instead, they chose a mode of engagement with Irish relief that suited their own needs. This mode was dangerous. They risked harm at Smith's hands by refusing his call to "give up one meal a day." Moreover, their collective possession of fifty dollars was evidence of illicit activity, as enslaved people in Alabama were prohibited from profiting by their own labor.[6] Giving up this money also meant that they would be unable to spend it elsewhere, on food, clothing, or even, possibly, manumission.

These men and women, whose names have not survived in the historical record, were among innumerable people from many walks of life who became involved—in ways both small and consequential—in the international project of Irish famine relief in the 1840s. In the twenty-first century, it is commonplace for governments to muster humanitarian responses to overseas crises and for individuals to participate in crowdfunded campaigns to help the distantly suffering. International aid is a booming business, and while pundits might debate the wisdom and morality of individual causes, there is often consensus that, when confronted with overseas crises, "something must be done."[7]

This was not the case in the 1840s. *Aiding Ireland* explores the Irish famine as a moment when such ideas about international obligations in the face of disaster were just beginning to emerge. To explain this phenomenon, I examine a range of attempts to relieve Irish suffering, including awareness-raising, policy, and communal or individual donations. These various forms of relief were useful because they could easily be deployed in arguments about local politics; they included claims about political identity in Ireland and the United States, critiques of the obligations of empires to subjects, calls for the reform of trade and landholding practices, and resistance to oppressive structures and governments.

The Irish potato famine was a local event with global impact. Described in Ireland at the time as "an drochshaol" (the bad times) and more recently as "an gorta mór" (the great hunger), it has also been called genocide, ethnic cleansing, and liberal policy gone horribly awry.[8] The famine was also a watershed moment for global demography—an event that prompted thousands of "emigrants and exiles" to leave Ireland for Europe, the Americas, Africa, and Asia.[9] These migrations lay the groundwork for a global Irish diaspora still evidenced today.[10] Whatever its causes and consequences, the famine occupies a central place in the British, Irish, North American, and Atlantic historical imaginations.[11] *Aiding Ireland* contributes to these understandings by arguing that, in addition to its role in shaping society both within and beyond Ireland's borders, the famine must be understood as one of the first truly global humanitarian relief efforts. This book explores how that happened, and why it matters.

Blight and Famine

In a world of abundance, it is difficult to imagine that an entire class of people might have been as reliant on a single food source as the Irish peasantry were in the 1840s. Ireland, in the nineteenth century, was governed by Britain. Much of it was rural. Most residents of the countryside were tenant farmers who tended small parcels of land rented from non-resident British landlords.[12] These rural men and women relied almost exclusively on the potato as a food source.[13] As landlords in Ireland began to dedicate more and more of their holdings to the production of grain for export due to its greater profitability, Irish tenant farmers were pushed to marginal land, where they occupied parcels that were so small and barren that potatoes, which yielded a high return on very small areas of rocky or hilly terrain, were the only supportable crop.

Into this already food-insecure environment came the particularly virulent "rot" of 1845. In the autumn of that year, farmers began to report "a blight of unusual character" spreading through their potato fields.[14] The blight, later identified as the fungus *Phytophthora infestans*, was brutal. Potatoes putrefied overnight, and rot appeared as if by magic in tubers that seemed perfectly sound a few days before.[15] At the time, agricultural experts assumed that the disease was the result of too much moisture.[16] Thus, early attempts to fight the crop failure focused on ways to dry the potatoes in the hope that more arid conditions would slow the spread of disease.[17] Despite these efforts, in the first year of the blight, more than half the potatoes harvested were unfit either for human consumption or for seeding the next year's crop. In 1846, farmers lost three-quarters of the meager crop that they had managed to sow after the 1845 harvest. In 1847, instances of the blight were few and scattered, but the damage had already been done. The losses in 1845 and 1846 meant that seed potatoes were scarce, and crop yields were small. Irish people began to starve.

Conventional estimates suggest that the rate of Irish mortality in 1847 was more than three times what it was in 1841.[18] Of a prefamine population of roughly 8.5 million, more than 1 million people died of starvation or related disease, and 2 million more emigrated from Ireland.[19] For those who remained and survived, the impact of the crop failure was far reaching. Fertility was depressed, rates of mental illness increased, and local economies were ruined.[20] The famine quite literally changed Irish landscapes—agricultural, demographic, economic, and political.

The Relief Landscape

Efforts to ameliorate Irish distress, including government policies, ad hoc relief efforts, and private donations, rapidly followed the onset of the blight and were widely discussed in Britain, Ireland, and abroad.[21] In 1845 and 1846 the British government implemented a number of reform measures designed to help feed the starving Irish. Parliament arranged for the distribution of grain at reduced prices. The British prime minister, Sir Robert Peel, campaigned to repeal the Corn Laws, a legal structure that set a minimum price for the sale of British grain before foreign grain could be imported. This meant that it was impossible to import cheap grain from elsewhere in Europe and effectively prevented impoverished Irish people from buying cheap food. Politicians in both Britain and Ireland encouraged local elites to initiate and fund public works projects like improving roads, dredging harbors, building piers and draining swamplands, measures intended to create alternative jobs for unemployed farmers while strengthening the Irish economy.[22]

Successive British governments were not so sympathetic. Lord John Russell, Peel's successor, scaled back the distribution of food and relied on workhouses to provide aid to the most destitute of the famine's victims.[23] These workhouses were notoriously miserable, designed to be a last resort before death. While some starving Irish did go to workhouses for relief, many more tried to eke out a living and ultimately starved or succumbed to disease on their rented lands.[24]

Private relief efforts were intended to supplement what many observers and commentators viewed as an insufficient official response. Some groups mounted campaigns to establish soup kitchens to distribute hot food free of charge.[25] Others donated money or supplies. These private donations came from both sides of the Atlantic Ocean and beyond;

between 1845 and 1852, established groups such as the Quaker Society of Friends solicited contributions in Britain, Ireland, and the United States, as did organizations created explicitly to meet the challenge of the Irish famine, such as the British Relief Association and the Irish Relief Association. At the same time, thousands of individuals around the Atlantic world convened local ad hoc committees to aid Irish victims of famine. Relief committees in American cities held dinners and gave fundraising toasts; workingmen's organizations held rallies; church groups passed collection plates; and groups of individuals, from enslaved Black people in the United States South to displaced Indigenous nations west of the Mississippi, contributed what little they could muster. Interest in Irish relief spanned the globe.

The scale of participation in Irish famine relief was unprecedented. At the turn of the nineteenth century, most charitable donors undertook what Robert Gross has called "concrete, direct acts of compassion" with "discrete ends."[26] These charitable acts were generally practiced on people close by or with close connections, so that the organizations and individuals involved in dispensing aid might immediately see the results of their benevolence.[27] Charities held fundraisers to help sufferers in their cities, churches took up collections for destitute members, and individuals gave to friends and family members who had fallen on hard times. For example, in the late eighteenth century, people of Scottish descent living in England were regularly expected to help fellow expatriate Caledonians in distress.[28] Similarly, before the US federal government's "Indian Removal" policy fundamentally disrupted their governance structures, members of the Cherokee Nation turned to tribal communities in times of need.[29] When, in the early nineteenth century, the US government embargoed trade with Britain, driving up food prices, elite New Yorkers formed committees to raise funds to provide emergency relief to their poorer neighbors.[30] Across the North Atlantic world in the eighteenth and early nineteenth centuries, providing relief to those within one's community was established practice.

In the decades before the famine, new trends emerged, and philanthropy began to move beyond merely local causes. Some people expanded their philanthropy to regional contexts. For example, fires in St. Johns and New Brunswick, Canada, prompted residents of Boston who had commercial ties to those cities to raise thousands of dollars for food and supplies.[31] In this period, some governments began to occasionally collect funds for distant crises. In 1812, the US government authorized $50,000 to purchase provisions for residents of Caracas, Venezuela, who had been subject to a devastating earthquake.[32] At the same time, a burgeoning interest in humanitarianism led to the establishment of groups and institutions concerned with effecting sometimes far-flung structural change through broad reform movements.[33] These included missionaries' attempts to spread Christianity and promote nascent human-rights campaigns on issues such as cruelty to children, prostitution, drunkenness, and intolerable conditions for the hospitalized and incarcerated.[34] These efforts connected groups with those in need outside of their immediate vicinity, but they did not generally inspire widespread giving from diverse strangers. Those who contributed to missionary efforts tended to be coreligionists; those who gave to reform societies tended to be members of the middle class who supported one cause, or a handful of causes as part of their professional and social lives.

None of this, however, could compare with the outpouring of interest in Irish famine relief in the 1840s. Newspapers from places as far flung as Mexico, France, and India printed reports of the Irish crisis.[35] People with no previous personal interest in Ireland began to comment on the best way to relieve Irish suffering. As if by common agreement, thousands of people from hundreds of locales collectively sent millions of dollars to help the Irish. Although there were major players in the relief efforts—such as the Society of Friends—interest in Irish famine relief could truly said to be crowdsourced and crowdfunded.

The Uses of Famine Relief

No part of the story up to this point, though, is novel. Scholars of the famine have long marveled at and sought to explain the extent of Irish famine relief efforts. While these explanations shed light on some parts of this phenomenon, they do not account for the full breadth of Irish relief efforts.

Some scholars have argued that the famine garnered this kind of philanthropic attention because Irish suffering was uniquely catastrophic. It is clear, however, that the scale of the famine, though devastating, was no different than famines that had struck Ireland in the past or famines that occurred elsewhere in the British Empire.[36] In fact, writing in 1851, William Wilde (the father of the more famous Oscar Wilde) noted that, from his perspective, the crop failure of the 1840s was one among eleven instances of "scarcity" or "distress" that had already disrupted rural Irish life in the first half of the nineteenth century.[37] Nor was it the case that in this particular famine, Ireland suffered more grievously than elsewhere.[38] Ireland was not the only country impacted by the potato blight in the 1840s. The disease *Phytophthora infestans* appeared in potato fields across Europe and even in the United States. The Netherlands and Belgium experienced significant "excess mortality"—deaths beyond what would have been expected in a normal year—due to crop losses.[39] Scotland, too, was affected by the disease; in 1846, three-quarters of the districts in the western Highlands reported that crops had been completely lost.[40] Although other countries did begin to recover more quickly than Ireland for a variety of reasons, it would not have been evident in the early years of the famine—when there was the greatest international interest in Irish relief—that this would be the case.[41] While the Irish were not the only group in need of aid, they garnered overwhelming humanitarian attention nonetheless.[42]

Other scholars point to extensive prefamine diasporic networks in Britain and North America that may have driven public interest in the situation in Ireland and thus donations to Irish relief organizations and associations.[43] As the famine progressed, more people emigrated from Ireland to these same areas, solidifying connections between Irish people overseas and at home. During the famine more than three hundred thousand Irish women, men, and children immigrated to Britain, joining the approximately four hundred thousand who resided there prior to 1840.[44] For some, this was merely a stopover on the way to the United States, Canada, or the Antipodes; others took up permanent residence in British cities and settled into working- and middle-class urban life.[45] Those who immigrated to the United States also initially settled in cities. By 1855, there were twice as many Irish men and women in New York as there had been in 1845, and Irish-born people made up almost one-third of the city's total population.[46] Similar communities developed in other Atlantic port cities, including Boston, Quebec, and Philadelphia.[47]

These Irish social networks certainly did drive interest in famine relief and did direct money to sufferers in Ireland. However, most Irish emigrants seemed more interested in supporting specific Irish friends and relations than they were in contributing to relief efforts that might be directed to any part of Ireland. Generally, their remittances home were sent directly, separate from more public transnational fundraising efforts and attempts in the mainstream press to generate interest in the best mechanisms of Irish relief.[48] For newly emigrated Irish men and women, there would have been little point in funneling remittances through an organization when they could just as easily be sent to a specific relation in need. Tellingly, many of the donors to private famine relief organizations seemed to have no direct personal connection to Ireland.

Another explanation often posited for interest in Ireland in the 1840s is that a confluence of new media technologies encouraged people to start caring about distant sufferers. It is certainly the case that the nineteenth century saw increased interest in relief efforts far from home, and that this was driven by greater access to global news. Ireland was no different: famine news circulated widely because of changing Anglo-American publishing conventions, which increasingly catered to non-elites and even nonreaders. In many respects, the news consumers of the 1840s were radically different from their counterparts a century before. In the early eighteenth century, newspapers around the Atlantic had been designed for and consumed by elites.[49] In the early nineteenth century, the press underwent an "age of egalitarianism," moving away from elite audiences toward a broader public.[50] By the 1830s, technology in both Europe and the United States made it possible to print newspapers that could be sold for one cent per issue—a marked contrast to the six cents that was charged for the average newspaper in the first third of the century.[51] This "penny press" emerged to fulfill the needs of a reading public that was more urban, less bourgeois, and, according to some scholars, more democratic than it had ever been before.[52]

This news traveled speedily and widely. In the late eighteenth century, it could take more than a week for news to travel from the west coast of Ireland to Dublin and months for it to cross the Atlantic. By the 1840s, accounts of the famine, carried by horse, mail coach, or rail, could cross Ireland in as little as four days.[53] From Dublin, the London and British provincial papers might receive copies of Irish newspapers and print news from Ireland as soon as two days later. Steamships might take only two weeks to deliver news from Europe to Atlantic port cities, and it might take only another week to reach the interior of North America. In the nineteenth century, it was common practice for city papers to extract news from provincial papers closer to the source; papers also frequently reprinted snippets from other papers. This allowed those that were far from the site of an event to print news about it despite the unlikelihood of having a reporter on the scene. While this practice was doubtlessly frustrating for publishers, who saw their hard-earned reporting shamelessly copied, it did give papers around the Atlantic access to international news.[54]

Some scholars of the famine argue that knowing about Irish suffering prompted people around the world to give. In his formative work on international philanthropy, Merle Curti notes in passing that people who organized famine relief meetings were "aroused by reports of prevailing conditions."[55] According to this narrative, people were motivated simply by hearing vivid descriptions of Irish suffering.[56] Historians of humanitarianism have complicated this argument, contending that the rapid and extensive circulation of news actually reshaped emotional responses to faraway suffering by facilitating imagined connections between the reader and the written subject.[57] Linking global capitalism to changes in moral conscience; some argue that emergent global capitalism fostered the ability to envision and react to crises at a distance. When people were able to imagine their goods or funds doing work for profit in far-off locales, they also became able to imagine funds and actions doing humanitarian work at that same distance.[58] Others contend that antislavery campaigns oriented toward boycotting slave-produced goods made clear the global consequences, such as the suffering caused by slavery, of local actions like buying sugar.[59] While these various frameworks might explain the rise of abolition, neither awareness of the crisis nor the ability to imagine the distant impact of actions explains widespread famine philanthropy. If that were the case, many more distant crises—including other famines of the 1840s—would have prompted the same scale of donations as did the one in Ireland.

Certainly, some famine philanthropists were shocked by the vivid reporting on Irish suffering, and some Irish émigrés raised money and spread awareness, but assuming that these factors explain the reaction to the famine produces a series of circular arguments. For instance, did newspapers continually publish on the famine because individuals were gripped by it, or did readers become engrossed because of their ability to understand and sympathize with its victims through news? In the end, while international reportage; the development of capitalist and abolitionist mindsets; the particularities of Irish distress, immigration, and extant relationships between Britain, the United States, and Ireland all contributed to the global phenomenon of the response to the famine, they are not sufficient to account for the fact that so many people with so little personal connection to the starving Irish became involved in famine relief.

This book proposes an alternate explanation. It contends that the Irish famine could be put to many and varied political uses, and that those uses drove interest in relieving the Irish in particular. This was a dramatic story of suffering, taking place in the heart of the British Empire, in the midst of contests over land, nationalism, trade, and imperial rule. These contexts positioned the famine to become something greater than itself, a cause célèbre that could be rhetorically situated to take on multiple, conflicting meanings simultaneously. The famine was a site upon which myriad differing—and often diametrically opposed—groups could project their own experiences and goals. Arguments about the best way to achieve famine relief, in turn, were reflections of these myriad interpretations. In this context, the famine operated as what Ernesto Laclau calls an "empty signifier": a word or concept that, because it cannot be wholly incorporated within a particular framework or set of ideas, loses a firm connection to one specific meaning and can thus be given different meanings by different people. Empty signifiers, like famines, often signal the failure of dominant systems to manage complex pluralities.[60] This is not to suggest, of course, that the famine did not have devastating consequences; for its direct victims, it meant dispossession, hunger, illness, poverty, exile, and death. For others, however, the famine itself and the relief efforts that went hand-in-hand with it, became identified not only with the suffering of the Irish but also with the needs of communities around the world.

The politicization of famine relief was enabled by the fact that the famine signaled a fundamental failure of governance and elite obligation.[61] Irish landlords had failed tenant farmers; nationalist politicians had failed Irish non-elites; the British government had failed its Irish subjects; and the British Empire had failed those it cast as "savages" whom they meant to uplift and civilize. Each of these failures provided a framework that allowed donors and commentators on philanthropy to see the famine through their own narratives and use it for their own goals. Writing and commentating on the famine in newspapers, and raising money and donating to relief, thus became political acts.

This argument, of course, calls for an understanding of politics and political action that is more expansive than voting and holding office. Around the Atlantic in the nineteenth century, political culture was becoming more popular. Despite this change political power was still formally limited to men who were of age, white, and, in many cases, property owners. Throughout the late eighteenth and early nineteenth centuries, however, those who were excluded from formal political action increasingly found new venues for engagement with power. Studies of protests, public demonstrations and even violence have demonstrated that rhetorical forms of politics provided women, people of color, and others typically excluded from political discourse with opportunities to resist or critique state power.[62]

Aiding Ireland reads engagement with Irish famine aid as part of the political tool kit available to people in the nineteenth century. It argues that relief—both donations and calls for interventionist action—was used to level political, economic, and social critiques.[63] This interpretation draws on scholarship about contemporary giving that demonstrates how charity, philanthropy, and aid today are mechanisms through which to express contentious politics. People raise funds to help each other when governments fail to address their concerns. This kind of fundraising is often prompted by exclusion from political power. As Shawn Teresa Flanigan has noted, giving becomes a way to express grievance, often as a suite of political actions.[64]

Philanthropy-as-resistance has been most frequently documented between people who share an identity. For example, the activist and scholar of philanthropy Jean E. Fairfax has documented how Black philanthropic projects operate "as connectedness to the brothers and sisters who exist at the margins of our society—the oppressed, the angry, the despairing."[65] Similarly, Stella Shao argues that Asian-American foundations emerged to meet the needs of ethnic groups excluded from political power.[66] Still others note that philanthropy and aid can connect members of national and religious diasporas. The Northern Irish Aid Committee, for example, famously fused fundraising in support of the Provisional Republican movement in Ireland with Irish American ethnic politics in the United States.[67] As these examples illustrate, aid, charity and philanthropy can be—and often are—used as a part of broader political campaigns. In *Aiding Ireland* I contend that this utility is not just a contemporary phenomenon, and that its value is not limited to people with obvious shared identities. The act of giving, encouraging others to give, or advocating for particular relief policies often produced rhetorical connections to the suffering Irish. Just as creating philanthropic organizations in the twentieth century had the power to build solidarity or call attention to government failures, public engagement with famine relief in the nineteenth century allowed people to claim Irish suffering as their own. Public opinion about Irish famine relief was shaped in the space between accounts of Irish distress and the rhetorical needs of newspapers, aid organizers, politicians, and other public commentators.

Each chapter of this book examines a particular moment of political action. They illustrate how narratives of Ireland's crisis shifted as they moved farther away from Ireland, and as famine relief was put to different political uses. Viewed through the lens of the political utility of relief, the famine becomes not only a local catastrophe or demographic event but also a complex node of meaning speaking to class, race, land, colonialism, economics, governance, and war. Commentators, politicians and philanthropists used the press and other public venues to shape public opinion about the famine and famine relief. In politics, "public opinion" comes with much conceptual baggage, most of it concerned with the relationship between beliefs and voting patterns, and with the effect of voting patterns on politics. Certainly, some of the groups described in this book were seeking to influence policy.

However, a greater number were concerned with articulating a vision of Irish relief that was not necessarily connected to direct political action.

Certain of these understandings were reflected in the records of famine relief groups. Some of these records, like the Society of Friends' General Central Relief Committee, the Irish Relief Association, and Charleston's Hibernian Society survive archivally, memorializing discussions about the best way to mobilize interest in famine relief. Most Irish aid groups, however, were ad hoc and ephemeral, and their records have long been lost. Newspapers provide an opportunity to understand how a wide range of people—the editors and writers who shaped the news, and the people who read it—came to understand the political utility of famine relief. Some articles directly proscribed particular perspectives. However, public opinion was also shaped through what communication scholars call "media frames": the broader contexts and saliences that people drew on when interpreting the news.[68] By bringing together of records of giving, public commentary, and the broader frames and contexts in which people learned about and formed opinions on the famine, I am able to reconstruct the information environments that conditioned the politicization of famine relief around the North Atlantic world.

Each chapter is located in a specific community and political context and details political uses to which the famine was put. In Dublin, where many commentators were able to afford distance from the crisis, both the famine and possible relief measures were immediately used in debates about Irish political identity. Commentators in British industrial cities mobilized famine relief in service of debates about free trade. In London, at the center of British imperial power, politicians, and the people who wrote about them, used the issue of Irish aid as an opportunity to test ideas about imperial obligation. As news of the famine moved across the Atlantic, famine relief took on ever-more varied and malleable political meanings. For New York politicians with national aspirations, the famine provided an opportunity for the United States to consider its role as an imperial power and to differentiate itself from Britain through moral exceptionalism. For tenant farmers in central New York State, aid to the rural Irish intersected with the politics of land stewardship and reform. Enslavers and proslavery activists in the

United States appropriated Irish suffering and relief to bolster their own claims of marginalization at the hands of the federal government. At the same time, a group of free and enslaved Black people in Richmond, Virginia, used famine aid to critique the dehumanization of slavery and insist on their own moral agency. Finally, in perhaps the most surprising instance of Irish famine philanthropy—one that persists in the popular imagination today—members of the Cherokee and Choctaw Nations in what is now the state of Oklahoma used famine relief as a part of a set of claims to political autonomy.

Together, these chapters demonstrate that the Irish famine was more than an unprecedented crisis, and that famine relief was more than the extension of older charitable norms to people at a distance. Rather, engagement with famine relief became a way of interacting with unknown suffering others as proxies for donors' and commentators' own political identities and objectives. The famine's impact on Irish politics and society, and on demography around the world via the Irish diaspora, is already well documented. In *Aiding Ireland*, I argue that the famine was also an event that reverberated politically far beyond Ireland's borders. As the story of Ireland's suffering became the business of the world, the question of relief—who should provide it, in what way, and at what cost—circulated broadly as well. As they made use of famine relief, politicians and commentators around the North Atlantic inextricably linked philanthropy with politics in ways that persist into the present.

1

The Irish Nation

Rumors of a European potato blight began to appear in Ireland's most prominent newspapers in August 1845. One report from the English county of Kent noted that potatoes had suddenly turned "completely black."[1] Another, from the Netherlands, described entire fields that began to "die in the course of the night" and were wiped out in a matter of hours.[2] By September, papers were full of stories that detailed the blight's spread across England and its increasing toehold in Ireland.[3] As summer shaded into autumn, magistrates, constables, members of the coast guard, and other government officials in cities and towns throughout Ireland cataloged spreading disease and increasing losses.[4] Though the long-term consequences of the crop failure were not clear in these early months, it did seem certain that a considerable portion of rural Irish food stores would be lost that fall.

At the end of October, a group of Irish politicians formed a committee to investigate "the alarming accounts of the failure of the potato crop."[5] They met at the Mansion House, the official residence of the lord mayor of Dublin, and called themselves the "Mansion House Committee." These men sought to expand Irish political power, though their particular aims and strategies differed. Some, like Daniel O'Connell and Henry Grattan Jr., wanted to bolster the political rights of Irish Catholics and achieve Ireland's political independence from Britain. Others, like the lord mayor of Dublin, John L. Arabin, were members of the Protestant gentry, whose families had dominated Irish politics until 1801, and wanted to reclaim that power.

These men claimed that the British government had failed Ireland, and that, if government policy did not change, Ireland was likely to succumb to "the dreadful scourge of anticipated famine and pestilence.[6] They also agreed that the crop failure constituted a uniquely Irish problem that affected all sectors of Irish society. At an early meeting of the Mansion House Committee, Daniel O'Connell argued that the blight had the power to impact alike "the lives of the rich who are threatened to be attacked by the contagion of the disease" and "the lives of the poor who have no other subsistence but the potato." At the same meeting, he cast the potato failure as a "national calamity."[7] In making this claim, O'Connell unambiguously put famine relief to his own political use: he linked the immediate subsistence crisis to debates among Irish politicians and political commentators about who should be included within the Irish nation and, consequently, who should be able to exert control over Ireland's political future.

A few days after O'Connell's remarks, in October 1845, men representing the Mansion House Committee presented a petition to Baron Heytesbury, who held the office of the lord lieutenant, the British government's primary representative in Ireland. Drawing on information that they promised was "both accurate and extensive," and that was "derived from sources altogether unaffected by any political party motive whatsoever," the committee sought concrete actions that would make it easier for Irish men and women to buy food.[8] These included suspending taxes on foreign food imports, prohibiting food exports out of Ireland, limiting the oats allotted to the British army's horses, and temporarily suspending the distillation of grain into spirits. They asked that the British government extend a loan to Ireland, "chargable upon Irish resources," that could be used to support "increasing the quantity, and decreasing the price of food."[9] They also called for government investment in public improvement schemes that would simultaneously develop Irish infrastructure and make employment more readily accessible to Irish tenant farmers who were unable to sell their crops to buy food for their families.[10] Their requests reflected desired changes in British government policy that would ultimately be paid for by Irish capital. Notably, despite every indication that Irish crops would soon be decimated, they did not ask for charitable aid from Britain.

This focus on government action and repayable loans rather than outright philanthropy reflected the committee members' views that charity was a way for Britain to maintain political supremacy in Ireland. Shortly after the Mansion House Committee met with the lord lieutenant, *The Nation*, a paper that supported a radical break from Britain, elaborated on the link between charity and political oppression, writing, "From England we may always expect Charity, but that is just what we should most deeply regret to see the People receive. It is to the last degree de-grading—it creates an obligation and gives an excuse for the commisera-tions of conscious superiority. We have heard but too much, from time to time, of the last great national alms we received at English hands, not that we were ungrateful, but it was expected that our gratitude should be more loquacious. No; let the English legislature put our own resources into our hands, and we shall not ask any charity."[11] For Irish nationalists, British charity was a cudgel. Rather than solicit funds freighted with co-lonial expectations, they argued that the Irish people should be allowed to gather and direct national resources to meet this "national calamity."

However, the meaning of "national" was very much in question. There was little consensus in Ireland in the 1840s about what the bound-aries of Irishness were, who belonged in the Irish nation, or who should lead it. Some saw Irish national interests as congruent with the interests of those who could vote, serve in office, and shift official policy—in other words, men who were largely of the Protestant aristocracy. For these politicians and political commentators, access to political power was the true marker of Irishness, and that access was fundamentally mediated by Britain. Others saw the boundaries of the nation as cir-cumscribed by the ability to exert influence, but not necessarily bound to formal politics. For these thinkers, Irish political power lay in Irish Catholic people undertaking political action, including action not sanc-tioned by the British government. Still others adopted a more capacious romantic nationalism, locating Irish national identity in shared heritage and experiences and hoping for political solidarity across Irish people, regardless of class or sect.

In the century before the famine, politicians and political commen-tators argued for various and competing models for the Irish nation. These models had first gained and then lost traction among Ireland's political classes. Over this same period, Ireland's autonomy from Britain had waxed and waned, as did the political access of different groups within Irish society and the power of informal or extragovernmental political structures. These shifts and fluctuations produced different cultural com-munities and political coalitions. In the 1840s, these groups used the crisis precipitated by the blight to promote their diverse views of and agen-das for Ireland's future. Specifically, thinkers and commentators repre-senting these political positions filtered their arguments about Ireland's political identity—rooted in Catholicism, Protestantism, or a shared historical past that transcended sectarianism—through claims about who was to blame for the famine and who should be obligated or entitled to provide relief.

These understandings were structured by the colonial relationship between Britain and Ireland. Debates about the Irish nation were centered in Dublin; newspapers published there were designed to influence the opinions of metropolitan elites and of Irish men and women outside of the capitol, as well as people outside of Ireland. In the decades before the famine, arguments about Irish national identity and political leadership played out in these papers. They continued to play a decisive role in shaping notions of Irish identity throughout the course of the famine and, indeed, until the Irish war for independence in the early twentieth century.

These papers were the sites of several debates over relief and the meaning of the Irish nation. The first of these took place just before the famine, in response to recommendations made by the Devon Commission, a British body tasked with determining the causes and remedies for rural Irish distress. In the following months, papers debated whether potato failures would result in a famine, and how relief was to be adjudicated in response to "famine panic." After politicians and political commentators agreed that the rural Irish were indeed suffering from famine, the papers were venues for debates over who was best poised to administer aid. This conversation was complicated by the rise of extragovernmental relief organizations that stepped in to provide aid when it became clear that government relief would be insufficient. Each of these debates reflects the use of the famine as a deeply compelling tabula rasa upon which to project competing images of the Irish nation.

Defining the Nation

The contours of these debates turned on the deep history of the colonial relationship between Britain and Ireland. English commentators had long characterized the Irish as backward, bestial, and depraved, as part of bids to control Irish land.[12] One example of rhetoric denigrating Irish character used for political gains was the *Laudabiliter*, a possibly apocryphal, but nevertheless much-referenced, document purportedly written by Pope Adrian in the twelfth century, granting the

English king Henry II full authority to rule Irish people, due to their inherent inferiority. The document, along with the subsequent policies that relied on it, was frequently used to justify English conquest of Ireland.[13] From this early period, English arguments that Ireland should be subject to English rule turned on the assumption of Irish "savagery."

English elites claimed that the Irish were hopelessly primitive. Given this, early English colonial policy focused (as it would in North America) on settlement. The Irish themselves might be irredeemably backward, but successive groups of English settlers could, the Crown hoped, secure Irish land and make it fruitful.[14] This was not a straightforward occupation, however. English governing elites worried constantly that the depravity of what they called the "native" Irish would threaten the stability of Anglo-Irish settlements. The 1367 Statute of Kilkenny attempted to mitigate against Irish cultural contagion, which elites believed caused English settlers to forsake "the English language, dress, style of riding, laws, and usages" and instead "live and govern themselves according to the manners, dress, and language of the Irish enemies."[15] The statute was part of a pattern of legislation by which the English government sought to preserve Englishness among the settlers, reinforce their allegiances, and distinguish—in ways that have been read by scholars as protoracial, if not explicitly racist—between people of English and Irish descent.[16] It reinforced claims of Irish inferiority while arguing that Ireland and the Irish would benefit from adopting English culture and practices. From this early period, Irish identity was contested.

Throughout the late sixteenth century, the English Crown continued to use a combination of settlement and military force to expand its control of Ireland and replace Irish inhabitants with English ones.[17] While these new settlers might not have considered themselves as acting on behalf of a coherent English empire, they behaved in much the same way as other settler colonists in the period.[18] They cleared and built homes on land deeded to them by the English monarch, often displacing the Gaelic-speaking, Catholic Irish who lived there; they worked to reestablish English laws, customs, and practices and expand them into the Irish countryside.[19] Despite their participation in English colonial projects, members of this group who lived in Ireland for a long time eventually came to view themselves as Irish. They became the Irish Protestant aristocracy, which complicated notions of Irish identity that had previously delineated between "native" Irish and English settlers. However, because their power relied on their relationship to England, and, later, to imperial Britain, they also needed to differentiate themselves strongly from the Gaelic Irish. Thus, they turned to the same tropes that their forbearers had used, which cast Gaelic Irish character as degenerate in order to solidify their own place at the top of Irish society, increasingly articulating an elite Irish political identity that was separate from and equal to Britain.[20]

When, in 1603, the English and Scottish monarchies united to produce the political entity of the United Kingdom of Great Britain, Irish plantations were used as models to "plant" new colonies across the Atlantic ocean in North America and in the Caribbean.[21] Though Ireland's proximity to Britain marked it as different from transatlantic colonies, British attempts to settle Ireland throughout the seventeenth century paralleled attempts to establish colonies farther afield.[22] As would be the case in these new colonies—and as had been the case in the fourteenth century—governance of British settlers in Ireland proved challenging. In the seventeenth century, British colonists in Ireland continued to form alliances and intermarry with the Irish and, according to Jane Ohlmeyer, deliberately built an elite social stratum that capitalized on the political and military power of connections to Britain, but which sought to consolidate power on the ground in Anglo-Irish hands. This power, centuries in the making, solidified into the form of the Irish peerage, a Protestant Anglo-Irish aristocracy who identified as Irish and sought political self-determination, but often acted as proxies for Britain against poorer, Catholic, and Gaelic-speaking Irish.[23]

For much of the century before the famine, Ireland was governed by these elites, who sat in a parliament that met in Dublin, but was effectively controlled by London. This control was partially managed by a resident lord lieutenant, who oversaw "undertakers," members of the Irish Parliament who agreed to shape policy in exchange for patronage.[24] Additionally, the British Parliament in Westminster retained the ultimate right to legislate for Ireland.[25] In the tradition of those who came before them, the Irish Parliament's elected and hereditary members considered themselves to be the true representatives of Irish national interests, which were synonymous with Protestant political supremacy.[26]

These men, along with fellow members of the Protestant Irish aristocracy, wielded considerable control over the lives of average Irishmen
and women, who remained predominately Catholic. The Irish Parliament passed laws that sought to outlaw the practice of Catholicism,
though these laws were sparsely and inconsistently enforced.[27] It also
limited Catholics' incomes, made it difficult for them to inherit inter-
generational wealth, and barred them from voting or holding office.[28]
In doing so, Anglo-Irish elites worked, as their forebearers had done, to
exclude the Gaelic, Catholic Irish from political power.

In the latter decades of the eighteenth century, however, several
factors came together to inspire non-elite Irish men and women to
push back. First, Britain passed laws restricting the sale of Irish products to all places except for Britain and colonies under British control,
effectively subordinating the needs of Irish producers to those of British producers.[29] In response, protestors began to publicly agitate for
Irish economic independence. In doing so, they linked Irish politics
to commercial interests and sought to exert power through economic
disruption. The second factor was the involvement of France in the
American Revolution, which prompted fears among the Irish Protestant elite of an invasion against which Britain was incapable or unwilling to defend. In the face of this imagined threat, Protestant men
across Ireland joined volunteer militias committed to protecting Ireland from a French invasion. By the end of 1781, over eighty thousand
men had joined the Volunteer movement, identifying themselves as
Irish "patriots."[30] The British government agreed to increase economic
and political autonomy for the Irish Parliament, in the hopes that a
small increase in political agency would quell opposition to British
legislative control. This move effectively demonstrated that Irish men
and women who were excluded from formal politics could nonetheless
impact political policy.[31]

Only a few years later, similar types of extrapolitical action would
swing the pendulum away from Irish autonomy. Irish Catholics were
still excluded from the electorate and from public office. Throughout
the 1790s, groups advocating for Catholics' political rights formed
across the island. The most famous of these was the Society of the
United Irishmen, founded by middle-class liberals in Belfast in 1791. In
response to overt political pressure and covert threats of violence from

these groups, the British government approved and the Irish parliament passed legislation allowing Catholic men to hold some public offices and to vote in municipal and parliamentary elections. While these small concessions were as far as the British government was willing to go toward Catholic political equality, they were not sufficient for many Irish Catholics. In 1798, the United Irishmen, as well as "Defenders"— rural groups who undertook violence against Protestants whom they saw as furthering Catholic oppression—sought to ally themselves with the French and invite an attack on British forces in Ireland. In the face of this threat, the British prime minister, William Pitt, proposed, as Protestant elites had long feared, that Ireland could not be trusted to govern itself. The Act of Union of 1801 abolished the Irish Parliament and added Irish representatives to the British Houses of Lords and Commons instead. Irish governance was once again firmly in the hands of the British Parliament, and political power in Ireland was in the hands of a relatively few Protestant Irish MPs who found themselves in a minority among British parliamentary representatives.[32] The Act of Union called into question Irish political identity long associated with the Irish Parliament.

This new political configuration did not seamlessly incorporate Ireland into Britain. While Ireland was governed from London, much legislation still treated it as a polity separate from the United Kingdom.[33] Furthermore, this new governance structure had been implemented with force, mirroring the power struggles that had played out between Britain and its other colonies.[34]

Because Catholics were still excluded from sitting in Parliament, the Act of Union further alienated most Irish people from those who governed them. Responses to the act varied. Some Irish political thinkers advocated for the repeal of the Union entirely and the return of Irish governance to Ireland; others focused on expanding political access within the framework of the Union. Daniel O'Connell, who would later be a member of the Mansion House Committee and who would call the famine a "national calamity," advocated for both of these positions in the three decades after the Act of Union. In 1828, drawing on both his political connections as a lawyer and the clout of his wealthy Catholic family, he stood for office as a member of parliament for County Clare.[35] He won and used his victory to successfully achieve "Catholic emancipation," overturning the laws that banned Catholics from sitting in Parliament. However, in return for wealthy Catholics serving in the highest political offices, Irish leaders agreed to increased economic qualifications for voting, which meant that middle-class Catholics continued to be excluded from politics. This Irish constituency was thus sympathetic to O'Connell's next political project: the repeal of the Act of Union. The repeal movement was extremely popular, as evinced by widely attended meetings (called "monster" meetings by both O'Connell and the popular press) and numerous contributions to the "repeal rent," donations that O'Connell pledged to spend in political advocacy. This was a Catholic Irish identity, focused on independence from Britain.[36]

In the midst of these contestations over whether Irish national identity was Protestant or Catholic, rich or poor, another group of Irish political activists came on the scene. The decade before the famine saw the rise of a group that hoped to transcended sectarian divisions. The so-called romantic nationalism of the Young Irelanders was of a piece with other nationalist movements across Europe and North America that sought to forge connections with imagined historical pasts pre-dating the nation-state and uniting diverse ethnic groups. In Ireland, this group included Charles Gavan Duffy, Thomas Davis, and John Blake Dillon, who founded the newspaper *The Nation*, as well as men who wrote for it, such as John Mitchel, Thomas D'Arcy McGee, Charles Patrick Meehan, and Thomas MacNevin.[37] Although the name "Young Ireland" had originally been intended as derisive and infantilizing, these literary and romantically minded young men ultimately embraced it, using it to signal their departure from what they saw as the outdated politics of O'Connell. Their core belief was that "we [the Irish] ought to be united, not alone because we have mingled our blood with each other, but because we inhabit the same country, and possess one common interest."[38] Young Irelanders advocated for the repeal of the Act of Union and a more inclusive understanding of the Irish nation that would include the Protestant propertied classes and be less bound to the interests of the Catholic church. The leaders—in particular, Thomas Davis—hoped to include both landlords and tenants under the umbrella of cultural Irishness. However, this approach would only work if the landlords could become what Davis called "national," and if they would reform their policies to help, rather than hurt, their tenants.[39]

This history essentially describes the evolving conflict between three frameworks of identity: Protestant nationalism linked to political supremacy; Catholic nationalism, which sought to give monied Catholics access to political power previously hoarded by Protestants, but which also increasingly tolerated the political involvement of middle- and lower-class Catholics; and romantic nationalism, which endeavored to unite all Irish people. This was the context in which Irish thinkers and commentators approached the issue of famine and famine relief: it shaped how they saw it, as well as suggested how they might use it to promote their own narrative of who truly belonged to Ireland.

The Irish National Press

Ireland's politicians and political commentators lived in a very different world than the rural Ireland that was decimated by the famine. Most politically engaged Irish men spent some, if not most, of their time in Dublin, which, in the 1840s, felt distant from the rest of Ireland and was both literally and figuratively proximate to British structures of power. Writers of the time described Dublin as the "second city" of the British empire.[40] Its streets were peppered with statues celebrating English leaders. These included statues of monarchs erected before the Act of Union, as well as statues of British politicians erected in the early decades of the nineteenth century. Dublin's urban landscape was an ongoing reminder of colonial rule, collectively enacting symbolic ties between Britain and Ireland.[41]

The wealthy and fashionable of the city tended to be members of the Protestant elite with connections to the British officials who operated out of Dublin Castle. Other politicians similarly used Dublin residences to bolster their political power; even Catholic politicians like O'Connell maintained expansive and expensive city townhouses.[42] This consolidation of politicians in Dublin is important because, as Sean Ryder, a scholar of Irish media, has noted, reports of rural distress that circulated in Ireland's capital were not merely collections of facts, but were curated in ways to bolster or undermine political power.[43] The men who wrote for, edited, and published Dublin's three major newspapers in the 1840s—the *Dublin Evening Mail*, the *Freeman's Journal*, and *The Nation*—used these papers to hone arguments and promulgate ideas about Irish national identity.[44] Their real and experiential distance from the famine allowed the crisis to function as an arsenal of evidence for various political positions, rather than as a daily, lived catastrophe.

By the 1840s, the Dublin press had long been viewed—by both the people who wrote for it and those who read it—as a political tool. At the end of the eighteenth century, the British government in Ireland had sought to purchase, with a view to suppressing, any opposition newspapers. They were largely successful. Those papers that did not cease to publish significantly moderated their criticism of the government. As the nineteenth century wore on, however, newspapers that publicly supported an independent Irish nation began again to gain traction.[45] In the 1840s, as both Catholic and romantic nationalism gained in power, the indisputably propagandistic Dublin newspapers provided space for Irish politicians and political commentators to promulgate their ideas, which were reported by Ireland's bourgeoning professional journalists, drawing on text submitted directly by politicians and through articles reprinted from other newspapers.[46] The press of the period, therefore, offers a window into how Irish thinkers presented the famine to the public.

The oldest of Dublin's major newspapers, the *Freeman's Journal*, had been founded in the eighteenth century by Irish Catholic Charles Lucas. In the course of his life, Lucas was a vocal advocate for Irish parliamentary independence and, later, a member of the Irish parliament for Dublin city. The men who edited and wrote for the *Journal* after Lucas were vocal opponents of the Act of Union, and the paper served as an official venue for support of Daniel O'Connell in his campaign for Catholic political rights. In 1846, *Mitchell's Newspaper Press Directory* – a trade publication intended to present "a more dignified and permanent record" of the British press – characterized the *Journal* as a staunch advocate for "'national' Irish principles."[47] By the late 1840s, it was in many ways an establishment paper representing middle- and upper-class Catholic interests, opposed to British and Protestant rule.

Shortly after the passage of Catholic emancipation, men who supported the Act of Union and the interests of Irish landlords founded the *Dublin Evening Mail*.[48] The *Mail's* editors and journalists wrote for a Protestant audience and represented in particular the values of landed property in Ireland. Although this position meant that the *Mail's editors* were virulently opposed to absentee landlords who did not attend to the needs of their tenants, and whom they saw as unfairly shirking the responsibilities of the landed classes, more of their vitriol was reserved for the repeal movement, especially for O'Connell. The paper had trafficked in sometimes-extreme anti-Catholicism in its early years, but by the mid-1840s it had more or less become the official paper representing the Protestant ascendancy and British rule in Ireland.[49]

In 1842, the Young Irelanders founded a nationalist paper to rival the *Freeman's Journal* and called it *The Nation*. Its editors intended "to create and foster public opinion in Ireland—to make it racy of the soil."[50] *The Nation* took a harder line than O'Connell on both Irish independence and the acceptability of violence in achieving political aims. While O'Connell eschewed violence, the editors of *The Nation* saw it as useful in particular circumstances. *The Nation* also published literature and poetry alongside news, in order to act in "the service of mankind in politics."[51] This approach was meant to foster a unified national culture and to work against rhetoric from both O'Connell and the Unionists, whom the editors of *The Nation* cast as seeking to divide the Irish people and turn them against one another. Charles Gavan Duffy, one of the paper's founders, contended that, despite "all the nicknames that serve to divide us . . . there are in truth but two parties in Ireland; those who suffer from her National degradation, and those who profit by it."[52] For Duffy, and for others who wrote for *The Nation*, Irish national identity lay in shared historical oppression, and political power should be the possession all Irish men and not limited to formal political spaces.

The political ideas circulating in the *Dublin Evening Mail, Freeman's Journal,* and *The Nation* would have been readily accessible to upper- and middle-class Dubliners, as well as to Irish people outside of the capital and even to people outside of Ireland. The papers did have different audiences, however, if only because of price. The *Freeman's Journal* was the cheapest, at 4 d. per issue. At 6 d.—the cost of two loaves of bread and only slightly less than a laborer on the public works might make in a day—*The Nation* and the *Dublin Evening Mail* were priced beyond what many Irish people could have afforded.[53] However, as was the case for newspapers around the North Atlantic in the nineteenth century, many people read—or were read to from—these papers but did not subscribe to them. The papers themselves would have been available in reading rooms and other social spaces, and perhaps as many as ten different readers had access to every paper sold.[54] As they did with other issues of the day, Irish politicians and political commentators used the press to shape readers' understandings of the famine and famine relief. In the 1840s, these were instrumental in four debates when political commentators used the famine to shape the public's perception of Irish identity: the Devon Report on food shortages before the famine; disagreements about the extent of the famine in early years of the crisis; discussions of government relief once the extent of the famine had been established; and the emergence of extragovernmental relief organizations in the face of the inadequacy of the government response.

The Devon Commission

Politicians and political commentators were able to use the press to frame the failure of potato crops in 1845 in political and national terms because of the ground laid by political commentators during earlier subsistence crises. In the 1830s and 1840s, Irish farmers, politicians, and political commentators were preoccupied with food shortages related to the "land question," which capaciously included problems stemming from inequities between landlords and tenant farmers, the legal structure of landownership, investment in improvements, and the relationship between these systems and poverty in rural Ireland. Many—including both ardent nationalists and representatives of the British government—believed that Irish farming and landholding practices were hopelessly regressive, and were the cause of much starvation and poverty among farmers, and financial precarity among landlords.[55]

Perspectives on whose interests to prioritize when resolving the land question predictably mapped onto debates about who should hold political power in Ireland. O'Connell and other nationalists sought to represent the interests of Catholic tenant farmers and cottiers. Irish politicians who advocated for the continued Union between Britain and Ireland tended to sympathize with landlords, both because landowners in Ireland tended to be members of the Anglo-Irish elite, and because nationalist violence tended to threaten private property. Even those landlords who were not part of the British political establishment typically saw a stronger relationship with Britain as the best way to protect their interests. The British government was concerned with resolving the land question in large part because rural discontent over poverty could lead to more widespread anti-government agitations.[56]

Solutions to the land question were political in nature. In 1838, the British Parliament passed a poor law for Ireland, modeled on the English Poor Law of 1832, which prohibited "gratuitous" outdoor relief—that is, aid freely given—with no work or supplication on the part of recipients. It divided Ireland into unions, administered by local "guardians of the poor," who tended to be both propertied and wealthy. Each union built a workhouse, funded by taxes on Irish landowners, which would be the primary means of providing sustenance to the Irish poor in exchange for their labor. Entrance to these workhouses was determined by a "workhouse test," which was designed to ensure that only those who were the most desperate would avail themselves of state support. The only way to appeal to the Irish government for aid was to enter the workhouse.[57]

When this didn't solve the problem, the Conservative prime minister of Britain, Sir Robert Peel, convened a commission, led by the Earl of Devon, a politician and an Irish landlord, to explore possible improvements to the relationships between Irish landlords and their tenants and, in the process, to identify and ameliorate the causes of rural Irish discontent. In February 1845, the commission released its report. Among other findings, it noted that the rural Irish were living with what seemed to be permanent food insecurity, and that Irish laborers and cottiers were incapable of deriving "from their small holdings a sufficient supply even of food for their subsistence."[58] The committee traced this insecurity to a lack of employment for Irish laborers, persistent poverty, and the "unimproved state of extensive districts"—that is, the lack of investment in or development of land in ways that would make it more productive.[59] It suggested several remedies, including the recommendation that landlords should implement land improvements, and that tenants who themselves improved their holdings should be compensated.[60]

Unsurprisingly, this series of negotiated solutions didn't satisfy any political group in Ireland. Conservatives writing in the *Dublin Evening Mail* contended that, while the report "contains many valuable recommendations" that would improve the lives of landlords, some of the remedies suggested by the commission had the potential to place an undue burden on landowners. In one author's opinion, this problem derived from the fact that Lord Devon was "utterly ignorant of 'Ireland and the Irish.'"[61] The *Mail* suggested that landlords, not tenants, were those most in need, and it held the British government responsible for their aid. For the *Mail*, failure to attend to the needs of landlords was the same as failing to attend to the needs of Ireland.

Nationalist opinion was even more critical of the Devon Commission's report. O'Connell and his allies argued that the commission had failed not because it put too much of a burden on landlords, but because it did not suitably account for the needs of tenants, who were obviously the economic heart of Ireland. Nonetheless, O'Connell frequently used the words of the Devon report itself to argue against the Act of Union. One of the set pieces in his speeches at repeal meetings included the reminder that "these are not my words—they are the words of Lord Devon's Commission, who have declared, after the closest investigation, that the Irish labourers are ill-fed, ill-clothed,—that their only food is the potato, and their only drink water; that the houses of many are pervious to rain, and possessed but little shelter against the wind, that a bed or a blanket in many districts, was a luxury almost unknown, and that the only property possessed by the majority of my countrymen is the pig sty and dung heap."[62] This piece was repeated in many of O'Connell's speeches that were reprinted in the Irish national press, often accompanied by articles arguing that the British government was in the business of bringing famine to Ireland. One, in *The Nation* from June 1845, contended that the "Union was the assumption to legislate for us by a country which filled our soil with martyrs, and our statute-books with penal laws—which, finding the persecution of the sword insufficient, created famine by an elaborate process of desolation for the avowed purpose of exterminating us."[63] If this continued, O'Connell wrote (presciently, as it turned out) that he feared that "the people will slip out of my hands and the hands of those who, like me, are for peaceful amelioration."[64] In other words, should Britain and Irish landlords continue to ignore the rights of Irish tenant farmers and fail to implement structural solutions, people would die of famine, and the struggle could turn violent.

John Mitchel, a Young Irelander, was more critical still. In his 1861 history, *The Last Conquest of Ireland (Perhaps)*, Mitchel argued that the Devon Commission's purpose was to "devise the best means of getting rid of what Englishmen called 'the surplus population' of Ireland."[65] For Mitchel, attempts in the early 1840s to mitigate rural Irish suffering were merely a cover for the extermination of Irish people and the consolidation of power in the hands of men who held land in Ireland, but lived in England.[66] Similarly, the *Freeman's Journal* accused the commissioners of believing "that the good of Ireland has no other meaning than improving the properties of Irish landowners."[67] For these nationalists, the Devon Commission's report was evidence that any discussion of rural Irish relief must center the needs of the people actually living on and working the soil. Since the British government could not be trusted to provide that relief, politicians (in the case of O'Connell) and extrapolitical actors (in the case of Mitchel) would need to step in.

"Famine Panic"

The rhetoric crafted in debates about the Devon Commission shaped discourse in the months after the potato blight appeared, as various groups tried to assess the extent of its impact. While the *Freeman's Journal* described the loss of potato crops as an "emergency" in November 1845, just months after diseased potatoes began to appear, the *Dublin Evening Mail* repeatedly argued that nationalist politicians were exaggerating the extent of the disaster in order to fabricate a "famine panic" that would make the passage of their policies easier.[68] In order to ascertain the extent of the crisis, Prime Minister Peel appointed a scientific commission to explore the cause and extent of the blight, as well as possible ameliorative measures. The members of this commission were Lyon Playfair, a Scottish chemist; Dr. John Lindley, an English botanist; and Sir Robert Kane, an Irish chemist.[69] Peel was particularly concerned about their opinion because he feared the "tendency to exaggeration and inaccuracy in Irish reports."[70] Arguments about the severity of the famine, and whether it was a famine at all, were proxies for debates building on those in the aftermath of the Devon Commission about whose suffering mattered, who in Ireland should be the focus of relief policy, and who should fund that relief, if it was found to be necessary.

Eyewitness accounts of the consequences of the blight differed. Some were positive, if cautious. In Ballyshannon in County Donegal, one report noted that the potato crop was "fully equal to last years['s], which was considered an excellent one. Some few instances of failure, but nothing to affect the crop in a general way."[71] Other accounts, however, warned of an extensive portending crisis. In Clontarf, outside of Dublin, "large fields or gardens that presented the most luxuriant and healthy appearance are now found to be more or less disease."[72] In Donegal, another report described the crop as "very bad: one half supposed to be rotten or tainted, and painfully, those easiest sown." A report from Louth was more alarmist still, warning that "it is now ascertained that within a few days the disease has increased alarmingly and that, on the average one third of the general crop will be lost."[73] Still other reports urged caution until more information could be gleaned. From Kerry, one warned that "a report on the actual state of the crop cannot yet be made with accuracy" but that "recent symptoms are discouraging."[74] Another, from Carlow, expressed concern, but warned that "until the general crop is dug out a decided opinion cannot be formed."[75]

As the commission collected these reports, newspapers emphasized those that best served their interests. In October and November 1845, the *Freeman's Journal* reported meetings from places like Fermoy, Mayo, and Cavan, all describing the extent of "the disease in the potato crop."[76] *The Nation* similarly noted that "the reports from every district in Ireland published in the provincial, and metropolitan journals this week, with the single exception of the county Cork have not tended to dimmish the apprehension that the greater portion of the potato crop is utterly destroyed."[77] Meanwhile, the *Dublin Evening Mail* cited "all the intelligence we could find on this most important and, to this country, most vital subject" and concluded that the majority of the potato crop would be saved.[78] In the fall of 1845, whether there was a famine at all was a real and pressing political question.

Dublin's politicians and political commentators made use of these competing claims. O'Connell and his allies saw attempts to downplay the severity of famine as a refusal to prioritize tenants in national politics. When, at the first meeting of the Mansion House Committee, O'Connell called for action, he highlighted the Devon commission's findings "that nearly half of the labouring population of this country have no other resource than the potato." He called for the return of an Irish parliament, so that "Irish money should be kept at home" and "applied to prevent starvation in Ireland."[79] With this, O'Connell rhetorically claimed rural tenant farmers as Irish political subjects. In purporting to speak for these famine sufferers, O'Connell also asserted that those who protected tenants' interests should hold political power in Ireland—a perspective echoed in an article published several weeks later in the *Freeman's Journal*, attacking the *Dublin Evening Mail* on the grounds that denying the extent of famine posed a danger to the rural Irish. "We perceive with regret," the article stated, "that endeavours are now used to persuade the government that there is no dearth to attend to—no scarcity apprehended. This is the object of the *Mail* of last night in an article prompted by the worst and most dangerous spirit."[80] An article in the *Mail* issued a strongly worded rebuttal, which included the first contention that reports of the famine were driven by party politics: "the 'Famine' panic sought to be created by a certain party in Ireland is a cry of faction, and not a cry for food."[81] For the politicians and political commentators whose perspectives were voiced in the *Mail*, calls for rural aid were a ruse, designed to help politicians like O'Connell consolidate power.

In much of the Irish national press in the latter months of 1845, the famine was a set piece in the larger game of politics. Through the end of 1845, the *Mail* continued to assert that "the whole movement was political—that the cry was that of party," and that the famine had been constructed as a way of undermining Peel's government.[82] Throughout 1846, when the other papers were reporting potato fields "having turned completely black," the *Mail* persisted in its campaign to establish the falseness of the famine.[83] One article cited experts who had "not been greatly struck by any appearance in starvation or misery" and argued that "there is not more than the usual, if so much, appearance of misery or destitution throughout the country."[84] After Peel's government began to acknowledge the extent of the crisis, the *Mail* rescinded its support of him, referring to "Sir Robert Peel's famine and fever mirage."[85] This opposition had much to do with the measures that Peel's government implemented in response to the famine, including the establishment of relief committees that were funded by rates levied on local landowners. The position of the *Mail*, and the politicians and political thinkers whom it represented, was that, while there was scarcity there was no famine, and while government relief in the form of public works would be a "wise and wholesome measure," radical constitutional shifts such as the repeal of laws that set the price of grain for all of Britain, or changes to Ireland's poor law, were not.

Finally, in August 1846, the *Mail* could not deny the fact of the famine any longer, reporting, "We have no hesitation, therefore, in stating the fact of a very general and well ascertained failure of the early crop of potatoes."[86] *The Nation* was particularly gleeful about this admission: "God forbid that we should be found, like our contemporary, the *Dublin Evening Mail*, shutting our eyes against the clearest evidence of the universal nature of the malady and continuing to hold out false hopes to the people, until famine has actually entered their dwellings."[87] For papers in Dublin, in the early years of the famine, proving or disproving the famine's existence was considered a political prize.

Government Relief

As the famine progressed, the British government's relief efforts continued to reflect debates about which Irish people should be prioritized, and who should have the power to dictate relief policy. The relief policies supported by the British government and its representatives in Ireland acknowledged the need for intervention and sought to place the economic burden for that intervention on tax-paying Irish landowners. Landlords, especially those in residence in Ireland, objected to relief schemes that could potentially bankrupt them, and that had the potential to provide for what they saw as unjust claimants on relief funds. Nationalists, on the other hand, both those who identified with O'Connell and those whose sympathies lay with Young Ireland, argued that if Irish funds were to support Irish relief, then the political power to dictate relief policy should lie with Ireland as well.

Once the extent of the crop failure became clear, Sir Robert Peel established a famine relief commission to organize the distribution of food across Ireland, in combination with local poor law and ad hoc relief committees. The commission was staffed by current and former members of the Irish administration, as well as Catholic elites.[88] While it implemented these measures, Peel's government renewed its opposition to gratuitous aid outside of workhouses. It also required that government funds be matched by donations by local elites and published the names of landlords who refused to contribute.[89] These measures were driven by the sheer extent of starvation. However, Peel was concerned that instituting government relief might relieve landlords of their responsibilities to attend to rural suffering; members of the commission were similarly concerned that "Irish notions" would overtake relief policy, subordinating the immediate and targeted need to administer aid to the needs of nationalist politics.[90] One of the relief commission's early plans proposed using destitution, rather than ability to work, as grounds for dispensing relief. The British government in Ireland would have far preferred relief efforts that did not require increased taxes on Irish ratepayers; they did not want their insistence that Irish landlords pay for Irish relief to be used by nationalists to argue that because all of the funds were coming from Ireland, then the dispensation of those funds should be governed by Irish politicians. In other words, they didn't want their actions to be fodder for the cohesions of an Irish nationalist identity.

The government proposed a relief scheme that relied on local charity, but allowed landlords some control over who received aid. Local committees, populated by landlords, drew up lists of destitute laborers and raised funds to help them purchase food from government depots. In 1846, the British Parliament passed legislation intended to simultaneously stimulate investment in public works and provide employment for tenants unable to farm their land.[91]

The question of who would administer famine relief in Ireland, and how it would be administered, continued to be politicized as the famine worsened. It even impacted British politics. In 1846, Robert Peel resigned after his successful repeal of the protectionist Corn Laws and his failure to pass legislation to help landlords suppress agrarian violence that caused a split within the Conservative party.[92] Peel was succeeded in July 1846 by Lord John Russell, a Whig who attempted to solve the Irish crisis with legislation that would require "Irish property to pay for Irish poverty" with limited help from the British government.

Landlords naturally wanted to know how relief funds would be raised, given the famine's disruption to their rental and agricultural income. Politicians and political commentators who were themselves landlords, or who represented landed interests, argued that those interests must be safeguarded above all else and, from that position, critiqued the government's relief measures. Before Peel stepped down, the *Dublin Evening Mail*, perhaps unsurprisingly, called for "the resident gentry [to be] allowed to wield, in all power, the magisterial functions with which they are vested" while the "loyal and peaceable yeomanry of the country" would be "enrolled and armed against the disturbances of the peace."[93] Within the framework of Anglican-Irish identity suggested by the *Mail*, landlords should be able to organize the countryside as they saw fit. Though this might include dispensing aid in select instances, the *Mail* emphatically argued that charitable relief was both a drain on landlords' coffers and detrimental to Irish society. In late 1846, it characterized "well meant measures of relief" as the "ultimate demoralization of the people."[94] It also critiqued the enforced "benevolence" of landlords, which had "burdened their estates with debt of about 7,000,000£ sterling" while failing to make significant improvements on the land and instead "answering only a very limited extent the purpose of giving relief to the destitute."[95] A letter from "An Ulster Landlord" printed in the *Mail* in November 1846 lamented that, in "trying to keep my tenantry from sinking into destitution, I am employing large numbers, paying them with borrowed money," and that "it is unjust and impolitic to join landlords of different characters in a common taxation."[96] The article cautioned that if landlords were not supported in providing relief, then the countryside would descend into further starvation and violence. One month later, in an article that seemed to represent the views of its editors, the *Mail* invoked common Irish interests, in opposition to British legislation, and argued that the interests of landlords were congruent with the interests of the nation. The article called for "combined action amongst the Irish people in matters as to which there really existed very little difference of opinion" and asserted that "the Irish population and Irish members [of parliament] ought, in a body, be prepared with the general principles which should regulate" relief legislation in the next session of parliament.[97] For those whose views the *Mail* represented, Irish national interests and the interests of landlords were one and the same.

Catholic and romantic nationalists also used these governmental relief efforts to argue for their concept of Irish political identity. An August 1846 article in the *Freeman's Journal* rejected the idea of English aid, writing that "our people demand employment, but not at the expense of England. They disdain all eleemosynary aid. They require no gratuitous benefactions and make no appeal to the charitable dispositions of England." The article cast British relief measures as extravagant and unnecessary, contending that the Irish required "only a small portion of the spoil which has been lavishly extorted from their industry."[98] *The Nation* also opposed Russell's efforts. In August 1846, it described the new modes of relief as ones in which "the police" would be "the chief agents of the English government in Ireland." The paper, like the Mansion House Committee the previous year, called for freedom for the Irish to invest in Ireland, asking, "How are industry and enterprise to grow up, when men are taught to rely upon receiving Government task work by which they may earn government rations? How are manly independence and public spirit to take root amidst a nation of beggars?"[99] Despite their political differences, the *Mail*, *The Nation* and the *Freeman's Journal* each concluded that Irish relief required Irish political autonomy, As the British government feared, contributors to these papers argued that Irish aid could only be borne by Irish shoulders if British economic and political control over Ireland was curtailed.

Extragovernmental Aid

At the same time that the British government was attempting to mitigate Irish suffering legislatively, nongovernmental organizations began to step in to provide additional relief. In the early years of the famine, three major relief organizations were housed in Dublin. These groups articulated an alternative to British relief through taxation and, consequently, represented a different perspective on who was best positioned or best able to aid the starving Irish. Each solicited aid from different donor communities and administered aid differentially, in doing so offering yet another interpretation of the ways that relief was linked to Irish national identity and obligation.

The first of these committees to form was the Irish Relief Association, in September 1846. This group was a reorganization of an 1831 committee devoted to helping distressed "peasants" in the west of Ireland. The 1846 reformation was led by the Duke of Manchester, the Earl of Roden, the Marquis of Downshire, and the Archbishop of Dublin, all of them Unionists who saw the future of Irish national politics as intertwined with the continued ascendancy of Protestants. Their political perspective was reflected in their discussion of the donors to their cause. The report, published in 1848 as the Irish Relief Association was winding down its operations, celebrated that "one of the most gratifying results of that painful crisis is that Irishmen have been taught how deeply the heart of England sympathized with their afflictions."[100] This sentiment reflected the fact that considerable contributions totaling £8149, 14 s., 11 d. were made by people living in England. For the Irish Relief Association, a connection with England had been instrumental in the work of ameliorating Irish distress.

However, despite an expressed desire to maintain connections to Britain, the men who administered the Irish Relief Association expressed a desire for national cohesion as well. They collected funds directly at the association's offices on Upper Sackville Street in Dublin, through the bankers La Touche & Co. on Castle Street, and from members of the Protestant clergy, who themselves solicited funds from parishioners. These donations came from across Ireland, though political elites were well represented. The association's final report noted that the men who collected donations "most sincerely do they hope that the day is not far distant when the gentry and peasantry of Ireland will come to a right understanding of their relative position, and of their mutual dependence on each other, and be convinced that the interests of the one are involved in the welfare and prosperity of the other."[101] In many ways, the sentiments of the Irish Relief Association with regard to their own fundraising mirrored those of Young Irelanders, who believed that Irish should come together to help each other. However, unlike either O'Connell's followers or the Young Irelanders, the association saw Irish unity as inexorably tied to England. They hoped that Irish tenants would come to appreciate the challenges of landlordism, would recognize their place at the bottom of the Irish social hierarchy, and would eventually see that Ireland ultimately benefited from a close relationship with England.

The Central Relief Committee of the Society of Friends formed shortly after the Irish Relief Association reconstituted itself. Quakers fit uncomfortably into the typology of Irish nationalism. As members of a non-Anglican church, they were subject to many of the same legal restrictions as Catholics in the eighteenth century.[102] They were also doctrinally opposed to intervening in violent conflict, thereby excluding them from militarized political agitation in 1798. They were highly critical of the British Government's famine relief policies as well. On November 13, 1846, a "meeting of men + women friends residing in Dublin + its vicinity" was called "for the purpose of considering what steps are to be taken by us, as a body, towards the relief of the widely spread distress now existing in this country."[103] The committee was ultimately comprised of twenty-one men (the women friends called for in the original appeal for participants either did not attend or were not selected) whose "commercial pursuits had brought them into intercourse with distant parts of the country."[104] This committee immediately contacted Quakers in London and in New York, who set up related committees in their respective cities.

In many ways, this committee codified efforts that were already underway across Ireland, spearheaded by Quakers in their own localities. It endeavored to supply food and clothing at no cost, instead of the subsidized schemes suggested by the British government.[105] It solicited direct reports from the Irish countryside, in order to ascertain "the real state of the more remote districts" as well as appropriate venues through which "to open suitable channels of relief."[106] The committee also corresponded with "benevolent persons in all parts of the country" as they administered relief, including interlocutors from auxiliary committees in Cork, Kinsale, Tipperary, Clare, and Waterford, as well as individuals in Donegal, Mayo, and Armagh.[107]

Like the Irish Relief Association, the Central Relief Committee collected funds from Quaker meetings across Ireland, including "Friends in Dublin and its Vicinity," as well as from "Irish families of every class, who stretched to the utmost their means, and denied themselves their usual comforts, that they might be able to relieve some of their destitute neighbors."[108] While the names of individual donors to these collective donations were not recorded, the parishes, churches, and denominations they represented reflected a diversity of Irish men and women.

Shortly after the formation of the Central Relief Committee of the Society of Friends, the Marquis of Kildare inaugurated the General

Central Relief Committee for all of Ireland. This group mirrored the Mansion House Committee, by including a range of nationalists who shared critiques of British governance but disagreed about the mechanisms or parameters of Irish independence. This committee solicited donations from across the British Empire, and the funds they raised were reported in the *Freeman's Journal*.[109] Among their donors were men who were familiar with or involved in debates about Ireland's political future, such as Edward Twistleton, the Poor Law commissioner resident in Dublin, who came to believe that the British government was drastically overspending in Ireland and gave £100.[110] Nationalists were also well represented. Michael Staunton, a Catholic newspaper owner, served on committees of O'Connell's Repeal Association and donated both to the Central Relief Committee of the Society of Friends and the General Central Relief Committee. Charles Patrick Meehan, a Catholic priest who was alternately aligned with both O'Connell and the Young Irelanders, and Reverend John Walsh, of Dublin's Augustinian Friary, who attended repeal meetings throughout the 1840s, both gave. James Rooney, a merchant and occasional participant in repeal organizing, and John Kehsan, a city alderman and merchant, gave £1 and £5, respectively. Henry Grattan Jr., a member of the Mansion House Committee, MP for Dublin and later for County Meath, and the son of the Henry Grattan who had campaigned for Irish legislative independence in the eighteenth century, gave a total of £50 to the General Central Relief Committee in the later years of the famine.

Members of the Irish gentry also gave. Among the attendees at a January 1847 meeting of "Peers, Representatives and Gentry of Ireland" calling for the government to "advocate such measures as may appear calculated to raise the social, material, and moral condition of the people, to save society from the ruin by which all classes in the land are now threatened," were Luke Corr, a wine merchant and member of the Irish gentry; Cecil Lawless, the MP for Clonmel; and others.[111] These men appealed to the British government as a collective of Irishmen, temporarily centering national identity as a part of appeals for aid, which they cemented with private funds. The work of these committees shifted the responsibility for relieving the starving away from the government and onto other Irish people. In this way, they conformed to the Mansion House Committee's early contention that if the Irish were able to accrue sufficient resources, they would be the ones best positioned to aid their countrymen and women.

The early rhetoric of these various Irish relief associations might give the impression of a cohesive Irish identity, manifested through philanthropy. Indeed, in the early years of the famine *The Nation* had appealed to the "Protestants of Ireland" that "we have one common enemy at our doors—Famine."[112] After establishing the common interests of Irish Catholics and Protestants, the editorial went on: "The country where our laws are made is suddenly left without a responsible government, at the very moment when the gravest of all duties which devolve upon a government are pressing to be discharged—with hunger threatening the poor—murder and social disorganization frightening the rich."[113] In these early months, *The Nation* had attempted to make an argument for a far-reaching definition of the Irish nation, in which the interests of the landed elite and cottiers alike were linked, and that tied famine relief to those shared interests. According to *The Nation*, "The one great political lesson, yet to be learned in Ireland is, that we can do one another justice if we will."[114]

The *Freeman's Journal* also repeatedly called, in the early years of the famine, for a coordinated effort between the landed and the peasant classes. In August 1846, the *Freeman's Journal* said of the famine that "the evil being one of magnitude, can only be met by the most vigorous and well-considered efforts" by both "those who hold the reigns of power" and those who did not.[115] According to the *Freeman's Journal*, the perspective that "the interest of the tenant and the interest of the landlords" are "not only things different, but opposed to each other" had contributed to the present state of Ireland.[116] Appeals to national conviviality continued throughout 1846 in both nationalist papers, in calls for abandonment of feuds that pitted "landlord against tenant, tenant against landlord—class against class, interest against interest."[117]

The more conservative writers in the *Dublin Evening Mail*, however, tended to view philanthropic efforts as an attack on the Protestant aristocracy. Just as the *Mail* was slow to accept the extent of the famine because its editors initially believed that the entire narrative of starvation was a political ploy, so, too, did the *Mail* come to describe relief as a conflict between those who were in "possession of property" and those who had "the active desire to possess it at any cost."[118] In early 1847, it criticized the "miserable delusions" of "the ignorant peasantry" who believed that "because the Government and their landlords have undertaken to provide for a sudden (it is hoped) temporary calamity, the same system of eleemosynary relief must be continued."[119] This is not to say that the people who wrote for and edited the *Mail* disapproved of private philanthropy, freely given. It cast the Irish Relief Association as "the most efficient confederation ever formed in these countries for the benevolent purposes on a large scale" and appealed to readers to "call the attention of the humane and opulent" to that organization's calls for donations.[120] For the *Mail* and its readers, depriving landlords of political power and requiring them through British laws to fund relief efforts both resulted in financial losses and exacerbated the problem of rural Irish starvation. This broadly reflected a Unionist perspective on Irish politics: that famine relief should protect Anglo-Irish landlords, who should in turn hold Irish political power.

Due to this attitude, as well as other factors, in the later years of the famine, sympathy for Irish landlords in the nationalist press abated considerably. In March 1848, *The Nation* remarked that "we are tired of exhorting men to duty who have neither sense of shame, faculty of preservation, nor spirit of resistance. Here, last week, they have had an instance of Imperial arrogance enough to rouse the dead founders of their houses into action."[121] Four months later, the paper officially renounced the cause of national conviviality, noting that, though "we had a vision of universal Ireland arising in her unity and strength to assert her rights as a nation among the nations," the Irish landed class had behaved "at best" like "some scornful patron who fed [the Irish people] like his dogs with human contempt, at worst a pack of wolves ready to devour them for a meal."[122] In failing to engage in the work of relief, nationalists argued, Irish landlords and their allies had effectively revealed that their interests were not the same as those of the majority of Irish men and women. Famine relief had been a test of Irish landlords' ability to consider shared national identity. In failing to meet the needs of non-elite Irish men and women, they had, according to Young Irelanders, forsaken their right to be considered as part of the Irish nation and, consequently, forsaken their claims to political power.

Private relief efforts might have provided an opportunity for different Irish political interests to come together, realizing the romantic nationalist dreams of Young Irelanders. Ultimately, however, a coalition was neither practically nor rhetorically sustainable, as Irish leaders and political commentators increasingly saw the issue of famine relief as useful in promoting varying visions of the Irish nation. Whether there was a famine at all, what action the British government ought to take, and who should be obligated to contribute funds to aid suffering Irishmen and women were all filtered through the dominant political frameworks of the time. Nationalists specifically critiqued British policy as charity and hence as a tool for control. Unionists often argued both that Britain was obligated to aid Ireland—particularly landlords—and that Ireland benefited from its association with Britain. Romantic Nationalists hoped for national conviviality, but were often stymied by class antagonism.

When news of the famine crossed the Irish sea this politicization continued. Instead of the issue of Irish national identity, however, commentators saw the issue of famine relief as a way to achieve long-desired legislative reforms.

2

Food and Free Trade

At the same time that Ireland's major newspapers were debating whether the failure of the potato crop would cause a famine, the Anti–Corn Law League was holding meetings in Manchester. Thousands of people from Manchester and neighboring towns attended; hundreds more were turned away at the door.[1] The Anti–Corn Law League had been founded in 1836 to oppose laws that purported to regulate grain prices within Britain, but that had come to serve as protections for domestic British products. While these laws safeguarded the profits of British farmers, they in turn made grain more expensive for British purchasers (the term "corn" expansively included many different kinds of grain). The Anti–Corn Law League campaigned for these laws to be repealed and for British grain to be traded freely. The League's members numbered in the thousands, including financiers and people with social influence, as well middle-class merchants and laborers.[2] It sought to bring together all residents of the British Isles who were victimized by restricted trade.[3]

At a meeting in late October 1845, Richard Cobden—radical MP, famous orator, and advocate for Corn Law repeal—explicitly incorporated Ireland into the League's project.[4] In front of thousands, he took the floor and "started at once into the object of the meeting," which was "to point out the remedy for the famine which threatened our own island, and to avert the misery, starvation, and death of millions in Ireland." According to Cobden, "the natural and obvious remedy" to this distress "was to open the ports."[5] For Cobden and other Anti–Corn Law League members, it was clear from the start that the famine would soon impact Britain, that restrictions on the sale of food would cause distress across the British Isles, and that abolishing the Corn Laws would mitigate against the forthcoming misery. In short, they saw famine relief and free trade as one and the same.

Cobden's arguments at the Manchester meeting were part of a loose Liberal consensus that linked Irish food shortages to free trade, free trade to British economic welfare, and British economic welfare back to the need for a government policy that would allow Irish people to feed themselves without becoming a burden on the state.[6] Liberal politicians' use of the famine as part of a suite of arguments for free trade has been well documented by historians, who point out that their interest was often more political than humanitarian.[7] Rather than focus on men like Cobden, this chapter instead explores the ways that Liberal rhetoric shaped debates about humanitarian obligation outside of formal political spaces, in Liberal-leaning newspapers published outside of London which deployed the famine as part of their arguments about British economic policy. Just as writers for *The Nation*, the *Freeman's Journal*, and the *Dublin Evening Mail* had used the question of who was obligated to provide Irish relief as a touchstone for debates about Irish national identity, Liberal and Liberal-adjacent newspapers like the *Liverpool Mercury*, the *Manchester Guardian*, and the *Glasgow Herald* used the possibility of Irish starvation to argue for a fundamental realignment of British economic policy, away from protectionism and toward laissez-faire capitalism.

British Liberals are often characterized as having privileged their commitment to laissez-faire capitalism over the needs of the starving Irish.[8] Residents of provincial British cities that experienced large-scale famine emigration are frequently represented as extremely hostile to Irish immigrants.[9] While these characterizations are broadly true, this chapter argues that co-opting the famine in debates about the Corn Laws produced a short-lived moment in which commentators in the provincial Liberal and Liberal-adjacent press were able to rhetorically cast the Irish as members of a wider British community in an attempt to argue that the welfare of all Britons was the proper concern of British government. In doing so, they positioned humanitarianism toward the Irish as synonymous with British interests. In other words, using famine relief for politics had unintended humanitarian consequences.

Politicians and political commentators who lived and worked in Britain's growing industrial cities had a particular stake in an expansive understanding of the constituency to which the British government was responsible. In 1845, male, propertied residents of cities like Liverpool, Manchester, and Glasgow had only recently gained political representation. Despite this expansion of the franchise, in the 1840s the British Parliament still seemed primarily focused on the concerns of Londoners and landed elites. Newly enfranchised men, including Cobden, were hungry for legislation and governance that recognized the needs of middle-class merchants, tenants, industrial workers, and other Britons who were neither Londoners nor substantial rural landowners. The repeal of the Corn Laws was one such piece of legislation. The extremity of Irish distress was a useful example of the kind of relief that trade reform could offer. Commentators in the Liberal and Liberal-adjacent press put famine relief to two rhetorical uses. The first was in arguments for the repeal of the Corn Laws; the second was part of a call to reform the Irish Poor Law. In each case, the need for relief of the Irish was effectively deployed in arguments for government reform and the expansion of the concept of Britishness.

Provincial Papers and Liberal Politics

The ways that the *Mercury*, the *Herald*, and the *Guardian* reported on the famine were shaped both by the cities in which they were published, and by the cohesion of reform-oriented Liberal politics. In the late eighteenth century, as a consequence of the industrial revolution, Manchester, Liverpool, and Glasgow, formerly ancillaries to London, became booming industrial cities at the center of British economic activity.[10] They underwent a transformation from small towns, provincial in every sense of the word, into the most populous cities in Britain, excepting London.[11] As these cities grew, their residents began to feel left out of the British political system, and they started to critique the structures of political distribution that allotted boroughs in the "home counties" surrounding London two members of Parliament to represent twenty-three people, but allotted no members to represent the residents of the rapidly growing industrial cities. Residents of these cities also began to protest property restrictions that left many self-styled middle-class men with no vote at all; they called for lower or no property restrictions on voting and for parliamentary representation befitting their populations.

In 1832, the Whig government led by Charles Grey passed the Great Reform Act, which lowered the value of property qualifications for voters from £100 to £10, expanded the British electorate from approximately 400,000 to approximately 650,000, and redistributed parliamentary seats from "rotten boroughs"—districts with few voters, in which uncontested elections tended to deliver power to the local gentry—to the industrial cities. For the first time, many voters in these cities felt that their political interests were being directly represented. What's more, those who still did not have access to the vote, including the women who had been explicitly excluded from the franchise under the Great Reform Act, felt empowered to agitate for political power.[12] Richard Cobden and many other Liberal politicians came into office in the Act's aftermath. The 1832 expansion of the male electorate heralded the beginning of an era of reform and the rise of a Liberal coalition that would shape British politics for decades to come.[13]

Political agitation also shaped journalism. The major newspapers of these cities encouraged new voters' interest in popular political participation and redefined themselves in the course of the movement for government reform.[14] The campaign for the passage of the 1832 act was instrumental in this transformation, as it convinced newspaper editors not only of the power of their publications but also of the necessity for a wide variety of British interests to be expressed in the political arena.[15] The *Guardian*, the *Mercury*, and the *Herald* were all products of this political moment.

The three papers differed in some ways, but they agreed in their promotion of Liberal economic policies. The *Liverpool Mercury*, founded in 1811, was a Liberal newspaper in a broadly conservative city that aimed to represent local and regional issues, news from London and abroad, and mainstream Liberal political opinions. Its readership spanned Liverpool, Lancashire County, Cheshire, and North Wales.[16] The *Manchester Guardian*, a reform-oriented paper published in an overwhelmingly Liberal city, had been founded after the British government attempted to censor accounts of the Petterloo Massacre, the British cavalry's attack on a crowd of pro-reform protesters in Manchester in 1819.[17] The *Guardian*'s editors and authors sought to more directly appeal to readers who would "warmly advocate the cause of Reform" and to "endeavor to assist in the diffusion of just principles of Political Economy."[18] The *Glasgow Herald* was in many ways a conservative paper, rejecting many of the demands of parliamentary reform, but in favor of the same economic interventions.[19] Founded in 1803, it was initially published and edited by Samuel Hunter, a Tory who saw part of the mission of the

Herald as conveying a conservative point of view to a city with strong Liberal sympathies.[20] The paper broke with conservative orthodoxy in its criticism of the Corn Laws, however, and in later years also came to support Scottish Nationalism.[21] These three newspapers were the most highly circulated publications in their localities, and the news and opinions they printed would have reached between six thousand and eleven thousand readers per week. Collectively, their editors and authors sought to sway the reading public to the cause of reform, particularly to the repeal of the Corn Laws.

Free Trade Ideologies

The Corn Laws were passed by the British Parliament in 1815 in order to regulate grain prices within the United Kingdom—including Ireland— and protect British domestic producers. They levied a tariff on foreign grain until British grain reached a set price, making it difficult for consumers to purchase cheap food but ensuring consistent profits for British farmers and landlords. Although landholders and MPs with agricultural constituencies supported the maintenance of a protectionist policy, by the 1840s successive prime ministers with a variety of political identities had come to believe that the Corn Laws should be gradually repealed to allow a free flow of goods throughout the United Kingdom. British merchants were keen to participate in international trade without penalty; factory owners thought that repealing the Corn Laws could make grain cheaper and reduce food prices, enabling them to stagnate workers' wages. Meanwhile, workers in England, Ireland, Scotland, and Wales hoped for access to more affordable food.

The Anti–Corn Law League drew these constituencies together through a commitment to the political philosophy of a group known as the Manchester school. These political economists, led by Richard Cobden and John Bright, advocated for free trade, unfettered access to commerce, and a spirit of rugged British economic individualism. Whereas the Corn Laws protected the economic interests of landowners, their repeal, these men argued, benefited a wider swath of Mancunian and, indeed, British society.[22] Cobden, the Manchester school, and the Anti–Corn Law League asserted that it was the responsibility of government to create conditions in which Britons could thrive economically, without restriction. Creating these conditions would require the government to briefly intervene in the workings of the economy, removing limitations to sustenance in order to allow the unfettered development of British—including Irish—economic welfare. In short, they believed that Parliament should correct ills of its own making and meet the needs of a more expansive British constituency.

Before the famine, Ireland was already a feature in Anti–Corn Law rhetoric. In the early and mid-nineteenth century, an increasing share of grain consumed in Britain was produced in Ireland.[23] This increase was a consequence of improvements in agricultural technologies as well as the marginalization of Irish tenant farmers. As Irish landlords increasingly relegated their tenants to poor land that could not support grain (but could support potatoes), they were able to continue to extract rents while devoting the best land to wheat production for the British markets outside of Ireland.[24]

In response to these conditions, reformers pointed out the danger that the Corn Laws posed to Ireland. By prohibiting the importation of cheap foreign grain, the laws made it impossible for many poor Irish men and women to afford any food other than the potato. One radical newspaper noted that the Irish tenants who labored in agriculture were effectively asked to engage in protectionism that punished them and "to join in reducing the price of the only thing they produce—for the purpose of cheapening the thing of which they never consume a particle."[25] In February 1842, in a speech opposing the Corn Laws in the House of Commons, Cobden referenced the state of the Irish tenantry, asking, "What is the state of the poor in Ireland?" and answering, "One-third of the people of Ireland are perishing for want of the common necessities of life."[26]

The Anti–Corn Law League sponsored a series of lectures across Ireland articulating these points that drew thousands of people and garnered tens of thousands of signatures for Corn Law repeal.[27] Daniel O'Connell publicly supported these campaigns, which were also bolstered by the combined interests of merchants, manufacturers, and workers who saw the repeal of the Corn Laws as essential to the future of Irish industry.

By 1842, foreign grain was selling in Britain for roughly the same price as British grain. The British prime minister, Robert Peel, used this parity to begin to argue for the gradual repeal of some tariffs on foreign imports. Peel believed that British economic security was linked to an increase in working class Britons' purchasing power, and that repealing the Corn Laws would mitigate tensions not only between landlords and tenants but also between industrialists and workers in Ireland and in Britain.[28] The potato failure, when it appeared in the autumn of 1845, tested these beliefs.

Corn Laws and Famine Relief

After the onset of the famine, the *Glasgow Herald* and the *Liverpool Mercury* consistently linked Irish hunger to the Corn Laws. On October 17, 1845, the *Mercury* reprinted the contents of a circular distributed by the grain merchants Fowler and Tunnicliffe, which reported that "yesterday's post brought us from parties in Ireland (on whose statements we can place complete reliance) very grievous accounts of the Potato crops!" The circular went on to note that "the only mitigating feeling which arises under such circumstances, is the conviction, that, considering our vast population, the glaring insanity of our makescarce bread law, with all its feltering, withering effect upon commercial enterprise, and all its biting tendency upon those whose means are scanty will become more and more apparent."[29] If any good was to come from Irish starvation, the circular noted, and the *Mercury* affirmed, it would be to reveal the absurdity of protectionist laws. Three weeks later, the *Mercury* commented that the result of relying on a protectionist policy was obvious when "the deficiency of this year's harvest, concurrently with the failure of the potato crop" had "necessitated a result to those foreign supplies." The article went on to note that Britons were "crying out for the total and instant repeal of the corn law," and that such a cry would soon become visceral, "without even waiting for the formalities of legislation."[30] The *Glasgow Herald* similarly proclaimed that "great efforts are made to persuade the people that famine is impending" in Ireland, "and that the opening of the ports"—a common metaphor for easing restrictions on the importation of foreign grain—"without a moment's delay" would be "the only means offered to prevent starvation and misery and disease."[31] The editors of and writers for both papers were quick to draw on the evidence of the famine in their campaign for Corn Law repeal.

The papers also emphasized the ways that a crop failure in Ireland would impact Britain. On October 20, 1845, the *Herald* stated that the "malady" had "made extensive inroads into the potato crop in several districts of Ireland" and, similarly, "to many parts of England and Scotland."[32] A few days later, the *Mercury* likewise warned that the crop failure threatened "to a greater or less extent in all parts of the United Kingdom." Without raising an alarm, the article also noted that there were "ample reasons to fear that the value of bread stuffs may rise to an extent to occasion some inconvenience to the poorer classes."[33] The following week, the *Mercury* linked the Irish crisis to food prices in England, reporting that "holders of Irish corn had refused to sell except at very high terms," and that Irish grain was no longer an affordable alternative to wheat grown in Britain.[34] The *Guardian* warned that, without "a permanent and also immediate change in our fiscal system," England would come to be known as a place where laws were "framed to make food scarce and dear—as the corn laws unquestionably do" and might in future be "subjected to famine by an act of parliament."[35] In the months between the onset of famine and the repeal of the Corn Laws, the Liberal and Liberal-adjacent press encouraged readers to see the Irish as a part of the British community and, consequently, to see Irish and British welfare not as separate, but as fundamentally intertwined. From this perspective, a more prosperous future for all Britons was contingent upon the repeal of "makescare bread laws."

In making the claim that the Irish ought to be included in the constituency of Britons, commentators acknowledged that their inclusion was not a foregone conclusion. This instability made it possible to leverage particular Irish interests while still attending to British needs. The reporting in these papers made it clear that the British broadly, and Irish people particularly, demanded government intervention and a fundamental reorganization of the relations between economic policies and the welfare of British and Irish subjects. Reformulating the question of Irish relief in terms of a cohesive British people in opposition to Parliament was an important aspect of arguments in favor of Corn Law repeal. This type of argument was familiar to writers and readers who only a decade earlier had fought for their own political representation. The people who produced and bought these papers were familiar with the experience of being excluded from politics, of being governed by a distant parliament, and of having their political agency undermined by decisions in London. They had this in common with the Irish as well.

The papers demanded not merely awareness of the problems caused by the Corn Laws, but government action as well. The *Manchester Guardian* called for Parliament to "adopt the only measures which give a hope of preserving the people from the horrors of famine" and to reverse the balance of trade by which "at the present time large quantities of potatoes are exported from the south and west of Ireland to the south of England, and to Rotterdam and Antwerp whilst the supplies of food coming into the country are quite insignificant."[36] Further, its editors argued, "we think it probable . . . that ministers, looking at the failure of the potato crop in Ireland, and the increased prices of all kinds of food in England and Scotland, may have come to the conclusion that something must be done" in the direction of free trade.[37] The *Liverpool Mercury* similarly expressed the hope that parliamentary action in 1846 would include "a larger and bolder measure of commercial reform than any way which we have yet witnessed."[38] The *Glasgow Herald* posited that "the efforts of the Government, aided by the benevolence of private individuals, [would] be required to avert the horrors of an impending national calamity."[39] The *Guardian*, however, took a different view, opining that private charity was not the solution to Irish distress: given "the present state of public feeling with reference to the corn-laws, we hardly think that it would do for the government to leave the people of Ireland to the chance of what may be obtained for them through the medium of a public subscription. Other and more decisive measures of relief must be adopted or the condition of the people in many parts of Ireland will be frightful indeed."[40]

By late 1845, dissatisfaction with the government's response to the Irish crisis had spilled from the pages of these radical newspapers into the streets. In addition to Cobden's meeting in Manchester, the *Herald* reported that "a public meeting of the citizens of Glasgow was held in the Merchant's hall," at which speakers argued that "looking at the present high prices of provisions, and their prospective scarcity arising from the destruction of that description of food on which so many millions of our fellow subjects depend for their food, we respectfully request that your Lordship will, on an early day, convene a meeting of the citizens to consider the propriety of memorializing Sir Robert Peel to issue an order in Council, for opening the ports for the admission of grains and other provisions, free of duty."[41]

At the same time, the Anti–Corn Law League undertook a vast campaign, much like it had done in the early 1840s, to educate the public on the virtues of laissez-faire economic principles.[42] It held meetings in London and across the rest of Britain, funded speeches by leading advocates for repeal, and arranged for letters to be published in sympathetic newspapers such as the *Guardian*. These events additionally reinforced connections between the famine and the necessity of repeal and between the economic well-being of Ireland and Britain. At one meeting Cobden claimed that the Irish famine was a "gaunt specter" that "set at naught all the contrivances and delays and moderation of statesmen."[43] W. J. Fox, an equally ardent free-trader, claimed that "Providence never yet sent a universal famine," and that "it is wicked—we might say blasphemous—that those who raise the price of corn should thus attempt to transfer the opprobrium of their own iniquitous doings to the Divine Government."[44] These arguments challenged the beliefs that the famine was either natural or divinely ordained; rather, Cobden and Fox argued, it was a product of bad government policy. By refusing to admit foreign grains tariff-free, the government was constricting the supply of food and putting it out of reach of those who were suffering. By 1846, the famine was deeply integrated into discourses about contemporary politics, in particular discourses about the responsibilities of governments to their subjects. Free trade could not be accomplished without a vote in Parliament (although readers were encouraged to participate in extraparliamentary events that were meant to nudge MPs in the right direction). Because government policy had made this a crisis, only government policy could provide relief to the Irish. If that relief took the form of Corn Law repeal, it would have the happy effect of aiding other Britons as well.

Although historians debate whether it was the high-political machinations of MPs or the actions of extraparliamentary groups like the Anti–Corn Law League that brought about the repeal of the Corn Laws, most agree that the acute crisis of the Irish famine hastened the decision.[45] In October 1845, Peel lamented that "the accounts of the state of the potato-crop in Ireland are becoming very alarming" and posited that "the removal of impediments to import is the only effectual remedy."[46] Later that year, before the full impact of the blight was truly felt in either Ireland or England, Peel wrote that it would be politically impossible to "vote public money for the sustenance for any considerable portion of the people [of Ireland] on account of actual or apprehended scarcity" while maintaining "in full operation the existing restrictions on the free import of grain."[47] He then recommended a variety of measures, including that either the Corn Laws be suspended and the ports temporarily opened, or that the Corn Laws be gradually reduced. In December 1845, Peel decided on the latter, announcing that the laws would be repealed over a period of three years.[48] Some members of the Conservative Party reacted strongly against this. Others supported Peel's actions. The party split, and, in the summer of 1846, Peel resigned, and Lord John Russell formed a Liberal government.

By the time, in 1846 and 1847, when Irish crop failures worsened, and when it became clear that Russell's relief measures were insufficient to mitigate death, writers for the *Herald*, the *Mercury*, and the *Guardian* had long since established a link between free trade, British economic welfare, and famine mitigation. This link would have consequences for the Liberal and Liberal-adjacent press's treatment of the question of further Irish relief.

Reforming the Irish Poor Laws

The gradual repeal of the Corn Laws began in 1846, but it was not enough to stem the increasingly worsening tide of the famine. In late 1846 and 1847, many Irish men and women were no longer able to eke out a living in Ireland. Others might have wanted to stay but were evicted by landlords who no longer wanted to depend on rents for their income. These displaced Irish began to emigrate, and the very tangible consequences of famine began to pour into Manchester, Liverpool, and Glasgow. It is something of a truism that the British response to the Irish famine was solidified by immigration, and that the rise of "Little Ireland" slums, the spread of fever and disease, and the inability of British public health systems to cope with thousands of new inhabitants provoked a "racial hibernophobia" that would color British opinions of the Irish well into the twentieth century.[49] While anti-Irish animus was a feature of British cities in the decades after the famine, in the

late 1840s, the major newspapers in British industrial cities continued
to emphasize Britons' obligations to Irish famine victims as a way to
improve life in Britain and in Ireland. Consequently, arguments about
the ideal way to relieve Irish suffering continued to be used in arguments for government reform.

Many British cities already had entrenched Irish populations at the
start of the famine. Some of these were permanent residents, while others were seasonal labor migrants who came to Britain to work but re-
turned to Ireland at regular intervals.[50] Irish immigrants were, like all
other residents of Britain, subject to the provisions of the 1834 English
and Scottish Poor Laws, which required local authorities to provide immediate relief to people in desperate need. They did not require officials
to provide long-term relief, however; in fact, they required that "able-
bodied" paupers be sent back to their home parish, to receive aid there.[51]

The waves of immigrants who arrived between 1846 and 1852 significantly expanded extant communities.[52] This expansion was most
dramatic in Liverpool. Between 1841 and 1851, the Irish population in
Liverpool nearly doubled. Of the 225,003 people who lived in Liverpool in 1841, 49,639 were Irish. By 1851, though the total population
had only increased by 32,052, the Irish population had increased by
33,674 people. Manchester and Glasgow experienced similar balloon-
ing of their Irish populations. In 1841, Manchester had 192,403 residents, 33,490 of whom were Irish. By 1851 the overall population of
Manchester had increased by 36,014 people, a considerable portion of
whom—19,014—were Irish. Although the Irish did not represent such
a dramatic proportion of Glasgow's increased population between 1841
and 1851, their community expanded by tens of thousands. Glasgow's
population increased from 308,275 to 390,373 between 1841 and 1851,
and the Irish population increased from 44,345 to 59,801.[53] This flood
of new residents increased pressure on already strained public health
resources, requiring as it did that thousands of new people be provided
with a temporary means of sustaining life while within the boundaries
of the cities.

These waves of immigration into Liverpool, Manchester and Glasgow
occasioned a shift in the content of news about Ireland, but not in the
framing of that news. With the issue of the Corn Laws settled, editors of and writers for the *Manchester Guardian*, the *Liverpool Mercury*,

and the *Glasgow Herald* began to take on the issue of domestic reforms that would materially aid victims of famine. Their reporting continued to rely on assumptions established by the papers' characterization of the repeal of the Corn Laws as essential for both Irish relief and British economic prosperity. This conceptual framework made possible the promulgation of solutions to the Irish crisis that relied on government obligation through intervention, rather than blaming the Irish themselves.

Between 1846 and 1849, almost every issue of each of these papers described the arrival of masses of Irish paupers. The language they used frequently referred to the Irish as a collective body, a framing that allowed the papers to focus on structural remedies instead of on the decisions of individual Irish people. For example, the *Mercury* described immigrants' entrenchment in Liverpool in an April 1847 article, lamenting that "for several days past the Union Workhouse in this town has been literally besieged by half-clad and miserable looking objects."[54] Similarly, the *Herald* cast immigrants as "daily being poured in upon the several parishes of Glasgow."[55] Although a descriptor such as "besieged" certainly had negative connotations, nowhere in these articles are individual Irish immigrants described as anything other than destitute unfortunates. One article in the *Mercury* described these men, women and children as "poor creatures" who had "paid their rent regularly" but were ejected by landlords nevertheless.[56] The *Guardian* reprinted an article from the *Liverpool Times* that described emigrants as victims of "heartless cruelty."[57] Even in an article concerned with the "pauper invasion of England," Irish immigrants were rhetorically cast as beleaguered, "pouring into Great Britain with hunger in their van and disease in their train."[58] If the Irish as a collective were an invading force, it was an unintentional one. Irish people were described as swept up in a harrowing process of famine, rather than as actively pursuing the invasion of British cities.

One of the most immediately obvious consequences of Irish immigration in these years was the incidence of "famine fever," or "Irish fever," and yet even this was portrayed as a collective British problem to be solved. Many of the emigrants had existed in a state of acute starvation long before they left Ireland, and the conditions of "little Irelands" within these cities was conducive to the spread of illness.[59] In the face of this, the *Guardian*, the *Mercury*, and the *Herald* expressed concerns both for the immigrants who arrived sick and for the communities that were forced to care for them. The *Guardian* printed a letter in May 1846 describing "an evicted Irish family . . . one of the exterminated families in Ireland" who was under the care of the Manchester overseers of the poor.[60] In January 1847, the *Mercury* described "the daily arrival of Irish paupers most of whom are landed in a miserable state of destitution, and require immediate relief."[61] Two weeks later, it reported the provision of outdoor relief to the "Irish poor" and described as "frightful" the "painful and most costly task to encounter, of keeping them alive, if possible."[62] In June of that year, the *Herald* warned of the dangers that "many thousands of disease and starving Irish" would pose to Glasgow.[63] What was needed, these papers suggested, was a better system of public health for Ireland and reform of the Irish Poor Law. Such a system would indirectly aid the cities who were currently administering aid to the sick and destitute Irish.

Poor Laws in Ireland and in England were designed to mitigate as much as possible the burden that poor people placed on the state. Between 1838 and 1847, the principle aim of the Poor Law in Ireland was to limit the number of roving destitute without a significant investment by the government.[64] It did not guarantee the rights of Irish subjects to relief under any circumstances except through workhouses. This policy was known as the workhouse test, because the conditions in workhouses "tested" the extremity of applicants' destitution; they were designed to be so miserable that only people in true distress would want to enter them. Only the non-able-bodied were entitled to outdoor relief, while those who were capable were forced to work for their food.[65] This conservatism was based on British officials' assumptions that the introduction of a wider-ranging Poor Law, one that offered relief to the able-bodied poor as well as the destitute, would simply invite the Irish to abuse the state's generosity.[66] The newspapers in these cities were concerned, however, with the temporary nature of relief measures, particularly because Irish paupers were coming to rely on Poor Law relief in British cities when they could not find sustenance at home. These papers advocated for a better-regulated, more expansive system of poor relief in Ireland, such that Irish immigrants could return to their own parishes, to be cared for by the own representatives of "Irish property."

From the period right after the repeal of the Corn Laws, arguments that "the Irish peasantry will, in all probability, again be without food; and government must provide for them," and that "the calamity must be regarded as continuous, and as such we must legislate for it" peppered *Guardian* articles concerned with Ireland.[67] Not only was the British government responsible for remedying the state of Ireland "with legislation," but the overseers of public health in British cities should also be concerned with the health of the Irish, in Britain as well as in Ireland. If the Irish Poor Law was not reformed, Irish paupers would continue to arrive in England and Scotland and become subject to British aid until they were healthy. Then they would be sent back to Ireland, only to return to Britain when they were not able to eke out a living with local support. Just as these papers argued that the British government had been responsible for relief via the legislative removal of the Corn Laws, so, too, did they contend that Parliament was responsible for passing legislation that allowed for the more effective relief of the Irish poor as their constituents. Such relief would also aid the residents of British cities who had undertaken the relief of famine immigrants.

In the meantime, however, these papers called on English and Scottish people to aid the Irish until such legislation was passed. It was, after all, the responsibility of city residents to prevent the immigrants from "imminent risk of starvation."[68] An article in the *Liverpool Mercury* argued that "we cannot compel the destitute Irish to return to their own land, unless the charitable aid they seek is from the parish." Moreover, "a good Poor Law must be the basis of all social amelioration in that country. The right to live *must, ante omnia, be secured to the peasant by law.*"[69] If the Irish Poor Law would not protect Irish peasants, then it fell on fellow Britons to provide succor. In late 1846, the *Manchester Guardian* again made reference to the "vast numbers of Irish poor [who] had begun to pour into this country."[70] However, the article went on, "in the present state of the Irish Poor Law there are no means of checking this heartless cruelty, for out door relief is not permitted in Ireland, and all the workhouses crowded to overflowing, the overseers of Liverpool cannot send the poor creatures back without exposing them to imminent risk of starvation."[71]

Critique was also leveled at Irish landlords. One of the most overt of these came in the *Mercury*, which argued both that "we have ever

contended that a good Poor Law must be the basis of all social amelioration in that country," and that "death by starvation is but legal murder,
so long as a shilling of rent continues to be pocketed by the landlord."[72]
Irish landlords were also blamed for the immediate conditions of the
cities. The *Mercury*, writing in mid-1847, claimed to speak for all residents of Liverpool, who "have now a duty to perform what it may
appear harsh in us to recommend to special and immediate attention,
but it is imperative upon all of us, no less from a politic consideration
for the poor destitute Irish themselves, than for our own safety and our
own emancipation from an oppressive and dangerous grievance, which
the selfishness of the Irish landlords has thrown upon us, and which the
apathy of Government has too long, and very shamefully, permitted us
to suffer."[73] It was in the best interests of the Irish, and of the citizens
of Liverpool, who would be freed "from an unjust load of taxation, and
from the deteriorating example of idleness and filthy habits, which has
squatted itself among our own humbler classes" for Irish Landlords to
become accountable to their former tenants.[74]

In 1847, Parliament passed the Irish Poor Law Extension act, which
recognized the right of every destitute person in Ireland to relief, regardless of whether they had entered a workhouse or poorhouse. It
permitted the provision of outdoor relief, including food, lodging,
medicine and medical attention.[75] After the act was passed, the responsibility to Irish paupers was transferred from Britain as a whole
and placed specifically on Irish shoulders, and provincial newspapers
began to be convinced that their former wards would be well cared
for under the new legislation. This transition has long been read as the
ultimate British government refusal to become involved in Irish public
health issues. Irish taxes would henceforth pay for all Irish relief, and
Irish commissioners would be responsible for the disbursement of that
relief on the ground. Perhaps best of all for Liberal politicians, Irish
paupers could more easily be sent back to Ireland to request aid from
their own parishes. However, the passage of the Poor Law Extension
Act was interpreted in the Liberal and Liberal-adjacent press not as a
limiting of government responsibility, but as the appropriate yet much-
belated introduction of coherent and adequate systems of public health
to Ireland, one that benefited Britain as well. This interpretation, like
the construction of Corn Law repeal, relied on the assumption that

provincial Britons and Irish people belonged to the same community, such that relief for a part was a cause of celebration for the whole. By focusing on the roles that the British government had played and could play in setting Ireland to rights, these newspapers were advocating for a narrative that cast the Irish as victims of government policy, the injustice of which should, ironically perhaps, be remedied by government policy.

In parallel with government policy changes, the Liberal provincial press celebrated private charity toward famine migrants. This charity was necessary, they argued, because of the slow government response to the problem. And yet it was laudable, reflecting positively on donors while making material improvements in immigrants' lives. As a member of the Manchester and Salford Soup kitchen, which provided food to Irish paupers, insisted, "Those hearts which have felt so deeply for Ireland, cannot be shut against the claim of the poor in their own streets. One effort more, and the committee trust in God prosperity and plenty will again gladden our land."[76] The *Mercury* applauded the citizens of Liverpool, noting that "they have exerted themselves to feed the starving thousands cast upon their shores from Ireland; they have opened their hospitals to the sick, and taken means to provide fresh accommodation for the increasing number of patients."[77] The *Manchester Guardian* echoed this perspective when it reported the arrival of "another large importation of Irish paupers, admitting to about two hundred, thirty of whom were in a dying state, and were it not for the prompt aid rendered by the humane and skillful, they would have died of starvation soon after touching English ground."[78] These celebrations of local humanitarianism resonated with discussions of Ireland during the campaign to repeal the Corn Laws: they imagined Ireland as part of a community of Britons, with responsibilities to one another, who were obligated to appeal to the government on behalf of a subset in service of better treatment for all.

While it might be surprising that narratives of free trade and the necessity of government support were so closely intertwined around the Irish famine, that very intertwining suggests the vital role that famine relief played in helping to define Liberal ideology in provincial Britain. It also suggests that the politics of free trade were fundamentally connected to the politics of British national belonging. The notion that free trade was but one way in which government ensured the ideal conditions for the social and economic development of the people of Britain broadly, including the people of Ireland, was a fundamental part of the ideology of thinkers like Cobden. It should come as no surprise that Liberal newspapers argued both that the British government existed to care for the British people, and that the Irish were a part of that British citizenry. As they argued for the British government to enact reforms in Ireland, however, editors and writers constructed a complementary interpretation of British responsibility in which all Britons were compelled to care and agitate for one another, until the government lived up to its own Liberal potential.

But this was not the only interpretation of the famine in Britain. For those directly involved in British imperial governance, many of whom were based in London, the famine was not an opportunity to consider Ireland in the context of Britons' obligations to one another, but rather an opportunity to probe the boundaries and limits of the British empire.

3

Imperial Obligation

In the 1840s, Ireland's place within the British empire was unsettled. Ireland was a part of the United Kingdom, but many of its governance structures were distinctly colonial. This uncertainty was reflected in discourse about famine relief printed at the center of the empire. After the worst failures abated, a December 1848 editorial in the *Times of London* lamented that, even after years of scarcity, "the enigma of Irish pauperism remains to be solved." Three years into the famine, funding for Irish relief was scarce, and the rural population was restive. In the face of ongoing need, the editorial asked, "Who is to pay? The empire, the island, the union, the parish, the electoral division the township or the landowner?"[1] The *Times* was not alone in questioning whether the famine was a problem for the British empire; it echoed the perspective of political commentators of the time, such as the Assistant Secretary of the treasury responsible for administering famine relief, Charles Trevelyan. In January 1848, Trevelyan had written in the *Edinburgh Review* that while some Irish commentators argued "that the calamity was an imperial one," he was not convinced. While "there can be no doubt that the deplorable consequences of this great calamity extended to the empire at large," he noted, nevertheless "the disease was strictly local, and the cure was to be obtained only by the application of local remedies."[2]

By asking whether the price of relieving Irish poverty and mitigating rural unrest should be placed on the shoulders of the empire at large, on Ireland, or on increasingly small subdivisions thereof, the *Times* and Trevelyan alike signaled that the question of the British Empire's obligation to the starving Irish, and Ireland's obligation to the empire, vexed those at the center of British power.

In fact, at the same time that Irish politicians and political commentators were arguing that famine relief was a matter of national identity, and as Liberal newspapers in British industrial cities were insisting that famine relief and laissez-faire politics were one and the same, government leaders and shapers of political opinion at the center of British governmental power were drawing on a range of interpretive frameworks to explain why the Irish were starving. Some emphasized the providential nature of the famine, arguing that it represented divine judgment.[3] Others turned to racialized stereotypes to explain Irish reliance on the potato.[4] Still others, mirroring debates among Irish nationalists, blamed Ireland's absentee landlords.[5] For people shaping opinion in London, these overlapping—and sometimes contradictory—interpretations were underpinned by Ireland's long and contested imperial relationship with Britain.

The language of empire proved extraordinarily flexible, allowing commentators to simultaneously deploy racist stereotypes, express righteous indignation at failed imperialism, and employ rhetoric of the British as oppressors. These were not the only narratives circulating about Ireland; neither was the famine the only rhetorical space in which empire was discussed. Nevertheless, the different and frequently conflicting ways that famine relief and empire were put into conversation in this period illustrate the continued utility of famine relief as an idea that could be used to bolster a range of political positions. Throughout the famine, for those at the center of British imperial power, famine relief and the politics of empire were inextricable.

Attitudes toward Empire

The contours, logics, and boundaries of the British empire in the nineteenth century were famously complex and at times ambiguous, even for the people involved in shaping imperial policy.[6] Many of the people at the center of British governmental power in the nineteenth century viewed Indigenous inhabitants, people who were transported and forced to labor in colonized spaces, and to a lesser extent, white settlers, as different from and subordinate to metropolitan Britons. They also believed that the interests of the empire were best served by attending to the needs of Britain first. This included the desire to extract as much from the empire for as little cost as possible. Imperial profits that relied on costly military interventions were less desirable than those that were produced more efficiently. If benefits accrued to the center of the British empire, these men believed, they would inevitably ripple out to the periphery.[7]

There were other perspectives on the British empire, however. An important alternative came from liberal humanitarians, who focused in particular on the question of imperial responsibility.[8] Their understanding was predicated on the idea that colonized people—and particularly Indigenous people—were inferior to Britons, but could be redeemed through colonial projects. Superior Britons were obligated to assuage suffering in the colonies, and, once elevated, colonized people would owe a debt of gratitude to the imperial agents who had helped them to prosper.[9] The campaign to abolish slavery and the slave trade in Britain and its colonies was a part of these Liberal humanitarian efforts, as were the efforts of missionaries to convert non-Christians and reforms that would encourage modern agricultural practices.[10] In his 1853 commentary on prime minister John Russell's colonial policy, Henry George Grey summarized this outlook: "By the acquisition of its Colonial dominions, the nation [England] has incurred a responsibility of the highest kind, which it is not at liberty to throw off. The authority of the British Crown is at this moment the most powerful instrument, under Providence, of maintaining peace and order in many extensive regions of the earth, and therefore assists in diffusing amongst millions of the human race the blessing of Christianity and civilization."[11] For Liberal Humanitarian thinkers, while empire was a vital structure through which to understand the world, it also needed to be shaped into a force for good.

For many of those debating famine relief policy in nineteenth-century Britain, Ireland was among the empire's colonial dominions and, consequently, subject to the responsibilities of the British crown. However, the fit was uncomfortable. Ireland had been incorporated into the United Kingdom in 1800. Irish representatives (albeit ones who were most likely to align their interests with those of Britain) sat in the British Parliament.[12] While some Irish people had access to direct representation, like many colonies they were still subject to the executive authority of the lord lieutenant, a resident imperial official acting on behalf of the crown.[13] The Ordnance Survey, a project to map Ireland undertaken between the 1820s and the 1840s, mirrored attempts to map—and thereby control—India in the same period.[14] The Irish constabulary was a "practical prototype" for policing Indigenous populations in colonial spaces.[15] The British barracks and garrisons built across the Atlantic world were planned according to a model developed by the British Army in Ireland.[16] While Ireland's mode of governance was nominally unionist, these features also marked it as a colonized space, subject to many of the same assumptions and expectations as colonies in South Asia, North America, and the Caribbean. Furthermore, its history was distinctly colonial, and many of the practicalities of Irish administration were at best a hybrid of the two. The men who developed imperial policy during the famine drew these long-standing ideas about colonialism and the special place of Ireland in the empire. They produced competing ideologies of empire as well as competing understandings of the obligations of the Irish to the empire, and of the empire to the Irish.

In the mid-1840s, the trope of Ireland as an undeveloped space that could simultaneously benefit from English influence and provide fertile ground for development was a thriving theme at the center of the British empire. This idea had coalesced in England in the medieval period and taken on a life of its own in the course of the long history of settler colonialism in the region. As noted in chapter 1, Protestant Anglo-Irish elites had a stake in continuing the rhetoric of native Irish savagery. Just as it had justified conquest in the medieval and early modern eras, in the nineteenth century it justified Anglo-Irish political control of the island. Michael De Nie and L. P. Curtis have chronicled the racialized stereotypes of Celts and Saxons, Catholics and Protestants, and even "apes" and "angels" that appeared in the British press, and in British politicians' discussions of Ireland.[17] The men who trafficked in these stereotypes imbued their solutions to the problem of the famine with hibernophobic racial language, casting the Irish as "paddys" who needed a healthy dose of Anglo-Saxon, Protestant, middle-class values. Articulating this perspective in 1799, using language that would persist throughout the famine, the *Times of London* wrote that "nothing can tend to humanize the barbarous Irish as a habitual intercourse with this country and the opportunities of observing the civilized manners of those who are from it."[18] Counterintuitively, however, this perspective on Irish inferiority led to three very different conclusions about the famine and imperial obligation.

What the Irish Owed the Empire

Some thinkers argued that degradation did not entitle the Irish to English relief. Rather, proponents of this perspective argued, the Irish people were responsible for lifting themselves up; only then would they be eligible for mutual imperial aid. This derived from a certain understanding of imperialism in which colonized spaces were meant to provide resources for the center, not be a drain on them. For example, Thomas Babington Macaulay, who had served as a Liberal MP for Leeds and Edinburgh and as a colonial administrator in India, wrote in the later 1840s in his popular *History of England* that Ireland "remained indeed a member of the empire, but a withered and distorted member."[19] This kind of language centered Ireland's utility toward, and obligations to, the imperial center: it reflected a dominant view among political leaders and the men who sought to shape political opinion that Ireland had failed to live up to its potential, was currently failing to serve the empire, and was, consequently, to be pitied and scorned. This pity and scorn, however, did not axiomatically lead to relief.

Macaulay was one among many current and former political leaders with this opinion about Ireland. He was joined by the men who actively worked on the Irish crisis, like prime ministers Peel and Russell, other current and former members of Parliament like George Poulett Scrope, and civil servants like Charles Trevelyan. These men, and their compatriots, held positions of power before or during the famine. When they were not in office, they were often involved in political debates, encouraging their friends, relations, and former colleagues to take or reject various policy positions.[20] Much of this persuasion took place in personal communication, but they also produced texts for public consumption, including pamphlets, historical treatises, and open letters. Britain's imperial relationship to Ireland, and the way that relationship shaped famine relief policy, was a frequent feature in this commentary.

These men were joined by other shapers of political opinion. In nineteenth-century London, even more so than other sites of news production, relationships between public discourse and policy were reciprocal. As was the case in most cities, newspaper articles were often the product of party connections or personal relationships among editors, writers, and politicians.[21] However, in London, the power of the press was amplified by the fact that the men who held positions of imperial political authority were often personal friends of the men who edited and wrote for newspapers, who produced framings of the news that reflected political positions. Politicians used the press both as a space to share their own ideas, and as a source of constituents' interests to which they could react.[22] The *Times of London*, for instance, was known among nineteenth-century newspapermen as "the thunderer" due to its role in urging parliament to pass the 1832 reform bill.[23] While the *Times* was atypically influential on government affairs, it was not the only paper that sought to shape national government policy. The *Morning Chronicle*, for example, was purchased in 1834 by men who sought a venue for Whig and Liberal political opinions that would challenge the power of the also-Liberal *Times*.[24] In turn, the *Daily News* emerged as a radical alternative to the *Morning Chronicle*. As Charles Dickens would write in the *Daily News*'s prospectus, the paper advocated for the principles of "progress and improvement" as well as "equal legislation."[25] In other words, its aim was not only to shape public opinion but also to shape government policy. Even weekly Sunday newspapers like the *Era*, *Lloyd's Weekly News*, and the *Illustrated London News*, which were intended primarily for working-class readership, circulated among London's political elites.[26] The *Illustrated London News*, for instance, was instrumental in shaping English nationalist and imperialist ideologies.[27] Similarly, Edward Lloyd's commitment to Liberal causes meant that *Lloyd's Weekly News* stood for Liberal politics throughout the 1840s.[28] In their own ways, the editors of these papers, alongside former and current government officials, attempted to shape policy toward Ireland.

A narrative of rural Irish degeneration appeared early in reports of the famine in London's newspapers. Much of this rhetoric was produced by the *Times*'s Irish correspondent, Thomas Campbell Foster, who had been sent to Ireland before the famine to investigate the state of destitution described by the Devon Commission. Through his reporting before and then during the famine, he serially disparaged the Irish.[29] In October 1845, he described rural Ireland as a place that "in the best of time exhibits a degree of degraded wretchedness such as will be in vain sought for in any part of England."[30] In November of that year, he argued that, in comparison with the English, "the Celt is the smaller, the less robust, and less upright of the two," but that these physical differences "may also serve to excuse his inferior habits of life."[31] In February 1846, Foster wrote that the Irish "are generally absolutely lazy and apathetic—too lazy to weed their land though they have nothing else to do,—too lazy to clean their cottages, with nothing else to do; or to mend the holes in their cottage roofs, with nothing else to do,—that their land is so wretchedly cultivated, their cottages are so dirty, and their hovels so miserable."[32] These themes were racialized, relying on the assumption of intrinsic differences between people of Celtic and Saxon descent. The particular themes of Irish degradation and unwillingness to work, pervaded Foster's—and, therefore, the *Times*'s—reporting on the famine.

Other papers echoed this trope of Irish degeneration. For instance, *Lloyd's Weekly News* described the Irish in similar terms to the *Times*, writing in March 1846 that "Irish nature lacks the essentials to hope for very great mental or social regeneration."[33] Even papers that did not explicitly make claims about Irish racial inferiority pointed to what writers and editors saw as fundamental differences between Irish and English people. The *Illustrated London News* printed regular reports of meetings in support of the repeal of the Act of Union. In the early months of the famine, these accounts were frequently paired with descriptions of agrarian violence, including "attempts at assassination," in which the intended victims were "literally covered in blood," and Irish peasants were portrayed as "barbarous murder[s]."[34] For the *Illustrated London News*, repeal, violence and savagery were the most salient features of Ireland. In the same issue that detailed the assassination attempts, the *Illustrated London News* also included a "sketch" of Kilkenny, which quipped that, in the past, English legislation had made it so "Kilkenny was sometimes emphatically called 'the English County'; a distinction which it has long lost."[35]

Politicians, too, described the Irish as constitutionally inferior to their English compatriots. In his retrospective analysis of famine policy, Charles Trevelyan wrote that the Irish were driven by "the principle of seeking the cheapest description of food at the smallest expense of labor," and that "the domestic habits arising out of this mode of subsistence were the of the lowest, and most degrading kind."[36] Without mentioning the empire, these kinds of descriptions nevertheless turned on imperial tropes that had been developed by English authors of preceding generations. The logic that enabled successive English—and then British—monarchs to claim the right to "plant" Ireland with productive citizens was the same logic that castigated the rural Irish for their own starvation.

For these commentators, and the public figures who agreed with them, the solution to the famine was for the Irish to improve themselves. This they saw in the context of Ireland's obligation to the empire. In the earliest months of the crop failure, Foster explicitly tied Irish improvement to imperial welfare, writing that, if the Irish were to improve, they would be able "to cultivate the land which we possess, and in the doing of that, to employ the people, to benefit the proprietors, to enrich the country and to increase the power and resources of the empire."[37] Perhaps foreshadowing his later castigations of Irish character, five days later he argued that "the poor, uneducated contented Irish peasant must not only be taught civilized habits, but forced into them," if only for the good of the empire.[38] After describing the "degraded wretchedness" of Mayo in October 1845, Foster went on to write that "the more prosperous and happy is Ireland rendered, as an integral portion of the British empire, the more prosperous and happy will be the British empire, therefore would I rather strive for her prosperity and happiness."[39]

Other papers also adopted the argument that relief from the famine must come through fundamental changes to Irish character, and that such changes were what Ireland owed to the empire. *Lloyd's Weekly News*, for example, argued in January 1846 that if political agitators in Ireland would quit their fundraising to repeal the Act of Union and instead solicit donations for actual aid to the starving, "the Saxons, who have often come to thy rescue, will esteem thee;" indeed, if the Irish were to cease agitating for repeal, "the empire, by unity and reasonable argument will succeed."[40] *Lloyd's* contended that Ireland had to earn its place within the empire, asking Irish politicians to "come, and receive the welcome of true Englishmen, into the House of Commons and prove yourselves the true and efficient representatives of the people."[41] Similarly, *The Era*, criticizing the leaders of the repeal movement for taking political advantage of the potato failure, asked, "What can be said of the leaders of a people who would endeavor to make famine the stalking horse for a dismemberment of the empire, and, who would, if they carried their insane schemes into execution, consign one-half of their dupes to all the horrors of starvation?"[42] The commentators who espoused these views believed that one of the most salient features of the British Empire was that it provided the colonized an opportunity and responsibility to learn from their colonizers in order to change their nature and habits and become productive members. The failure to do so on the part of the Irish, and the suffering attendant on it, bespoke a failure to fulfill their obligations to the empire, not the other way around.

What Landlords Owed the Empire

Of course the idea that the rural Irish were depraved was just one way to understand the relationship between "civilized" metropole and "savage" periphery. A second derived from the tradition of Liberal humanitarianism. This was part of the same reforming impulse in Britain that had led to the transformation of voting rights and arguments that it was the empire's obligation to uplift its subjects.[43] In the case of the famine, this often took the form of castigating the Anglo-Irish elite, particularly landlords, for failing to act as good stewards of their tenants. This argument dovetailed with a frequent refrain, both in the press and among politicians, that "Irish property must pay for Irish poverty." The landlords, as elites who benefited from their connections to Britain, were (conveniently) more obligated than were the unrelated—and uninterested—Englishmen to remedy Irish suffering. When politicians and commentators focused on landlords' civilizing mission, they often argued that the failures of Irish rural tenants were a consequence of the failures of landlords, and that landlords' imperial obligations compelled them to remedy their behavior.[44]

As the root of this perspective was the belief that the Gaelic Irish, though degraded, were not irredeemably so. Some pushed back against absolutist descriptions of Irish character and potential. One letter to the *Times*, penned by the pseudonymous Scotus, wrote: "The Irish are not unwilling to work. They can work as well, if not better than the peasantry of England or Scotland and would not be idlers if the spark of hope were kindled within them. Depressed as they are, their energy is often wonderful and from the constitution of the Irish mind, I am certain of this, that once risen, they will be a flourishing and great nation."[45] Newspapers in the periphery of British imperial power tended to push this narrative even harder. For example, the editors of the *Chambers's Edinburgh Journal* wrote on October 21, 1848, "We have no desire to enter into the question of races, now so commonly discussed; holding, as we do, that the Celt is as fully entitled as the Saxon to the good offices of his fellow-men in the attempt to change what is objectionable in his character."[46] Such perspectives revealed the potential for a change in the Irish character and the possibility of mutually beneficial relationships between Irish and British people that would ultimately continue to bolster and contribute to the British economy.

At the same time, the system of landholding in nineteenth-century Ireland was accepted by most contemporaries to be deeply flawed, rife with corruption, and constantly on the precipice of violence. In other words, Ireland was the picture of poor colonial management. Hereditary landowners complained that their tenants refused to pay rents, and they criticized government efforts to limit the "rights of proprietorship." Tenants argued that the lands they were leased were not sufficient to provide sustenance or income and called for compensation for improvements on land and greater security of tenure. They, along with British commentators, railed against "absentee" landlords who reaped the benefits of land ownership without exercising any of the responsibilities of a proprietor. British politicians proposed interventions throughout the early nineteenth century that would improve Irish agriculture and landholding practices.[47] This included the formation of the Devon Commission "On Occupation of Land" in Ireland that was often referenced by Daniel O'Connell. Even before the start of the famine, those at the center of British power viewed the Anglo-Irish aristocracy as a problem.

Although some articles castigated rural Irish tenants for failing to live up to the examples set by Englishmen, many articles—often in the same papers—focused on landlords as the best avenue for relief of Irish suffering. In early 1845, the *Morning Chronicle* asked, "Do not the Irish landlords, who have so deep an interest in the peace and prosperity of their country, employ the means at their disposal for the promotion of these objects?"[48] Two months later, the *Times* Irish correspondent explained that the mismanagement of Irish land was due to the fact that "the majority of landlords are non-resident" and were consequently unable, or unwilling, to exercise appropriate stewardship over the land or tenants.[49] The *Illustrated London News* charged that the owners of Irish "soil, who extract and receive rents higher than in any part of Europe, go untouched," while the burden for relief fell on those who actually occupied the land.[50] These characterizations of landlords were not confined to the press. George Poulett Scrope, the reform-minded MP who was concerned with social welfare, published a series of addresses on Irish governance in 1846. The first was a reprint of an address that he had originally published in 1834. In it, he criticized landlords for extracting "exorbitant rent" from "a peasant" tenant who "waters the soil with his sweat" but who could not produce "enough, even of the coarsest food, to support life and he and his family wast [sic] away from want and disease."[51] This observation held as true in 1846 as it had been when initially written in 1834.

Ultimately, the crux of the critique was that Anglo-Irish landlords were responsible for remedying Irish character, and were obligated to do so as agents of empire. This had been, after all, the justification for settler colonialism from the first days of the occupation of Ireland: to enable the British to civilize the locals. According to commentators, they were not merely failing but abdicating this responsibility. Thomas Campbell Foster, the *Times* Irish correspondent, wrote in 1847: "In Ireland, the rich man has been taught to think that the poor man has no claim upon him. The poor man, neglected by the law, has learned to vindicate his rights by its infringement. The one extorts and oppresses, the other cheats or assassinates, and the effect of which is that the good suffer for the bad. The tenant, demoralized by a sanctioned iniquity, evades the payment of rent. His lessor treats his own landlord in the same way, and thus many are deprived of the means of practicing that charity which is at once congenial to their natures and accordant with their station."[52] Similarly, an editorial in *The Era* asked, "How, then, can the Irish landowners wonder at the impending gloom—the harbinger of the coming storm—which now hangs like a funeral pall over their devoted island? Have they not for years been sowing that storm, and, by their cold, heartless, grasping cupidity, courted that catastrophe which is now come upon them?"[53] In other words, by acting cruelly and rapaciously, the aristocracy was not providing a civilizing example, and it was no wonder that their charges had sunk into brutality and poverty.

Thus, for some writing from London, the solution to Ireland's problems was to be found in the reform of the landlord class itself, to make its members more successful imperial stewards. Such reforms, in turn, had the potential to transform the rural Irish peasantry. Landlords were not just custodians of national soil, these commentators argued; they were agents of the British empire. Reforming the behavior of landlords would improve not only Ireland but also the empire as a whole, by creating a more efficient laboring rural population that was less inclined to rebellions and "outrages." When Foster criticized the rural Irish for being excessively tractable and content with poverty, he argued that lifting the tenantry up "is the duty of the landlords to see effected," and that doing so was both in the interests of, and consequently the duty of, the government.[54]

Foster repeatedly made this connection. In October 1845, he suggested that the government simply facilitate the emigration of as many Irish men and women as possible. Notably, many emigration schemes proposed that the Irish be sent to British North American or antipodean colonies, so as not to reduce the resources and manpower of the empire, but to redistribute them away from conditions that contributed to their depravity.[55] Moreover, he recommended that Irish lands be redistributed by allowing landlords to break up and sell portions of their estates. This would replace the "embarrassment of the landlords" with a system that would "cultivate the land which we possess, and in the doing of that, to employ the people, to benefit the proprietors, to enrich the country and to increase the power and the resources of the empire."[56] It would also "diffuse independent and enterprising capitalists throughout the country" and "strip from men who now flauntingly wear it, the tinsel garb of a nominal estate, without having either the means or the power to use and improve it."[57] Such a measure would remove irresponsible landlords and make space for enterprising newcomers who might provide a more industrious example for the local population. This approach would render Ireland "what it is capable of becoming—powerful and prosperous—the right arm, the proud participator, whether in peace or war, in the glories of the British empire."[58]

In one of his last letters from Ireland, Foster lamented the "utter neglect of all duties of the landlord" by the Anglo-Irish aristocracy, which was responsible for Ireland's condition as the "weakness and disgrace of Empire."[59] In response to these claims of landlord perfidy, an "Irish Western Landlord" wrote to the editor of the *Times*, contending that Irish landlords "do discharge their duties to all around them in an exemplary manner, under circumstances of discouragement, danger and difficulty, such as no other class in the British empire."[60] For landlords and their critics alike, the notion that landlords should act as part and on behalf of the British empire was commonplace.

Characterizations of Irish landlords as failed imperial agents also took place in parliamentary discussions of Irish relief. For example, in a discussion of "famine and disease in Ireland" in March 1846, Sir Robert Peel argued that relief to the starving Irish must come from the landlord class of Ireland. He offered a preemptive compliment, hoping that there would be "an undoubted claim upon the landed proprietors, who will not fail to come forward at this period of general distress. Without their aid, without the local efforts of those who are acquainted with the particular circumstances of the district, the intervention of the government would be useless." He concluded that Parliament must be "satisfied that the landed proprietors of that part of the Empire will not fail in their duty in this instance, as there have been many cases in which they have shown a disposition cordially and effectually to unite with Government."[61] Members of Parliament also argued that the actions of landlords were key in providing aid to Ireland.

These characterizations continued throughout the famine. In March 1847—in the midst of a series of debates about how landlords, local governments, and the Irish Poor Law should contribute to rural relief—Sir William Clay, the Liberal MP, asserted that Parliament should be in the business of creating conditions that would allow Ireland to "maintain its own people from its own resources," which included taxing landlords to fund relief schemes. This, he suggested, should be, "in the long run, the permanent condition of the empire."[62] In an article published in April 1847, the *Illustrated London News* castigated in particular landlords' representatives in the British Parliament. Reacting to the insistence by Irish representative Thomas Spring Rice, Lord Monteagle, that food only be distributed through the poor houses, the *Illustrated London News* wrote, "Monteagle speaks as Irish landlords always have spoken, as they have always acted; and the consequence of their speaking and acting is that Ireland is the scandal of our name and century, the source of weakness to the Empire, a fearful drain on its resources, and the abode of every horror of the worst periods of the middle ages."[63] If landlords did not rise to the occasion and provide relief, they had failed both their rural denizens of their country, and the empire.

What the Empire Owed to Ireland

In contrast to arguments about whether the rural tenants or landlords were most responsible for lifting Ireland from conditions of famine, a final theme in discussions of famine relief at the imperial center emphasized the British Empire's imperial harms and obligations. One way that those obligations manifested was through donations. Relief committees, such as the British Relief Association and the Quaker Central Relief Committee, also relied on the concept of the civilizing mission to appeal for funds. The General Central Relief Committee for all of Ireland solicited contributions "from all parts of the empire."[64] Although this appeal was targeted more broadly than London, for Londoners already accustomed to thinking about the famine as an imperial crisis it would have resonated with their understanding of imperial obligation. Appeals that referenced donations from the West Indies or from Calcutta might also have played on the prejudices of Londoners, suggesting, as they did, that these people—some of them nonwhite—from the peripheries were better imperial citizens than the Britons themselves.

In fact, denizens of the empire did respond to the appeal for aid. Donors from India, South Africa, Canada, and the West Indies contributed a small but much-vaunted amount to Irish relief efforts. The Calcutta Relief Fund made two separate donations, totaling £6,000, which were widely publicized in 1846, and both the General Central Relief Committee and the British Association reported that just over 2 percent of the donations they received came from abroad. One of these was from "Negroes belonging to the Congregations under the charge of the Moravian missionaries in Basseterre, Bethesda, Estridge and Bethel, in St. Kitts, per the Rev. G.W. Westerby"—a donation marked "for Ireland only."[65] While some of these donations might simply have come from individuals with personal interests in Ireland—or might have been forcibly collected from servants or enslaved people to suit the philanthropic impulse of their employer, religious leader or enslaver—they suggested to some in London that the empire was concerned by the Irish crisis, and readers of the major London newspapers certainly were made aware of that concern. In doing so, as Aoife O'Leary McNeice has demonstrated, the relief associations were reinforcing arguments about the value of empire.[66] Additionally, these narratives also introduced the idea that those within the empire were obligated to help one another, and perhaps that individuals from far-flung parts of the empire could be better stewards of Irish welfare than the leaders of Ireland themselves.

Another way that the question of imperial obligations manifested was in arguments that Ireland's current state, though admittedly degraded, was traceable to the generations of English conquest. These arguments were made most forcefully in the provincial press, but were also adopted in London. The *Chambers's Edinburgh Journal*, the popular general-interest periodical published in Edinburgh, repeatedly expressed the view that Ireland was coequal with Britain.[67] According to its editors, it was the fault of abusive historical relationships, rather than something intrinsic to the Irish, that prevented the country from thriving. "What a noble country might it not have been," pondered one article, "if exposed to a different course of circumstances since the period when it shone a star of light in an age of medieval darkness." It went on to lament that "all the Archaeologists can do is wander amidst its glorious ruins, and search for traces of refinement which centuries ago was laid ruthlessly in the dust."[68] In another classical allusion, the *Journal* described England as Rome and Ireland as ancient Greece, "the spot whence it derived not a little of its civilization and which it afterwards mal-treated in requital."[69] The *Manchester Guardian* echoed this sentiment, noting that "the social and economical condition of Ireland becomes more and more difficult and perplexing subject. The evils of ancient misrules are so inveterately mixed up with the present character and circumstances of the people of that unhappy country, that, do what we may—act in obedience with the strict laws of political and social economy, or disobey those laws in order to follow a course more in accordance with generous impulses towards a suffering and unfortunate people, and in either case the result appears equally disastrous."[70]

Both publications also argued that the Irish were capable of rising above their degradation, given a different environment. In January 1848, *Chambers's Edinburgh Journal* made this point in asides concerned with Irish character, such as one that noted that "the Irish character, when properly directed, is as capable of advancement as any other in the world," or a commentary on the utility of Irishmen in constructing vital public works projects: "The ordinary notion of the Irish being disposed to idleness may be true, for anything we know, in the land of their birth; but from all we have heard or seen, they are anything but lazy when mixed with English and Scotch, and have a fair prospect of remuneration."[71] This mirrored an argument that the *Guardian* had made in 1846, suggesting that different environments made it possible for Irish men and women to thrive. That editorial affirmed that "no sooner do this class of Irish reach America, and are let loose to shift and provide for themselves, than they begin to acquire a knowledge of their comparative helplessness (in part occasioned by the stunted and perverted habits of their former life) and the necessity which now impels them to an entire change in their general conduct."[72] Another article in the *Guardian* recounted the experience of an Irish pauper woman, who when faced with the death of her husband and the brutality of her landlord, emigrated to England where she "(thanks to the soup charity) is greatly recovered, appears to be rather a superior woman of her class (for it was with evident reluctance that she told where she was at present staying.)"[73]

Some London papers echoed these sentiments. For instance, a letter to the editor of the *Times* in 1845 opined, "It appears obvious that the population of Ireland could never have been reduced to its present degraded condition but from proximity to a richer country, viz. England."[74] In other words, the empire's extractive nature could not but result in the impoverishment of its neighbor. A similar viewpoint appeared in the *Morning Chronicle*; in contrast to the *Illustrated London News*'s depiction of rural violence, a report from the *Chronicle*'s correspondent in Dublin noted that, "in all quarters, the peasantry, although suffering extreme privations, exhibit the most patient endurance. The measures for their relief have been long delayed by technical difficulties and official forms. Many of them are actually starving, but still there has been no attempt at a popular outbreak."[75] This suggests that the author of the article felt that, in this context, unrest and rebellion might have been a reasonable response to government mismanagement, and that the rural Irish exhibited extreme forbearance. Governments that allowed their subjects to starve had not fulfilled their duties and could realistically expect popular violence. The fact that the peasantry was not resorting to such actions spoke to their character.

The idea that rebellion might be a consequence of Irish mistreatment surfaced in the writing of politicians as well. In the 1846 reissue of his 1834 pamphlet, George Poulett Scrope wrote that pacifying Ireland and averting an Irish rebellion would result in "the integrity of the empire secured."[76] Unlike many of his contemporaries, however, who saw violence or coercion as a means to pacification, Scrope wrote, "The answer [to the Irish problem] is—by doing simple justice to the people of Ireland: by fulfilling the frequent promise of the Sovereign—the late solemn pledge of the Legislature—by removing their just causes of complaint."[77] Scrope's perspective—that Irish grievances were justified, and that a change in Britain's imperial behavior was warranted—was supported by other leaders and shapers of political policy on Ireland. In 1844, in a debate about the state of poverty in Ireland, Thomas Babington Macaulay described Ireland's relationship to England as being produced by a "conquest." For Macaulay, this conquest was racialized; he described it as "the conquest of race over race, such a conquest that established the dominion of the Mahrattas in Bwalior, or that of the Spaniards over the American Indians."[78] This mode of conquest, he said, "was the first great cause of these disorders" of Irish poverty and rural distress.[79]

This language was echoed by Irish MPs in parliamentary debates during the famine. For example, on February 1, 1847, while debating the expansion of the Irish Poor Law, William Smith O'Brien, the Young Irelander and an MP for Ennis in County Clare, argued that it was clear that the famine "should be viewed as they would view a war—as an event calling for an appeal to extraordinary resources and extraordinary exertions."[80] Smith O'Brien wondered "whether or not England, as a portion of the empire, should share in the burden which had devolved on the empire," but he said that "he nevertheless had no hesitation in asserting that the Imperial Parliament was bound to make a national effort to alleviate the misery of the inhabitants of one section of the United Kingdom."[81]

Similarly, on March 15, in another debate on the Irish Poor Law Bill, Sir Denham Jepson-Norreys of Mallow, County Cork, encouraged his English colleagues "to recollect that since the conquest of Ireland by Henry II, that country had not been in a prosperous condition." He asked them to consider why, when Ireland was in extreme distress, English members of Parliament had asked how it was that "while we have progressed in prosperity and happiness, these people, whom we call our brethren, and a part of the United Empire, should be in the miserable state," rather than "are we not answerable for the condition of these people?" Norreys mounted an energetic defense of his fellow Irish landlords, asking of British MPs, "have not the Irish landlords been your tools? Did we not conquer Ireland for you? Did not we maintain it for you? What is it that has put us in the position in which we now stand?"[82] For Irish MPs like Norreys and Smith O'Brien, it was clear that England's conquest of Ireland was the cause of the current rural distress, and that, insofar as Irish landlords were responsible for rural distress, they had been acting on behalf of the empire. For a range of commentators at the center of British imperial power—including English and Irish politicians as well as those who sought to shape political opinion through pamphlets and the press—the British Empire, and the Englishmen who controlled it, were obligated by the lengthy and extractive Anglo-Irish relationship to undertake famine relief projects. For these men, it was not a question of Irish people evolving to meet the needs of the empire, but the empire's obligation to the people of Ireland.

And yet, for many of them, it was clear that Irish independence was not the answer. Although some, like a letter writer to the *Chronicle* in 1847, argued that "that the less a government or a legislature interferes beyond the removal of obstructions and securing of perfect freedom, the better," most viewed Ireland as an intrinsic part of the empire, if not the United Kingdom itself.[83] A letter to the *Times* in March 1846 contended that fair treatment for Ireland would help to "constitut[e] a mighty empire, to perform a mighty part of the history of the world."[84]

Predictably, nationalist politicians did not agree that independence was not the solution to Ireland's imperial problems. Ireland's role in the empire became even more pressing after Young Irelanders attempted a rebellion in 1848. Radicalized by the ongoing famine and by popular uprisings in Europe, in late 1847 and early 1848 Young Irelanders began to form nationalist "confederate clubs" intended to establish a structure of resistance that could be deployed in a countrywide rising against the British. The goal was "to destroy the English interest in this country, root and branch, to institute a national government" and "by our own laws and arms, to restore the country in its full integrity and glory to its own brave people."[85] By March 1848, the British government had arrested prominent Young Irelanders on charges of sedition.[86] In late July, the lord lieutenant suspended habeas corpus in Ireland.[87] A few days later, a handful of Young Irelanders, led by William Smith O'Brien, were confronted by a police force in Ballingarry, Tipperary. The two groups exchanged gunfire for two hours, before police reinforcements arrived, effectively ending the nascent rebellion.[88] Writing well after the initial panic of famine had passed, but while much of Ireland was still suffering the effects of five years of starvation, the English political thinker Lord Sidney Goldolphin Osborne could not have helped but to have the attempted uprising on his mind when he wrote to the *Times*, "I, sir, hold Ireland to be a hardly separable part of the British empire, a part we could only lose with pain and with detriment."[89] Even in debates over the best way to remedy historic wrongs, Ireland's value to the empire was paramount.

For those shaping and debating the empire's policies, the question of imperial obligation was a vital frame for debates about Irish relief. At the same time, Irish relief was deployed in debates about the contours and obligations of empire. People who were—or who aspired to be— at the center of British power alternately argued that relief should be located in Ireland until the Irish lived up to their imperial obligations, that the Irish were too degraded to ever effectively contribute to the empire, and that Irish landlords had failed to act as imperial stewards. Just as they could be deployed to argue for Irish peoples' obligations to the empire, so, too, could they be deployed to argue for the empire's obligations to Ireland. These uses illustrate how flexible ideas of both relief and empire were in this period: at the center of British imperial power, famine relief and the politics of empire were mutually constituted.

As news of and debates about the famine moved farther away from sites of actual suffering, ideas about famine relief became more malleable, and suited to an ever-wider range of political positions. When these ideas crossed the Atlantic ocean, they were applied to local politics in myriad and innovative ways.

4

American Power

In 1847, British imperial officials were not the only people preoccupied with ideas of empire. Across the Atlantic, in another metropole, a group of men gathered at the offices of Prime, Ward & Co. to discuss Ireland and to "devise efficient measures for the relief of the starving poor." Prime, Ward & Co. was a company of international bankers which occupied premises on Wall Street, in New York City.[1] The firm's offices were the proximate major financial institutions of the day, including banks, New York's Customs House, and the New York Stock Exchange. They were at the center of networks of people, funds, political power, and information that connected New York and the United States with the rest of the world.

The men who gathered at the Prime, Ward & Co. building on February 10, 1847, embodied these connections. They included Myndert Van Schaick, a former city alderman and current state senator; Robert Minturn, one of the most prominent merchants in the city; Jacob Harvey, a Quaker broker with ties to the Society of Friends in Dublin; and John Jay, a New York lawyer and abolitionist who would help found the Republican Party. These men were joined by other successful New York businessmen and politicians whose offices were scattered throughout lower Manhattan.[2] The attendees knew each other socially; they served on committees together. Several had been appointed to serve as New York state commissioners of emigration, a group tasked with safeguarding immigrants from fraud and abuse.[3] They competed for the same elected offices and served on the boards of the same charities. They were the politically connected of nineteenth-century New York, with interests that spanned the United States and the Atlantic Ocean.

Their stated goal was to make a plan to "collect and transmit funds and provisions" to Ireland, but their interaction with the famine went far beyond a simple philanthropic mission.[4] As merchants and traders with transatlantic connections, they were ideally poised to undertake the work of soliciting and transmitting funds to Ireland. As current and former politicians, they were also keenly aware of the uses to which famine relief could be put in the politics of New York City and the United States.

Indeed, the political scene in New York City in the middle of the nineteenth century was so fragmented and the famine so distant that famine relief could be and was appropriated for a variety of political causes. The dominant political parties—Whigs and Democrats—and the multiple divisions therein co-opted accounts of Irish suffering as well as philanthropic efforts in service of many different political projects of the day; the factions within each party were quick to seize on any contemporary story that suited their needs. The many different uses to which the famine was put also suggest that accounts of Ireland were being divorced from the actual starvation of actual people. Famine relief's very malleability, the fact that it was accepted as an appropriate example for so many different political causes, highlights the ways in which disasters, and responses to them, could take on symbolic character in the mid-nineteenth century.

New York City was situated at the center of transnational news networks, which mediated local and national politics through the partisan press. Of particular interest to New Yorkers was the debate over the appropriate use of US power on the global stage. This issue was deeply entangled with the historic relationship between the United States, Ireland, and Britain, as well as with growing impulses for reform, both at home and abroad. Commentators used famine relief to position nascent US imperialism against the British Empire. In doing so, conflicts over domestic political power spilled over into discussions of foreign relief.

Networked News

In the middle decades of the nineteenth century, US cities were clearinghouses for news, New York City exceptionally so. It was an important node in networks that carried information about the famine and famine relief across the Atlantic and around the country. This news was mediated by various sources between Ireland and New York. Rural Irish newspapers printed accounts of suffering in their localities. Some of these reports were reprinted or summarized by the Dublin press.

Both rural and urban Irish newspapers were sent across the Irish sea to British port cities, where they might be further excerpted or reprinted. Contemporary journalists and scholars described this style of journalism as "scissors and pastepot," given its liberal borrowing, often without citation, from other papers.[5] This practice of borrowing and reprinting news was so common that in November 1846 a writer for the *Cork Constitution* complained: "Some of our Dublin Contemporaries frequently quote from other Papers articles of news which have been pilfered from the *Constitution*." They went on to lament that "the pilfering process is continued from month to month, an acknowledgement being sometimes conceded to perhaps one paragraph to cover the dishonesty practiced on the others."[6]

By the start of the famine, steam packets that crossed the Atlantic on regular schedules, connecting American and European ports, had become commonplace. They carried British and Irish newspapers, each containing slightly different collections and reframings of Irish news. In 1845, fifty-two transatlantic packet lines sailed regularly from New York City, and three ships each week carried news in and out of New York.[7] Over the course of the famine, New York City newspapers explicitly drew on periodicals from Cork, Dublin, Galway, Limerick, Tipperary, Belfast, Antrim, and London and probably drew on other, uncited publications as well. These practices meant that the news of the famine that reached New York represented a variety of voices, mediated through a range of publications. The New York press then pulled from, distilled, and reframed these accounts for their own readers. During the 1840s, articles from New York City newspapers often "went viral" across the United States.[8] News was both transmitted through the city and made in it.

A Political Hub

As was the case in Britain and Ireland, the framing of this news was shaped by local politics. The Whig and Democratic parties dominated politics in this period and vied for popular support. At the same time, factions within those parties were fighting to define party politics itself. As was also the case across the Atlantic, these parties and factions used newspapers to garner partisan support. Some thought that workers and non-elite voters should drive politics. Others thought that monied elites were better positioned to determine the future of the United States. Still others thought that a technocratic central government was the best approach. Some advocated for a combination of these modes. It was in this context, rife with debate over government and responsibility, that the issue of famine relief became a way of talking about how the United States should reach beyond its borders.

The histories of the parties and their factions were entangled with the history of New York City. The Democratic Party had coalesced in the 1820s, with the political rise of Andrew Jackson. Jackson, who emphasized his status as a war hero, initially ran as a politician opposed to political elites. As president from 1829 to 1837, he oversaw the expansion of the electorate to include all white men, regardless of whether they owned property. Jackson and his allies also argued that monied interests and hereditary elites had dominated and corrupted US politics, consolidating wealth for themselves while excluding poorer white men from power.[9] As the Democratic Party developed into the 1840s, it professionalized politics, normalizing formal political organizations, competition for office, and the development of political power through a consistent and loyal electorate.[10]

Jacksonian Democrats cast themselves as the party of men traditionally excluded from government and sought to make economic structures that had previously benefited only the wealthy more widely accessible.[11] On the eve of the famine, the national Democratic Party was primarily devoted to supporting the power of white men against what they perceived as government tyranny—activities that included, according to party platforms, preventing white settlers from displacing Indigenous people, prohibiting state governments from legalizing slavery, and creating a national bank overseen by urban, monied elites, which Democrats saw as a threat to the power and welfare of states.[12] For Democrats, decent white citizens, left to their own devices, would collectively promote the common good of the country.[13]

Within the party, factions debated the best path to that common good. Many of these factions were particularly active in New York. As the party became more established, political power consolidated, ironically, in the hands of a small number of wealthy men. In response to this consolidation, a faction called the Loco Focos formed in the 1830s, seeking to protect what they saw as pure Democratic ideals from the taints of corruption, antislavery, and the banking industry.[14] In New York, this populist faction was challenged by a coalition of politicians who came to be known as Tammany Hall. Famously corrupt, Tammany Hall Democrats seemed inclined to support whatever policies were most likely to accrue votes. In practice, this meant supporting the local and state banking interests which funded Democratic party operations, despite the platform's critiques of the banking industry.[15]

Democrats were also divided over the issue of slavery. In the 1840s, a small and radical faction began to argue against the expansion of slavery into new US territories. Its members were derisively called Barnburners, after a Dutch legend about a farmer who burned down his barn to kill the rats in it. Barnburners' opponents posited that this antislavery faction was willing to destroy both the US and New York economy in service of their radical ideals.[16] Barnburners were opposed by a proslavery faction known as the Hunkers. In the decade before the famine, Hunkers and Barnburners vied for control of the national Democratic party while Tammany Hall consolidated its hold on politics in New York City. These Democratic factions were joined in the 1840s by another, called the Young America Democrats, who advocated for territorial and commercial expansion, and who saw themselves as aligned with romantic nationalist campaigns in Europe, including the Young Irelanders.[17]

In opposition to the Jacksonian Democrats, the Whig Party emerged in the 1830s. Whigs claimed that government policy should work to benefit white men (and, according to some Whigs, white women) of all economic classes, but in practice they believed that policies that benefited monied interests would eventually benefit all of white society—a nineteenth-century version of trickle-down economics.[18] Because the Whigs emerged as an unstable collection of individuals opposed to Jacksonian Democratic principles, they experienced even more factionalism in the 1840s than the Democrats. Northern and Southern Whigs were often divided over issues of slavery. Urban Northern Whigs were sometimes more radical still, calling for a reorganization of the banking system in favor of private banks; for a limited freedom of religion in New York schools, in deference to New York City's rapidly expanding Catholic emigrant population; and for better education for New York's Black population. Other Whigs opposed these measures on the grounds that they were neither seemly nor genteel.[19] A large faction, which would in the 1850s break off to form the Know Nothing Party, was fiercely nativist, opposed to continued immigration, and particularly opposed to immigrant voters.[20] Know Nothings, who were especially powerful in cities, feared Catholic influence and produced Protestant propaganda claiming that, through immigration, the pope was looking to take over the United States.[21] As factions struggled within the parties, and as the parties struggled with each other on the national stage, they sought to accrue political power by mobilizing voters within New York City.

Control over news was central to these programs. Two newspapers dominated. The *New York Herald* had been founded in 1835 by James Gordon Bennett, who shaped the *Herald* into a Democratic party paper that often followed the Jacksonian party line, but which in the 1840s increasingly favored the expansionist ideology of Young America Democrats.[22] This meant that it supported US imperialism and the spread of slavery into newly acquired territories. This position was made most manifest in the later 1840s, when the paper argued for US annexation of Mexico (a position that would come to be entangled with the question of US governmental relief to the starving Irish.)[23] The Young America perspective was also represented in one of the *Herald's* innovations: a focus on both national and international news. For the first time in a popular newspaper, multiple columns were dedicated to news from Europe.[24] From its earliest days, the editors and writers for the *Herald* saw international news as a potentially useful political tool.

In contrast, the *New York Tribune* operated as the unofficial but widely accepted mouthpiece of the Whig Party, specifically the progressive, antislavery faction. Horace Greeley, a New York journalist and reformer who founded the *Tribune* in 1841, was opposed to many of the polities put forward by Jacksonian Democrats, and sought to counteract the sense that the Whig party was the purview of "an outgrown aristocracy."[25] In order to expand the reach of the party, the *Tribune* was priced as a penny paper. By the 1850s, it boasted nearly three hundred thousand subscribers, located both in New York City and across the nation.[26] Reporting on the famine in these papers was shaped by politics and politics was shaped by factionalism, as different groups vied for the heart of each party. Thus, although these two papers promoted specific ideological perspectives, the debates that were printed within their pages were framed by the tumult of ideas around them. They shaped understandings of the famine in New York City, and across the nation.

Imperial Dreams

Reports about the famine in New York often used the relationship among the United States, Ireland, and Britain as a way of talking about America's own imperial ambitions in the North American West, particularly with regard to Mexico. Some commentators used famine-struck Ireland as an example of the kind of governance to avoid; others argued that the United States would be better served by acting phil-anthropically on the global stage than it would engaging in rapacious expansion.

At the same time that Ireland was suffering from famine, the United States was engaged in a prolonged conflict with Mexico that began in the 1820s and 1830s, when white settlers from the United States began to relocate to the Mexican state of Tejas. These settlers brought enslaved people with them to Mexico, in the hope that the Mexican government would allow for the expansion of slavery; instead, the Mexican government did the opposite, seeking to limit slavery. In response, the white settlers, calling themselves the Republic of Texas, seceded from Mexico. In 1837, the president of the newly declared Texan republic, Sam Houston, suggested that the United States annex Texas as a slave state.[27] This request raised questions about how, and under what circumstances, the United States should intervene beyond—or even expand—its borders.

Politicians and political commentators from both the Democratic and Whig parties were initially skeptical of Houston's proposal. President Jackson supported the expansion of the United States but was concerned that the annexation of Texas would lead to war with Mexico.[28] Northern Whigs worried about the effect that new territory would have on eastern labor markets. While the prospect of another slave state was appealing to some Southerners, others feared that the sheer quantity of new territory would lead to a diffusion of the slave population, which would in turn detrimentally impact the Southern labor market. Moreover, Whigs worried that Texas's status as a slave state would further consolidate southern Democratic power.[29] In contrast, Southern en-slavers were deeply concerned by the prospect of Texas remaining a state in Mexico in which slavery was illegal, and of a vast free territory at the back door of the American South, a haven for runaway slaves. Democrats broadly supported annexation, believing that Texas was properly included in the Louisiana Purchase of 1803.[30]

Politicians in the United States were not the only ones thinking about what annexing Texas would mean for the United States. Many European diplomats and politicians hoped that an independent Republic of Texas would be a check on the growth of the United States.[31] In Britain, which was Mexico's most prominent foreign ally, politicians raised concerns about the impact of annexation on the British economy and British control in the region.[32] Allowing the United States to attack and annex Mexican territory with impunity would not only make Britain look weak but would also encourage further US expansion across the North American continent, possibly even into Central America.

The 1840s saw continued migration of white settlers to Texas and increased economic activity between Texas and the US Southeast. This created increased pressure on the federal government to accede to annexation, and, finally, in 1844, in the face of Texans' demands and growing domestic support, the US Congress agreed and promised that the United States would provide protection to Texans against Mexican retaliation. In response, Mexico declared war against Texas, and, in 1846, Congress approved a declaration of war against Mexico, thus forcing the United States to reckon with its imperial identity, much as Ireland and the famine had caused Britain to reckon with its own.[33]

It was against this backdrop that the issue of Irish relief was discussed for the first time in Congress in December 1846. Unsurprisingly, this discussion was interwoven with meditations about the cost of imperial expansion. Congress debated alternate measures to help the starving Irish. Senator John Dix of New Jersey first presented a petition from naval officer George DeKay, who proposed that the *Macedonian*, a British ship that had been seized by the US navy, be "fitted up for transporting supplies to the people of Ireland, and offering his services to the United States for that object."[34] DeKay's proposal was tabled, however, in order to accommodate the reading of an Irish relief bill, proposed by senator John Crittenden, that called for a half-million dollar appropriation to aid the suffering Irish and Scots. Many Democrats, and some Whigs, including Horace Greeley, the editor of the *Tribune*, opposed

the bill on the grounds that it was beyond the bounds of constitution-
ality to spend Americans' tax money on foreign causes. In March 1847,
to circumvent these criticisms, the citizens of Boston presented another
request for the loan of a US warship to Congress: they asked for the use
of the ship *Jamestown*, then in dry-dock in Boston harbor.

These three proposals—loan of the *Macedonian*, loan of the *Jamestown*, and the Irish relief bill—were debated simultaneously and were
largely supported by the Whig party, which argued that relieving Ireland was a better and less expensive use of government funds than pros-
ecuting the war with Mexico.[35] The Irish relief bill was defeated, but
the *Macedonian* and *Jamestown* schemes were adopted, providing useful
fodder for New York newspapers as they debated the wisdom of an ongoing war against Mexico.

New York City's major papers differed predictably in their support
for the war and invoked Ireland in their arguments for and against. The
Democratic *Herald* supported the war effort from the start, characterizing it as laying "the foundation of a new age, a new destiny, affecting
both this continent and the old continent of Europe."[36] The Whig-
oriented *Tribune* criticized the war as too expensive and printed without comment a speech of John C. Calhoun, the Democratic politician
and former vice president, who likened US expansion to other imperial
projects, some of which, he asserted, had been disasters for the metropole. In the speech, Calhoun cautioned that anarchy would follow if
a country of "free white Caucasian Men" expanded and made equals
of Texans, whom he described "a mixed-colored race, lower than the
Cherokee or Choctaw." Calhoun went on to draw a parallel to Anglo-
Irish relations, noting that "even Ireland is costing England and her
people heavily for having, seven centuries ago absorbed her. They are
this day a hostile people. Mexicans never will be reconciled to us."[37]
Despite his affiliation as a Democrat, Calhoun's words supported the
Tribune's perspective on the war with Mexico. Furthermore, Calhoun's
easy use of Ireland as an example of the dangers of imperialism points
to the ways in which US politicians were, even in the early years of the
famine, co-opting Ireland in service of national political issues.

The *Tribune* published its own articles deploying Ireland as an example
of annexation gone wrong. In May 1848, it printed an editorial that
posited: "If we go into this business of wholesale Annexation, Mexico

will become to us what Ireland and India now are to Great Britain—will compel us to keep up a large Standing Army, and very soon help us to a National Debt, and a variety and multiplicity of Taxes which even England cannot surpass."[38] In making these comparisons between annexed Texas and colonized Ireland, the *Tribune* argued that Ireland was in need of relief, and that its problems flowed from the relationship between Ireland and Britain. Both the *Herald* and the *Tribune* would go on to contextualize US foreign policy in terms of Ireland's need for aid.

In addition to making reference to Ireland's colonized status, commentators frequently tied debates over Irish famine relief to the question of funding for the war, often arguing that either Irish relief or the war could be funded, but not both. In staking one claim or the other, politicians and commentators argued for different understandings of US power on the global stage. Some Democrats adopted Ireland as a useful foil. In February 1847, New York senator Steven C. Johnson, a Democrat and Barnburner who was against the expansion of slavery, opposed "any public vote by Congress in Aid of Ireland," because "we are at war with Mexico." Robert Denniston, a fellow Democrat, agreed and went further, arguing that "Congress could not pay money for benevolent purposes abroad," but it could fund US interests via war.[39] For these commentators, aid and war were mutually exclusive.

In contrast, the Democratic-supporting *Herald* celebrated some measures of government relief. That paper noted that the dispatching of the *Macedonian* was particularly gratifying and ironic, because "the British government sent out the Macedonian with powder and balls to deal death among our sailors, but our tars took the king's ship away from the king's subjects, and now a Yankee sailor, by permission of an American Congress, goes back with the man of war deeply laden with the products of peace. Bread in return for cannon balls! Is not this good for evil!"[40] If the cost of Irish aid was borne by the British government, even at a remove through a captured ship, that was an acceptable use of funds. A few days later, an anonymous writer, using the name "Yankee Doodle," took a slightly different perspective, asserting in the *Tribune* that if a United States warship were sent on a humanitarian mission instead of to war, "history will dwell upon her first voyage with greater delight than if she were dispatched with instructions to bombard Vera Cruz."[41] With this comment, the writer suggested that the United States had a choice in deciding what sort of global power it wanted to be: one that pursued an imperial project in Mexico, or one that engaged in a philanthropic project in Ireland. Although this was manifestly untrue—the US Navy could accomplish both projects with existing resources, and the ships that the US government ultimately sent to Ireland were decommissioned—letters like this promoted famine relief as a useful alternative to US imperialism.

Throughout the 1840s, the *Tribune* continued to use the need for Irish relief to critique the war. In 1848, three months after the Treaty of Guadalupe Hidalgo officially ended the war and ceded vast swaths of western North America to the United States, one writer noted, "We are asked to show our sympathy for the shelterless, the distressed, the famishing" white settlers in still living in Mexico, "but when we were asked to incur a much smaller expense to save the Irish Millions from starvation, that was put down as unconstitutional."[42] A few months later, the paper continued to litigate the issue of whether it had been appropriate to devote resources to support the war, observing that some politicians had believed that it was "constitutional to compel Mexicans to come under our Government by force, as the English power compelled a part of Ireland to do." In this case, the paper created a parallel to what it viewed as unjust expansion, asking, "If American Republicans have the right to force Mexican Republicans by an invasion and the bayonet's point, to reestablish Slavery and come under a foreign yoke, have not English . . . the same right to invade and garrison and to compel Ireland to obey laws made in London?"[43] Throughout the famine, anti-war politicians and commentators in New York assumed that Irish relief was necessary because of British imperial impulses, and that both Britain and Ireland had suffered as a consequence. In doing so, they imagined a dire future if the United States continued to go down a similar path.

Courting Voters

New York politicians and the newspapers that served them also had pragmatic reasons to express concern for distant suffering. New York had always been a site of Irish immigration, but, in the early part of the eighteenth century, middle-class Catholic immigrants overtook

Protestants, and, in the decades before the famine, the character of Irish emigration shifted to include greater numbers of laborers and working-class immigrants.[44] These Irish communities became powerful political forces, and both parties courted their votes.[45] In doing so, they linked Irish relief to discourse about political power and how best to use it.

The Democratic Party had long relied on recently naturalized citizens to maintain their hold on political power.[46] For this reason, New York Democrats crafted a pro-immigrant, and particularly pro-Irish, posture.[47] This included gesturing at support for Daniel O'Connell's repeal movement and building relationships with branches of the Loyal National Repeal Association that developed in cities across the United States.[48] In response, the Whig-supporting *Tribune* worked throughout the famine to undermine Democratic support among the Irish. It suggested that Democratic politicians had voted against the Irish relief bill because they had "no sympathy for the Irish at home, as they can derive no political assistance from their votes while they remain there."[49] As the *Jamestown* and *Macedonian* were preparing to sail, the *Tribune* criticized Mace Moulton, a Democratic representative from New Hampshire, who, the paper said, claimed to be "friendly to human liberty everywhere, and anxious to alleviate the sufferings of the wretched" while simultaneously working to "destroy the bill which an American senate has passed in order to afford some relief to the suffering people of Ireland."[50]

The *Tribune* also brought this critique to local politics. Oliver Hungerford, a Democratic member of Congress from New York State, ran for controller of finances for the State of New York in 1847. Hungerford had voted against the relief bill, but supported the missions of the *Jamestown* and *Macedonian*. In its commentary on the race, the *Tribune* often trumpeted Hungerford's failure to attend to "the Starving people of Ireland when in their direst extremity."[51] In its reporting on the 1848 presidential election, the *Tribune* also encouraged Irishmen "who, having become American citizens, will to-day exercise their right of voting for a Chief Magistrate, of their adopted country" to vote according to politicians' positions on the Irish relief bill.[52] Irish relief was not only a useful political symbol; it also had electoral power.

The *Herald* used the famine to argue for a specific concept of the American nation and local politics. In 1847, it reported on a bill that would limit immigration to the United States, in particular impoverished immigrants seeking relief from starvation in Ireland. The bill's sponsor was a member of the nativist America party and represented New York. The *Herald*—predictably, as a Democratic publication—opposed such a bill, arguing that "it would be worse than unwise if any course should be pursued tending to discourage the emigration to this country of respectable citizens of the Old World."[53] For these papers, Irish relief was tied up with national policy concerning the extent of American power, policy that happened to play a role in the political calculus of the parties in New York City.

The Democratic attitude to the Irish nationalism spawned by the famine echoed its attitude toward the United States' imperial ambitions. In the early months of the famine, both the *Herald* and the *Tribune* reported repeal meetings, attended by "three hundred or four hundred of the 'Repeal Boys' assembled together . . . of every make, shape and character."[54] However, the *Herald* bore particular animosity toward O'Connell's movement. In November 1845, with little irony, the paper accused O'Connell of using the forecast famine for political ends, rather than working to mitigate the crisis.[55] It studiously reported the formation of "Young Ireland" parties in New York, whom it accused of "mixing repeal with hunger" in an attempt to benefit politically from Irish starvation. "Will repeal feed the starving peasant and his large family?" asked a *Herald* editorial. "No! Let us have a meeting of our people, without distinction, to raise money to buy food and 'repeal' can be talked of another time."[56]

The anti-war *Tribune* was far more celebratory of Irish nationalist politics. When it was accused by a rival Whig paper of organizing "parties to raise tribute for O'Connell and to bring about a repeal of the Irish Union with England," the paper responded that "we have done no more for Ireland than we would gladly do for" any other European country. The author went on to express surprise that support of "domestic legislative independence for Ireland" would be "a matter of division among Americans, supposing that they would all naturally incline to the side of Civil Liberty and the Rights of Conscience."[57] Opponents, in turn, interpreted this support as merely courting the immigrant vote in the city.

Irish nationalist politics came to the fore in the New York press in 1848, after the attempted, and ultimately failed, uprising.[58] Editorials in the *Herald* in the aftermath of the rebellion demonstrated a somewhat contradictory attitude to their approach to the American war with Mexico; they recommended that England sever ties with Ireland, rather than maintain a costly relationship. In an article entitled "Ireland Cutting the Gordian Knot," the paper wrote that "there is only one wise and safe course for the British government to pursue with regards to Ireland . . . that is—cast her off, leave her to herself, let her stand alone, let her manage herself and let her own concerns, just as she pleases."[59] At the same time, the paper criticized fundraising efforts in the United States to support a rebellion that would facilitate that same separation. In particular, US involvement in Irish political affairs was a cause for concern to Democrats. The *Herald* averred that "the cause of Ireland must depend on the Irish," stating that "if the Irish, English or Scotch or any other people mean to secure their rights and privileges they must rise up spontaneously and claim them in the same way as the Americans did their revolution, and as the French in their late revolution, have obtained theirs."[60] This arms-length approach to the Irish rebellion might have been politically expedient, insofar as it did not alienate too many Irish voters. However, it also demonstrated an ambiguous approach to imperialism and independence. It would seem that, insofar as the white settlers in Texas had declared and fought for their independence, Democrats felt comfortable accepting their petition for statehood and fighting Mexico on their behalf. They did not feel the same way about Irish peasants rebelling against a resident landlord class.

The *Tribune*'s attitude demonstrated more consistency. After the uprising, the paper continued its earlier trend of support for Irish nationalist politics. One month before the failed rebellion, it publicized a meeting of "the friends of Ireland and of humanity," which was intended to "take such action as may be necessary in the present imminent crisis of Ireland's affairs, and especially with reference to the arbitrary and inhuman conduct of the British Government."[61] After news of the rebellion reached New York, the paper published numerous calls for meetings in support of Irish nationalists and "lovers of Liberty."[62] Before the famine, the New York papers were familiar with Irish politics. During and after the famine, they readily weighed in on those politics, with the dual aim of cultivating electorally useful constituents and courting popular support at home.

Philanthropic Power Abroad

Although the Democrats and the Whigs disagreed about how US power should be used, they both believed that the country's power was on the rise. Both used the famine to argue for the country's exceptionalism, in ways that foreshadowed US claims to international moral authority in the late nineteenth and early twentieth centuries. For instance, the General Relief Committee of the City of New York, which had formed at the Prime, Ward & Co. building in February 1847, solicited funds through personal connections and through the press. Through the *Tribune* and the *Herald*, the General Relief Committee argued that US citizens were uniquely positioned to aid Ireland, due to the prosperity of the country and its emergent status on the world stage. At the same time, they argued, US support for Irish relief, either through individual donation or congressional legislation, would bolster the country's image abroad.

Many of the appeals for aid in New York, both those published by relief agencies and comments in the press, took as a given that the abundance of American soil could supply Ireland with food. One of the first mentions of relief in the *Herald* proclaimed: "Our country is peculiarly favored. Our harvests are superabundant. At present we have more than enough to supply ourselves, and the starving Irish too. . . . There is a heavy responsibility at present resting on America in this matter."[63] In 1847, the *Herald* suggested that those who were unable to give money should be convinced to give food, and if the relief groups would "send one or more active persons to the valley of the Mississippi, that inexhaustible land of plenty, with a view of calling meetings and canvassing the cities, towns and country places for contributions in provisions, breadstuffs, &c. Thousands of generous people in the West who might not probably have the money to spare, would give liberally of the produce of their rich soil."[64] The *Tribune* elaborated on this theme by noting that it would be difficult for US citizens to imagine the dreadful state of Ireland, because they had never experienced scarcity on so great a scale. In calling for American donations, they "state[d] generally that no one can truly realize, in a land of comparative plenty, how frightfully extensive and harrowing are the woes of Famine now endured in Ireland." Given this vast discrepancy between the land of plenty in America and of want in Ireland, the paper asked rhetorically, "Who can hesitate to give something to mitigate the sufferings caused by such a calamity?"[65] Such statements served not only as calls for aid; they also served to frame the United States as superior to the "Old World," blessed by plenty.

The requirement of US citizens to donate was made all the more immediate by the ease with which New Yorkers in particular were able to learn about the famine. The *Tribune* noted that, at a famine relief meeting, "one of the most enthusiastic assemblages ever gathered in this City," it was resolved "that the nearness to which the Old World and the New are brought by steam navigation, making the trans-Atlantic cry for food strong in our ears as though it came from some distant member of our own confederacy." Further, that nearness afforded "facilities for extending relief which cannot rightfully be disregarded."[66] The *Herald* echoed the *Tribune*'s sentiment a few weeks later: "The spirit of benevolence is as general as the information (thanks to the American newspaper press,) respecting the distress of our transatlantic brethren."[67]

However, simply noting that New Yorkers ought to give because they knew about Irish starvation did not seem to garner sufficient donations. If they had, it is unlikely that Irish relief groups would have employed more and more specific—and increasingly political—reasons that New Yorkers should feel obligated to donate. Each of these reasons was linked to the United States' growing power on the world stage.

The first was economic, calling for donations because of the degree of profit that many American farmers were making off of the Irish crisis. An advertisement in the *Tribune* called for "at least $1,000,000 [to be] contributed from this country to mitigate the present distress in Ireland," because "the calamity which has reduced so many of her People to utter misery has put money in our coffers—millions of dollars have been realized by our farmers, forwarders, millers, shippers &c. in the advance price of Grain over the price they would have received but for the failure of the harvests in Europe."[68] On the other hand, the *Tribune* wrote a month later, there was money to be made if large-scale Irish relief was accomplished: "By affording them relief, a new and vastly increased market for Indian corn and breadstuffs would be provided, in a country of eight millions of inhabitants."[69] Although Ireland's population was less than half that of the United States in 1840, the prospect of eight million new consumers would have piqued the interest of American merchants. Of course, a consumer sunk in poverty and starvation is not a consumer at all, so it would be necessary to get the Irish on their feet first.

This sentiment was echoed by several commentators of the time outside of New York City. George D. Prentice, the editor of the *Louisville Journal*, used a New Orleans famine relief meeting to remind listeners that Americans were making millions exporting food to Ireland.[70] Philip Hone, a former New York mayor, commented in his diary that he had felt "a little bad" about dining on "one of Mr. Ray's *pates de foie gras*" while there were landing in New York the "perfectly destitute" Irish, who had "no clothes, no friends, no object in view."[71] Others, including George Templeton Strong, a New York lawyer, were more pragmatic. Strong speculated that if the price of grain fell, donations to Ireland would fall as well, presumably because American merchants would no longer feel that Ireland was reciprocally aiding merchants through the purchase of foreign grain.[72]

In addition to economic opportunity, commentators noted that another reason for giving was that a boost in America's moral status could promote its geopolitical interests. Conflicts with Britain over the boundary between Oregon and Canada and over the legality of the war with Mexico caused editors of both papers to note that substantive donations to Irish famine relief were a bright mark on America's national character. The *Tribune* wrote in late 1846 that "the moral influence of a contribution of $100,000 from this Country for the relief of the starving Irish would be worth far more than the food which this contribution would buy. . . . The more unfeeling portion of the aristocracy of Ireland and Britain would feel rebuked and humbled by this exhibition of trans-Atlantic benevolence."[73] The *Herald* was blunter still, commenting in February 1847—the month that featured the most published appeals for aid to Ireland in both newspapers—that participation in famine relief would "confer a twofold benefit on us; it will prove to the world that Americans think on other matters besides the acquisition of money, and that our country is as inexhaustible as it is extensive, and that it is capable of being the granary of the world."[74] There was potential, these papers argued, for Irish famine relief to buy international approval.

To take its rightful place in the world, however, the United States had to overcome its isolationist tendencies. One way to do so was to use the historic contributions of the Irish to American society to argue that famine relief was a debt repaid. In part, this theme invoked contemporary debates over the value of immigrants in American society. Nativists were not only opposed to the presence of Irish bodies in America; they also built campaigns around criticisms of the Irish Republican movements, arguing that Irish Americans who were agitating for the repeal of Act of Union of 1800 between Britain and Ireland were subordinating American needs to Irish ones, and sowing discord between the United States and Great Britain.[75] Democrats and mainstream Whigs disputed this. In February 1847, the *Tribune* reprinted a speech given in Boston by W. E. Robinson, the editor of the *Buffalo Daily Express*, who claimed that "the spirit which animated the hearts of Irishmen required no change to fit them for American institutions under another sky beyond the sea. In 1776 George Washington was king—George III the tyrant in Irish hearts. There were 'Yankee clubs' in Ireland then, which were in correspondence with Washington. The Irish are natives of this country in feeling and in mind."[76] According to commentators like Robinson, in order for famine relief to demonstrate US leadership on a global stage, Irish revolutionaries needed to be coopted into claims of American revolutionary exceptionalism.

Whig and Democratic politicians and newspapers appropriated accounts of Irish suffering, and relief efforts, in order to bolster their own political power. The framings of the Irish famine in the party papers of New York painted a picture of the United States as ascendent, the beneficiary of providential favor, a land of abundance. The Irish had always been part of that story; they were colonial siblings with an equally complicated relationship with England.

Where the parties diverged was in what the United States should do with the power that it accrued. Would it follow the example of Britain and seek imperial conquest? Or would it use its power to aid those in need, those to whom the young country owed a debt? The abstract nature of this debate suggests that accounts of Ireland in New

York circles were divorced from the actual starvation of actual people. Famine relief was malleable, and, in many different political contexts, useful. This was facilitated in part by the distance between Ireland and New York, and the many different information channels that carried Irish news to North America. It also reflected widespread acceptance of the idea that famine relief could be put to political ends.

Elsewhere in New York, groups who explicitly rejected party politics adopted famine relief into their sometimes violent arguments for tenants' rights and land reform. In contrast to commentators in rural Ireland, who muted their call for reform in the face of the need for actual relief, these men were able to divorce the discussion of relief from the experiences of famine sufferers.

5

Land Reform

Osman Steele died on August 7, 1845, in Delaware County, New York. Steele was Delaware's undersheriff, and had been tasked with overseeing the sale of cattle belonging a man named Moses Earle. Earle was tenant of Charlotte Verplanck, who owned twenty thousand acres in central New York State.[1] For two years Earle had withheld his rent, believing that the money and labor he had invested in the land was more than equivalent to the rent charged by Verplanck.[2] Undersheriff Steele was instructed to put the cattle up for auction and use the money from the sale to pay Verplanck. This was no easy task. Steele's efforts on the day of the auction were stymied by the arrival of hundreds of "Calico Indians"—a name adopted by white New Yorkers who, dressed in calico and masks and armed with knives and guns, used both threats and actual violence to prevent landlords and their representatives from collecting rents.[3] Shots were fired by both the undersheriff's men and by the protestors. In the chaos, Steele was killed.[4] Local landlords and government officials moved quickly to punish the people they believed were the perpetrators. Two of the "Calico Indian" leaders were convicted of his murder and sentenced to death.[5] These kinds of encounters were commonplace in 1840s New York. They had been playing out since the late 1830s, as part of a conflict between landlords and tenants that came to be known locally as the Anti-Rent Wars.

The same landholding practices that set the stage for Steele's death in New York State had contributed to the conditions that allowed a single crop failure to become a catastrophic famine in Ireland. Like their New York counterparts, Irish landlords and their representatives were also experiencing escalating violence in the 1840s.[6] On November 31, 1845 in Kilkenny, James Costelloe was murdered in circumstances very similar to Steele's. Like Steele, Costelloe was tasked with recovering property owed to a landlord. In this case, a tenant named Martin Broderick was tending to two cows owned by his landlord Burton Pierce. When

Broderick failed to pay rent, Costelloe, acting on behalf of Pierce, re-possessed the cows. On the night of November 31, in retalition, an as-sassin shot Costelloe in the neck while he ate dinner with his family.[7]

These two acts of violence—which are but examples of more ex-tensive campaigns—highlight the ways in which questions about who owned land, who worked it, and who benefited from that work preoc-cupied people on both sides of the Atlantic in the 1840s. The circum-stances in which both Steele and Costelloe lived and died revealed deep and sometimes dangerous tensions between the interests of landlords and tenants. The histories of rural Ireland and central New York in the years before the famine mirrored one another. In both places, activ-ists called for "land reform," and tied that reform to landlord-tenant relations. However, whereas Anti-Renters in New York were able to use the suffering of distant Irish strangers to call for a radical reimagin-ing of relationships between landlords and tenants, commentators in some of the worst-affected parts of Ireland were faced with what one newspaper succinctly called "actual starvation."[8] The immediacy of that starvation, and the disease and death that followed in its wake, led Irish commentators who might in other circumstances have called for more radical political shifts to instead seek solutions through moderation of landlords' behavior. From places with similar histories, two very dif-ferent interpretations of the relationships between landlords, tenants and famine relief emerged, starkly illustrating how proximity shaped discourse around aid and reform.

Landholding Practices in New York and Ireland

The lives of tenants in rural Ireland and New York in the years before the famine were astonishingly similar. In both places, people who made a living from the land were overwhelmingly renters, whose relation-ship to the land was regionally distinct. In much of England and in much of the United States many renters farmed land that they would eventually purchase from banks or—in the United States—from the federal government. Others worked plots that belonged to family members, participating in hereditary ownership even if they did not hold deeds themselves.[9] Many tenant farmers in these places achieved financial stability, and were able to accrue capital that allowed them, or their children, to eventually purchase property.[10] This was not the case in central New York or in much of rural Ireland; there, most tenants farmed land to which they and their descendants would never hold permanent title.[11]

In New York's centrally located Delaware, Schoharie, Albany, Rensselaer, and Columbia Counties, much of the land had been owned for generations among a few families, like the Verplancks, from whom Moses Earle withheld his rent and on whose errand Steele was shot. Many of the farmers laboring on these estates in the 1840s were descended from tenants who began renting shortly after the American Revolution. This long history meant that the lives of the people who owned and those who rented the land were built on relationships freighted with inherited feudal expectations and obligations.

The doyens of New York's landholding families had been drawn to the colonial mid-Atlantic by reports of open space and fertile soil.[12] Some of these families had originally been granted tracts of land by the Dutch West India Company. Britain honored these grants after it claimed New Netherland in the eighteenth century, establishing a resident landed aristocracy much like that in Ireland. Also much like in Ireland, contracts in this part of New York State were based on medieval English property law. They passed from generation to generation, effectively establishing a stake in the land without ownership. By the late eighteenth century, most tenants' farms were productive enough that farmers were routinely able to pay rent. However, they did not produce enough surplus to allow tenants to accrue capital to purchase their own land outright at the prices that landlords set. Long-term, often multigenerational, contracts were tenants' primary sources of wealth and stability.[13]

This system suited landlords, who could expect a regular and predictable source of income. For a time it also suited tenants, who could plan for long-term commitments and improvements to their parcels of land.[14] These long-standing relationships also meant that tenants' financial obligations to landlords were often fluid. Farmers experiencing a shortfall one year could expect leeway to repay the debt in following years; landlords knew that farmers who came up short would want to preserve their relationship and were likely to eventually pay. However, this system only allowed for so much flexibility. The terms of contracts in New York State made it difficult for tenants to borrow money to fund revenue-generating enterprises. In practice, when tenants fell far behind in their rents, they often stayed behind.[15] This, combined with the length of these relationships, also meant that landlords often felt a sense of quasi-feudal obligation to tenants. They founded schools and hospitals, and some even provided charitable aid to tenants in need. In exchange for these benevolent acts, landlords came to expect deference from the people they rented to.[16] These features made the system of landed relations in this part of New York State simultaneously stable and exploitative in ways that closely resembled contemporaneous landholding practices in Ireland before the famine.

In the early nineteenth-century, the relationships between landlords and tenants began to degrade on both sides of the Atlantic. In New York, large, landed families began to eschew primogeniture, dividing their property equally among their children, resulting in smaller, less consistently productive estates. Landlords responded to this new uncertainty by demanding more rent, becoming less likely to forgive arrears, and retreating from traditional patrician benevolence. This more precarious system might have continued well into the nineteenth century, had a financial panic in 1819 not added additional financial strain. Suddenly, landlords who were previously cushioned from the worst effects of reduced rents could not get by, and they began to aggressively pursue overdue payments. Tenants who had previously been living hand to mouth were forced to deplete their already scarce resources. Whereas in the past these tenants might have been able to put off paying rent for a time, they were plunged into insolvency and became unable to maintain their leases. Their precarity worsened when landlords began to close off common lands, which had traditionally been used for grazing animals and collecting firewood, further reducing tenants' access to subsistence.[17]

This financial stress, and the consequent move to privatize the resources of formerly communal lands, mirrored movements that had long been at work in Ireland.[18] In the early nineteenth century, Irish landlords also had difficulties collecting rents and maintaining their benevolent obligations.[19] As was the case in central New York, Irish landlords often owned estates populated by tenant farmers living increasingly perilous lives on ever-shrinking plots. Irish tenants, like those in New York, were frequently unable to produce even enough food to feed their families, not to mention selling any surplus to accrue or grow capital. Some farmers had invested in improvements to their tenancies, but landlords were not obligated to compensate tenants for the work that went into making the soil more profitable.[20] External pressure meant that Irish landlords increasingly had little interest in their tenants' welfare, beyond their ability to pay rent. As tenants became ever more aware of landlords' abuses of power, they often retaliated through loosely organized political violence, agrarian outrages, and, in some cases, assassinations.[21] In both rural Ireland and rural New York in the early nineteenth century, to be a landlord was to live with the possibility of violent reprisal; to be a tenant was to live at the edge of destitution and starvation.

The politics of land in New York and Ireland were brought together by Thomas Ainge Devyr, an Irish radical whose work as a transatlantic political activist helped to cement the relationship between famine philanthropy and land reform on both sides of the Atlantic. Devyr was born in rural Donegal to parents who, "though in a small way of business, were very poor."[22] From his parents' circumstances, he inherited the belief that failed and toxic relationships between landlords and tenants were "the great blight, which, hanging over the land, keeps in a state of nature our reclaimable wastes, and blasts with comparative sterility our most fertile vales."[23] In the early 1830s, preoccupied by the "evil" that he traced "to monopoly of the soil by a few, and exclusion from it of the many," he became committed to land reform.[24]

Devyr was part of a long tradition of—often violent—land activism in Ireland. Extrapolitical groups used guerrilla violence to enforce their own standards of justice.[25] This included punishing landlords, or people working on their behalf like James Costelloe, when they levied extractive rents, repossessed property, or unjustifiably evicted tenants.[26] These groups sought to establish a shadow system of governance that would protect tenants' interests.[27] For instance, across southeastern Ireland in the 1820s, hundreds of threatening leaflets and notices were posted, signed by the pseudonymous "Captain Rock." These notices not only issued threats but also proposed legislative solutions to peasants' distress.[28] Although the "Rockite" movement dwindled in the later 1820s, agrarian resistance to landlords continued throughout the 1840s, and into the years of the famine.[29]

Devyr moved from Donegal to London, and then to Newcastle and on to Scotland, taking ideas about land rights and reform with him. In each place, he endeavored to prosecute "a war against Land Monopoly—a war to the death—the either one or the other should die."[30] In England, he joined the Chartists, a working-class political movement, and attempted to overthrow the British government in 1840. The rebellion failed, and Devyr faced charges of sedition. He fled to New York City, where he helped to establish the National Reform Association, a group dedicated to the ending private ownership of land.[31] Through the National Reform Association, Devyr was able to connect people interested in land reform to a transatlantic network of farmers and tenants that spanned the United States, England, and Ireland.[32]

This expertise ideally suited Devyr to the politics of land in central New York, where the combination of rising rents, shrinking viable landholdings, and vanishing public agricultural space echoed the Ireland that Devyr had left behind. Tensions came to a head several years before the famine. In 1839, Stephen Van Rensselaer III, the septuagenarian patriarch of Van Rensselaerwyck manor, had died. His estate was the largest in the region, spanning over one million acres. At the end of his life, Van Rensselaer had considerable unpaid debts, but was also owed back rent by thousands of tenants with debts of their own.[33] His sons and heirs, Stephen and William, who were saddled with these unwieldy financial obligations, turned to lawsuits against tenants with unpaid rents to extricate themselves. In response, tenants organized and resisted: they argued that landlords' original land claims were invalid, that laws protecting landlords turned tenants into feudal serfs, and that improvements that tenants made to the land should accrue to them rather than to landlords.[34] They asked that the rent arrears be forgiven and proposed a plan by which tenants could purchase their farms from the Van Rensselaer family. These solutions included provisions similar to those taken up by Rockites in Ireland a decade earlier.[35] The Van Rensselaer heirs refused.

As had been the case in Ireland earlier in the century, New York tenants then turned to more public solutions. They began to run Anti-Rent candidates for local office, organized petitions, and supported legislation that would allow tenants to receive compensation for improvements on their leased land. Tenants beyond the Van Rensselaerwyck estate, such as those who rented land from Charlotte Verplanck, joined the movement, which eventually spread to include ten thousand tenant families, living on nearly two million acres of land.[36] Parallel to this formal political effort, groups of masked "Calico Indians," like those who attacked Osman Steele, agitated to prevent the collection of rents, protect families who were at risk of eviction, and intimidate opponents.[37] Devyr, who became interested in the politics of land in central New York after he settled in New York City, was one of the principal architects of the civil disobedience, public protest, and violence that New York tenants used to assert their rights.[38]

The conflict escalated on the eve of the famine, both echoing and foreshadowing events in Ireland. Landlords or their representatives— like Osman Steele—seized and sold tenants' property in lieu of unpaid rents, as had happened to Moses Earle. Tenants stormed landlords' houses.[39] Some tenants committed murder. This was a conflict that aspired to undo the remnants of landed society in Central New York.[40] In the 1840s this political agitation began to pay off. Pro-tenant candidates for office swept local elections, and sought to enact laws protecting tenants and limiting landlords' actions. These included prohibiting landlords from selling tenants' personal property to recoup overdue rents and allowing the taxation of landlords' rental income.[41]

By the 1840s, tenants and tenants' rights activists in both rural New York and Ireland viscerally understood the ruinous consequences of land ownership being concentrated in the hands of a few. In both places, tenants' attempts to assert their rights had been stymied by people in hereditary positions of power. In both, some activists had responded with violence, while many had suffered from scarcity—and, in the case of rural Ireland, starvation. Despite these similarities, however, commentators in rural Ireland and rural New York differed markedly in their interpretations of landlords' role in famine relief. These different interpretations lay bare the pragmatic politics that underlay uses of relief on both sides of the Atlantic.

Relief by Landlords

The newspapers of County Cork, in southeastern Ireland, were in many ways ideal sites for the rhetorical intertwining of famine relief and land reform. Southeastern Ireland had emerged as a center of Irish intellectual life in the late eighteenth century.[42] Cork had become a hotbed of agrarian threats and violence during the 1820s. In the decades that followed, the neighboring counties of Killarney, Limerick and Tipperary became centers of rural unrest. In the 1840s, Cork became synonymous with some of the most harrowing effects of the crop failure.[43] Cork's status as the touchstone for famine misery was bolstered by local newspapers' extensive documentation of the extent of distress, the kinds of relief measures employed, and the successes and failures of those attempts. In the later years of the famine, one Cork author poignantly described the role of the city's newspapers, lamenting that "we again find ourselves set to our old shocking task of recording the sufferings of the people. We are again called on to bear witness."[44] Although this trauma might have led tenants' advocates to call for the legislative or violent overthrow of landed classes, instead it prompted them to advocate for reforms rooted in landlords' behavior.

Many of these calls for reform came from the *Cork Examiner*, which had been founded in 1841 by John Francis Maguire, an Irish nationalist and advocate for Catholic emancipation who would go on to become a member of Parliament and then lord mayor of Cork.[45] Under Maguire, the *Examiner* enthusiastically supported the tenants' rights movement and the repeal of the Act of Union. In many ways, Maguire's politics aligned with Anti-Renters in New York, although he was not nearly as radical as Devyr (few were). Despite these philosophical connections, when news of the famine first began to appear in the Irish countryside in the autumn of 1845, the *Examiner* did not marshal the language of land reform; instead, it initially focused on celebrating landlords who modeled behaviors called for by Irish tenants' advocates. This was reform of landlords from within, rather than through legislation or violent uprising.

This strategy was most notable in November 1845, when the *Examiner* printed a series of letters celebrating benevolent landlords. One commented that a "good landlord" had "noticed his intention of retaining all the potatoes grown on his estate for the support of such of his tenantry as may require them in the ensuing spring, and not permitting any to be disposed of or removed off the property."[46] Another reported on a landlord in Clare who, when his tenants told him that the crops had failed "he said to them—you have lost your seed and your labor. . . . I shall never ask you for a shilling of rent!"[47] Another still noted "a good a humane act on the part of a worthy resident landlord" who "nobly remitted the entire rent of all the ground in potatoes [that] had been planted" on his estate. The letter closed with a plea that "it is to be hoped, that other landlords will set in a similar manner." In September 1847, another letter to the *Examiner* celebrated the "most benevolent and most Christian conduct of Mr. James Walpole of Macroom for his very considerable and humane treatment of his conacre and other tenants." This letter's author went on to write that it was necessary to dispense "praise and commendation in these times of extreme destitution and distress in the kind, considerate and generous conduct evinced by a neighboring farmer towards his laborers and conacre tenants," and that he hoped "that others, encouraged and stimulated by such laudable and benevolent example will come forth and 'do likewise.'"[48] Pointing out virtuous landlords, this letter and other articles noted, was a way to encourage good behavior among the less virtuous.

Language encouraging benevolence among landlords also appeared in the *Cork Constitution*, the city's oldest and most conservative paper. Unlike the *Examiner*, the *Cork Constitution* tended to support the Protestant Anglo-Irish elite.[49] Its editors saw the paper as an advocate for the rights of landlords, much like the *Dublin Evening Mail*. These politics made it easy for the *Constitution* to emphasize landlords' central role in famine relief. One article in 1846 opined that landlords should not force the issue of rent, because "to insist upon" collecting "rent would be about as wise an enterprise as that of the philosopher who undertook to extract sunbeams from cucumbers."[50] An 1847 letter to the *Constitution* applauded acts of landed benevolence in language similar to that printed in the *Examiner*, noting that "Mr. Smith of Ballynatray has given up his fine pack of hounds, in consequence of the pressure of the times on the poor, and the praiseworthy determination of not feeding animals [during the famine] "with the food destined for human beings."[51] Like the *Examiner*, the *Constitution* recommended that landlords continue to act benevolently. Celebrations of their generosity were often accompanied by suggestions "that other landlords will set in a similar manner."[52] Both papers argued that the actions of local landlords could literally determine whether their tenants would live or die.

Both lauded the actions of "generous" landlords and chastised abusive ones. This shared approach reflected a certain pragmatism. Because they were so close to sites of suffering, the Cork papers could not afford to treat the famine as a metaphor or political trope; people were in need and landlords, if they behaved well, could help.

The Cork City newspapers encouraged landlords to support public works projects to "improve the social condition of the laboring classes of Ireland," as well as encouraged monetary contributions to local relief efforts, especially because many of the public works projects funded by the British government in Ireland actually benefited private land.[53] As the author of one letter to the *Constitution* wrote, "Let some of those whose property is to be benefited by all this outlay put their hands into their own pockets and furnish it."[54] While some landlords condemned the projects as slow or inefficient, others lauded improvements to the land—in particular, bog reclamation and improvements to Ireland's fisheries.

In addition to their calls for individual benevolence, these papers argued that landlords were uniquely able to provide or deny work opportunities, and thereby a livelihood, to the laborers in their midst. Their views on public works projects were more likely to sway policy than those of tenants. In many ways, articles and letters in both the *Constitution* and the *Examiner* were addressing landlords directly, calling on them to take action, and highlighting their role in the process of famine relief. Whereas other land reformers were able to argue that the removal—or, at least, significant curtailing of landlords—was the best way to achieve Irish relief, this was not a position that was tenable for commentators in close proximity to the crisis. For writers in the *Cork Constitution* and *Examiner*, failing to consider landlords as a possible source of aid would have been a betrayal of tenants living on the brink of death.

Cork newspapers' congratulations of landlords' behavior suggest that both contributors to and readers of the Irish press outside of Dublin, and in sites proximate to suffering, were aware of the ways in which landlords might mitigate the consequences of famine. In addition, this praise was likely meant to work against the perceived tendencies of some landlords toward eviction in the face of their tenants' misfortune. While some readers of the Cork City newspapers would not have been personally familiar with evictions and clearances, both papers discussed the perfidy of "peasant-exporting landlords."[55] Contemporary newspapers across Ireland and Britain referred to the removal of tenants who had not paid rent as "exterminations": a term that reflected the mayhem that evictions caused for people who were already destitute and who were forced by their removal to beg, enter the workhouse, and, in many cases, die.[56] Irish Catholic and Romantic nationalists adopted the term; for example, John Mitchel wrote in 1854, using language that became commonplace a decade earlier, that landlords practiced "extermination, that is the slaughter of their tenantry."[57] Throughout the famine, clearances and exterminations frequently featured in calls for land reform and tenant protections.

As the famine progressed, and as it became clear that many Irish landlords were not swayed by celebrations of beneficence and model behavior, the *Examiner's* strategy shifted to shaming, but still did not call for radical reform. On September 20, 1847, it printed a letter describing how "the agent of Sr. W. Wrixon Bacher, aided by his drivers and assistants, expelled from their cabins (situated in North street) three wretched families by the mode of leveling their dwellings to the ground. One of the parties is a widow with a large family." The letter writer used the example of this brutality to castigate landlords as a group. Rejecting any hope that landlords might give aid, it opined that at this stage of the famine "little is expected from this class—the oppressors of the peasant and tenant farmers."[58] Language in the *Examiner* shifted from celebrations of individuals to denigrations of all. An editorial in the same issue commented that "the landlords seemed determined to push matters to an extremity" and lamented that efforts to reform individual landlords had failed. The author marveled that "if ever the landlord heart of Ireland could be changed, by calamity, by sympathy with suffering, by a feeling for the oppression of others, threatened as they are themselves, surely such a social and moral change should have been the result of the year of calamity that has passed by." [59] Still another letter to the *Examiner* in October 1847 condemned landlords who engaged in evictions, nothing that "no cause can be alleged for this sweeping act of extermination, save a desire of removing the poor at any rate, and feeding upon that land sheep and oxen which God and Nature intended for the support of its indigenous inhabitants."[60] These descriptions of

evictions and castigations of the landlords responsible only became politically useful for the *Examiner* when more moderate recommendations
failed.

The *Constitution*, however, took a different approach to clearances. It
did not mention evictions, but celebrated removals undertaken with care.
In April 1847, returning to earlier modes of reporting, it lauded "a noble
example" of a landlord who provided "for the conveyance of the poor on
his estate in Sligo to our colonies in North America" a ship "in which the
comfort of the passengers has been so much studied: the berths for sleep-
ing are most spacious, the provisions are most plentiful and of excellent
quality."[61] Despite these expansive descriptions, the *Constitution*'s sense
of landlords' obligations is perhaps best summed up in a letter printed
in November 1846. Its author, E. H., opined that "those who (with their
ancestors) have lived in more or less luxury for the last two or three centuries on the sweat of the brow of the poor on their estates, ought to be
taught that the time has arrived when they, in their turn, must stir themselves aye, and labor too, in behalf of those who have hitherto labored
and will still labor for them."[62]

This was, of course, not the only rhetoric about famine relief that
circulated in Southeastern Ireland. As the crisis progressed, both of the
newspapers printed in Cork City began to call for structural solutions
amid their celebrations and castigation of landlord behavior. The *Constitution*, like the *Dublin Evening Mail*, hoped for government relief
for landlords, who were increasingly unable to pay their rents. The *Examiner* called for protections that would prevent tenants from being
evicted.[63] However, for neither paper was the question of famine relief
a proxy in other political arguments. Perhaps unsurprisingly, for these
prominent newspapers of Southeastern Ireland, those who were forced
"to bear witness" to famine suffering had no desire to politicize the
means of relieving that suffering.

Relief from Landlords

In New York, by contrast, Anti-Renters used the example of Ireland to
pursue their own local agendas, which reflected both opposition to land
monopoly and tensions within the Anti-Rent movement itself. After
the success of rural agitation campaigns, Anti-Renters quickly began to

diverge over both aims and tactics. Militants, including many of those who participated in "Calico Indian" acts of violence, sought to accomplish the dissolution of land ownership by any means necessary. Some, like Devyr, argued for the wholesale abolition of the landed class and of private property. Devyr and his compatriots hoped to accomplish that abolition through legislation, but were often sympathetic toward those who sought extralegislative solutions.[64] Another group did not see private property as axiomatically dangerous; rather, they believed that the breaking of landed monopoly was an opportunity for some tenants—the industrious ones—to leverage capitalism for their own economic security. They did not seek to overturn the social system of central New York, but merely to adjust it to be more equitable.[65] For each of these various perspectives, Ireland provided a useful example.

Even before widespread reports of the famine reached New York State, the *Albany Freeholder*, a newspaper that Devyr helped to found and for which he served as editor in 1845, pointed to Irish tenants as ideal examples of the abuses of large-scale landholding. According to the *Freeholder*, the problem with Ireland was that tenants were unable to reach their full economic potential. An article published in early 1846 mused that "from no man's life, perhaps, is hope more rigidly excluded than of the Irish peasant of a poor district."[66] This exclusion, the article argued, was a result of rapacious landlords. At an Albany anti-rent meeting reported in the *Freeholder* in early 1846, Ira Harris, who supported legislative reform rather than the wholesale abolition of the system of New York landholding, emphasized that Ireland was suffering under "her odious land system" which saw "2,000,000 of laborers at work at sixpence a day, and 2,000,000 more in a state of hopeless poverty and destitution."[67] Several months later, at a famine relief meeting, Harris opined that "so long as the entire of the soil is owned by absentee proprietors, and so long as the poor are burthened with taxation and tithes, so long must the people of Ireland be oppressed in their condition."[68] Harris's critiques of Ireland could be—and were likely intended by him to be—applied as equally to central New York as they were to Ireland.

Although the *Freeholder* acknowledged that external factors could result in destitution, it insisted that destitution in Ireland was amplified by perfidious landlords who chose not to offer aid. In echoes of the consequences for tenants of Stephen Van Rensselaer III's death, the *Freeholder* published a poem describing Irish recipients of charity who through "no fault of theirs—some link that broke / In credit's chain, some sudden stroke / By fraud—by malice hurled / a sweeping flood, devouring flame / or sooner harsh agent pushing came / and cast them on the world."[69] The *Freeholder* also proposed solutions, opining that "substantial relief will never come till there shall exist no great proprietors—but in their stead a multitude of small proprietors."[70] This was a structural solution to Ireland's problems, as well as to New York's.

Devyr was fired as editor of the *Freeholder* in 1845, largely because his firebrand tactics did not sit well with moderates.[71] He went on to establish the *Anti-Renter*, which was explicitly allied with the National Reform Association and held the radical position that landlords could not be reformed, and that private property itself was so toxic as to be untenable.[72] The *Anti-Renter* called for solidarity among tenants all over the world, in the process co-opting the state of the Irish tenantry for local Anti-Rent politics. When helpful, it drew directly from Irish newspapers; in late January 1846, it printed an excerpt from the *The Nation* that linked the exploitation of tenants to British colonial projects. Commenting on the colonization of New Zealand in the 1840, in which the government "gave permissions to British subjects to colonise (or plant) those islands," it drew attention to the harm caused to Indigenous New Zealanders, who, like the Irish, were subject to a British rule that seemed likely to favor settlers. The danger lay, the paper suggested, in the fact that "if any dispute should occur between the planters and the natives respecting possession of land (a not improbably contingency), they, the British government, by their military officers would adjudicate."[73] The *Anti-Renter* also contended that the Irish were being deliberately starved to death, as "a cheaper way of getting rid of their 'surplus population'" by "English land stealers."[74] In his idiosyncratic memoir, *The Odd Book of the Nineteenth Century*, Devyr made the point even more bluntly. He cast Irish landlords as robbers and murderers "who had always murdered on a scale of some 70,000 a year" and who, in 1847 "were now to murder by the million."[75] While Irish nationalists, like those who published *The Nation*, might have been primarily concerned with British misrule, Devyr argued that the colonial relationship begat another evil: that of the seizure and occupation of land, the conversion of that land into private property, and the application of capricious legal enforcement to the most marginalized. For Devyr and his contemporaries, the politics of Ireland and New York were the same. So, too, were the strategies open to tenants suffering under landlords' oppression.

Anti-Rent politics were not limited to the newspapers of central New York. Horace Greeley, the editor of the *New York Tribune*, was a frequent and strongly opinionated commenter on the issue of landlord-tenant relations and land reform. Greeley was frequently at odds with the Whig political establishment over his "radical" land politics, but he saw reform of the landed system as of a piece with his other reformist politics and impulses.[76] This perspective made him attractive to many working-class New Yorkers, who professed fellow feeling with producers in conflict with the elites who lived off their labor.[77]

The *Tribune* frequently made explicit the connection between Irish suffering and the failures of the landed class overseas as a way to critique the landed class closer to home. In the spring of 1846, when the potato blight seemed to be turning into a famine, and when advocates of more and less radical land reforms in New York were vying for the governorship of New York State, Greely's *Tribune* argued that the most important "two facts" about Ireland were "the extreme fertility of the soil and the destitution of the populace."[78] It sought to explain this apparent paradox, on the grounds that "the poor farmer in order to pay his rent is obliged to send his produce to market," to fetch whatever price he might "while the factor to which he sends it immediately then ships it to England where money is abundant, and where the produce will command a better price."[79] In short, the writer asserted, the profits of Irish tenant farmers were constantly stymied by their embeddedness in an extractive system of landed relations, whereby agents and landlords conspired to make as much profit on tenants' labor for as low a price as possible. In the pages of the *Tribune*, the dangers and "evils of Land Monopoly" were a persistent theme, compared in some cases to "those of Slavery, Idol-worshiping and intemperance, and every venerable wrong."[80] This language tied land to other reform movements of the time, in support of Greely's own politics of reform.

The *Tribune* continued this emphasis throughout the 1840s. One article from 1847 noted, "history teaches us that where the few monopolize the soil, the cultivators of the earth must be either serfs or slaves, or tenants more or less dependent, according to the yearly dues which they pay for the privilege of laboring."[81] Additionally, the paper noted, "were there no land monopoly and were the soil property distributed the rich and the poor would rapidly approach that happiest of all conditions which lies midway between them. There would then be an abundance of bread."[82] Framing the famine in terms of land monopoly allowed the *Tribune* to use Ireland as a cautionary tale. If the landlords of central New York did not support land reforms, they might find themselves in the same position as the landlords of Ireland.

Having established the dangers of land monopoly, of overzealous landlords, and of speculation, the *Tribune* explicitly tied the situation in Ireland to that in New York. In a mid-1846 article on the idea of "Land Tenure," the paper noted that "the recent anti-rent troubles would find parallels" everywhere, but were especially relevant to the Irish, since "this monopoly is the overshadowing curse of the famished millions of Great Britain and Ireland."[83] In February 1847, it acknowledged that while "general distress for food is by no means peculiar to Ireland, but pervades the Scotch Highlands and is measurably felt throughout Europe, in France and Belgium especially," Ireland exhibited the worst example of destitution, traceable to "the system which separates Capital from Labor by Social barriers—which makes of the owners and the cultivators of the Soil two distinct and isolated classes." The author argued that "the moral of famine" was that "Ireland to-day shows us what New York or New England probably will be, whenever our Population shall have become as dense as hers, and when the giant fortunes which the few are now rapidly amassing everywhere by Commerce, Speculation and Machinery, shall have fastened upon and monopolized the Soil."[84] Ireland was, in this case, deployed as a predictable and inevitable consequence of landlords' abuses.

Letters written to the *Tribune* also criticized the actions of politicians who were not acting to sufficiently protect the people from monopoly. One writer lamented that at the New York constitutional convention, and during a discussion of land legislation, "there are 53 lawyers by occupation, and if they were hired to breed strife and contention in the state, to engender and perpetuate litigation . . . they could not [as a body] have been more zealous in their vocation than I have found them here."[85] Similarly, in April 1847, under "foreign items," the *Tribune* reported accusations leveled in both the British House of Commons and *The Nation* that "very large numbers of Irish landed proprietors both resident and non-resident, had never contributed a halfpenny to the relief of the poor, starving people."[86] In highlighting the parallel perfidy of Irish and New York landlords, the paper was setting up the condition of Ireland as the worst possible outcome of current landholding practices in New York.

A letter writer noted in June 1847 that "the present position of Great Britain and a large portion of Europe proffers ample and inviting sources of thought for American Statesmen," and that while "there is no present danger of any extensive failure of food for our population, nor need any such apprehensions be entertained for years to come," nevertheless that there might come a day when the present New York and the United States might be seen in the past of Ireland, "and when that day does come" New York would "know, from what experience has taught."[87] The paper made that position explicit in July: "Every year's delay in this great matter leaves us a stride nearer to the fearful condition of Ireland." Further, the crisis in Ireland was feeding the imminence of a crisis in the United States: "Every ship load of needy emigrants from the old country puts fresh power into the hands of our land monopolizers to imitate those who are breeding famines in the best cultivated countries of the world, and they are not slow to avail themselves of it."[88] If Irish landlords had simply followed the recommendations of land reformers in the United States, the paper claimed, "there would have been no famine in Ireland last winter but for Land monopoly and absenteeism," and "such wretched poverty as poor Ireland suffers—such a frightful famine as she is now passing through—would then be unknown."[89]

In comments to a committee exploring legislative solutions to the landlord-tenant problem in New York, the *Tribune* commented, "Your Committee are aware that they may be told that the holders of property have the right to do with it as they please, and that therefore remonstrance or complaints are unavailing. This doctrine of the sacred privilege of property is at the very time being exemplified in unhappy Ireland."[90] Alongside relief in the form of landlords' behavior and donations from abroad, the newspapers that supported tenants in the Anti-Rent Wars advocated for solidarity among those who were victims of rapacious and extractive landlords. This constituted an understanding of relief that manifested in political support from across the ocean, because such political support might materially improve the lot of starving tenants.

The rhetorical and practical politics were brought together in New York in the later years of the famine. From 1847, reports of Irish distress were increasingly accompanied by warnings of escalating political strife and outrages. The outcome of landed abuses was made manifest in the Young Irelander rebellion of 1848.[91] Days before the rebellion erupted, the *New York Tribune* lay "the fundamental cause of Irish destitution" at the feet of those who had "rendered [Irish soil] the exclusive property of a few thousand persons, who are mainly alien in residence and feeling to Ireland, and who draw from her industry an enormous annual income which they expend" in Europe.[92] When the *Albany Freeholder* printed an article from the *Dublin Nation* calling for an Irish rebellion on the basis of "misery and famine and plague," it echoed the violence of the previous decade in rural New York, and threatened to be a harbinger for more.[93] Although the *Freeholder's* editors did not condone violence and, in fact, actively resisted it, the rebellion in Ireland provided a helpfully distant threat.

Who labored on the land, and who profited from that labor were pressing issues in both Ireland and the United States in the nineteenth century. Newspapers that supported Anti-Rent politics in New York were able to treat the Irish famine as a tabula rasa upon which to paint their own political goals. In fact, they often called for reforms that commentators writing in Cork, close to sites of abject suffering, shied away from. Near sites of "actual starvation," even those with long-standing interest in land reform shifted from calls to structurally reform the landholding system to those likely to be more effective—changing the behavior of individual landlords who had the power of literal life and death over starving tenants.

These examples starkly demonstrate how, as news of the famine and discussions of relief moved further from the site of crisis, it became easier to ignore the practical needs of Irish relief and use examples of Irish distress for local political ends. This malleability of famine relief would be proved among enslavers in the US South, who would go on to claim that they suffered as much as the Irish and to use those claims of shared suffering to argue for the continued subjugation of enslaved people.

Slavery

In March 1847, Dublin's Central Relief Committee—the Quaker group devoted to collecting famine donations and converting those funds into material aid—convened to discuss the mechanisms for distributing supplies and food "forwarded from America," and particularly from South Carolina.[1] After the meeting, Richard Allen, a Dublin Quaker, tailor, cloth merchant, and antislavery activist, wrote a letter calling his fellow members of the Society of Friends to account.[2] He reported that he was deeply troubled by the committee's willingness to accept "money sent by slaveholding communities."[3] Receiving such a donation, he argued, was fundamentally antithetical to the tenets of the Society of Friends specifically, and to Christianity more broadly.

Allen was a well-known commentator on humanitarian issues in the Irish press. Over the course of his life, he wrote numerous public letters, many aimed at convincing fellow Irish people of the evils of slavery, and he brought these epistolary skills to bear in his critique of the Central Relief Committee's decision to accept aid from enslavers. He noted that Quakers had succeeded, through nearly a century of campaigning, in branding slavery "before the world in its anti-Christian enormity."[4] He also recognized that he was asking a committee devoted to charitable relief to reject funds that might help "to save our own countrymen from starvation."[5] He acknowledged that such a rejection could open the Society of Friends up to criticism. He predicted that refusing donations from enslavers might cause "rage [to] take the place of apparent gentleness—cursing of blessing—that we may have to bear a great amount of obloquy both at home and abroad—that our motives will be impugned—that we shall be called hypocrites, and accused of aggravating the dreadful state of misery in this country."[6] He also admitted that enslavers were attractive donors; they could offer "thousands of pounds in money, and ship loads of provisions," and they seemed uniquely interested in Ireland, having been "awakened to feelings of sympathy towards our suffering millions, which have spread with wonderful rapidity."[7] Nevertheless, Allen argued that the funds from which their contributions were drawn were the profits of a system that made an enslaved person "chattel, robs him of his manhood, condemns him to heathen darkness, forbids him the use of the Bible, employs every possible means to degrade and deprave him, and classes him fully and unequivocally with the beasts."[8] It was because the profits of enslavement could not be disentangled from these cruelties—indeed, were the result of these cruelties—that Allen asked his fellow committee members to risk opprobrium and turn away "these blood-stained contributions to the sacred cause of suffering humanity."[9]

In addition to his concerns that the funds themselves were tainted, Allen feared that accepting these donations would lend moral authority to enslavers, because it would "stamp" them "with the seal of Christian fellowship" and "apply the flattering unction to [the enslaver's] soul." He feared that if "the Committee are willing to recognize" the enslaver "as a benefactor to our countrymen" and "take his money," then they would not be in a position to bear "testimony against his sins." Accepting money from such individuals might "in degree justify" enslavers' "pretensions to genuine kindness and compassion" and afford philanthropic credibility to politicians who "staked their political existence on the maintenance and perpetuation of slavery." It would, he added, "ratify their character for Christian benevolence," which would dishonor Christianity and the Society of Friends and be "detrimental to the cause of the slave."[10]

Ultimately, Allen's arguments were futile. The Dublin group decided that they would not turn away the substantial funds that enslavers offered.[11] From the perspective of those Friends who were eager to muster famine relief, enslavers from South Carolina were ideal donors: they were wealthy, and they were willing to donate because they had much to gain by associating themselves with humanitarian causes.

Donors to the Hibernian Society of Charleston, which was the body primarily responsible for soliciting and collecting famine funds from throughout the American South, did just as Allen feared. Enslavers not only tacitly benefited from the moral uplift of their beneficence but they also explicitly used famine relief to defend the institution of slavery. They, like many other donors, presented their contributions as evidence of their own righteousness—an argument of particularly importance to enslavers because of abolitionists' success in characterizing slavery as uniquely immoral.

Beyond benevolence as a moral cover for their actions, Southern enslavers seemed committed specifically to aiding Ireland for political reasons. These were donors with substantial resources to dispense who in the 1840s wanted to spend them on distantly starving strangers, Irish ones in particular. Enslavers and Southern politicians used discussions of famine relief to contend that the South was like the "Ireland of the North American continent," subject to the capricious overreach of a centralized government that had failed to attend to the economic needs of all within it.[12] This claim was in response to national debates over whether slavery should be legal in new states and territories. According to enslavers, any federal restriction on the expansion of slavery constituted a dangerous abuse of power. Throughout the famine, enslavers claimed solidarity with the Irish and leveraged the widely accepted subjugation of Ireland in service of arguments for the legality, morality, and geographic expansion of slavery. They also used the suffering of Irish peasants to argue for the comparative humanity of slavery, drawing on contemporary claims about slavery's benevolence. The cynical appropriation of Irish distress and weaponization of famine philanthropy to downplay the violence of the United States' slave system was exactly what Richard Allen feared when he sought to reject enslavers' "blood-stained benevolence."

The Charleston Hibernian Society

Though Allen generalized to all the South in his jeremiad, his letter singled out Charleston, and the very active relief committee that used the city as a base of operations to solicit donations from around the region. Charleston was the fifteenth most populous city in the country, and the fifth largest in the states where slavery was legal.[13] South Carolina was a top importer and exporter of goods in the 1840s, and Charleston was a commercial hub and its principal port.[14] Like New York City in the North, Charleston was central to the movement of information, commodities, and people to and around the South and a node in the intersecting networks carrying news down the eastern seaboard of the

United States from Halifax, Boston, and New York and across the Appalachian Mountains to the trans-Mississippi west.[15]

The Hibernian Society of Charleston, the members of which Allen implicitly targeted in his letter, was embedded in these transnational connections. As a result, it became a crucial avenue for famine philanthropy. Before the famine, Irish people had lived in Southern cities for generations. The earliest Southerners of Irish descent were Protestant merchants, who formed societies designed both to ameliorate loneliness and to provide much needed social support. The Hibernian Society had been founded by just such a group of Irish Protestants in 1799. Because these men came to Charleston with business connections, they were able to quickly integrate into the economic life of the city. Despite its upper-class Protestant roots, however, the Hibernian Society operated in the spirit of the Irish romantic nationalists, seeking to build connections among the Irish in Charleston regardless of political or religious affiliation.[16] In addition to serving as a cultural home for Irish emigrants, the Charleston Hibernian Society was a venue through which Irish, as well as non-Irish, elites could make business connections and accrue social and political capital. Being Irish was not a requirement of joining, and, as a result, by the 1840s the society had become a place where commercial connections were as important as ethnic ties.[17] Operating out of a magnificent Hibernian Hall at the center of Charleston's commercial district, by the start of the famine the Hibernian Society was an established and prestigious part of Charleston's social and commercial life.[18] The connections developed over generations by its members offered newer immigrants opportunities to integrate into Southern society.[19]

The Hibernian Society's connections to both elite Southerners and to Ireland made it an ideal organization for soliciting famine funds. On February 18, 1847, Major Alex Black, a Charleston businessman and enslaver, rose and addressed a meeting.[20] Black noted that the "original purpose" of the society was "the union of social and festive intercourse with sacred works of charity" in the city and environs of Charleston. Given this charge, he argued, the society should forgo planned St. Patrick's Day celebrations in favor of famine fundraising, opining, "Surely in a period when the cry of wailing lamentation and woe resounds throughout the land of our forefathers, when the birthplace of the fathers and founders of this benevolent institution is doomed to famine, pestilence, starvation and death—while Ireland is suffering under this national calamity, it ill befits the impulses and sympathies of the heart that we should indulge in feasting and rejoicing."[21] At the meeting and, later, in the pages of Charleston's newspapers, James Adger, the Irish Presbyterian president of the Hibernian Society, called for the establishment of a "General Executive Committee" to "organize the best and most speedy relief for the suffering poor of Ireland."[22] Henry Workman Connor, a Charleston financier, chaired that committee and immediately appointed representatives to "wait upon the citizens of their respective wards, and solicit from them such aid as is in their liberality under the circumstances."[23] The men soliciting funds typically had personal connections to Ireland. However, as was the case with Hibernian Society membership, there was no requirement that donors have a personal Irish connection. By the time the society met for its ordinary monthly meeting two weeks after Black's call for fundraising, Connor was able to report "the continued receipt of funds from all quarters," and that "the contributions from the city have been large and have been given in the true spirit of benevolence and charity." They were expected to "exceed $15,000."[24]

The Hibernian Society was different from other famine fundraising efforts. In most cities and towns in the United States, short-lived and ad-hoc committees solicited donations from people with no connection to Ireland, while local Irish fraternal societies collected funds from people of Irish descent to send to the communities from which they had emigrated. For instance, the major relief associations in New York, Boston, London, and Philadelphia were all created in response to the famine and dissolved when the crisis appeared to be over. Many of these committees were associated—either formally or informally— with Quaker merchants, but they were not fraternal organizations or sustained arms of the Quaker corporate body. In Charleston, however, the Hibernian Society collected funds from both Irish and non-Irish alike. Ward captains were tasked with canvasing different parts of the city and personally soliciting funds from Charleston's elite. Nor were the collecting efforts of the Hibernian Society limited to Charleston: while the General Executive Committee canvassed within the city, another group was tasked with "appeal[ing] to the benevolence of their friends and countrymen out of the city" in Georgia, North Carolina, and South Carolina.[25]

This second committee acted quickly to establish a rural charitable infrastructure. In some places, towns created local subcommittees to funnel money toward the Hibernian Society.[26] Additionally, just as Charleston committee members canvassed potential donors in different wards, in rural spaces Hibernian Society members circulated to solicit funds from different plantations. For instance, in late March and early April 1847, an agent of the society named Jonathan Robinson visited, and solicited donations from the Mulberry Plantation near Camden, South Carolina, a Dr. Reynolds in the town of Camden, and John Shaw of Sumter.[27] Robinson's circuit of Sumter and Kershaw counties included some of the donors that Richard Allen most reviled. Mulberry Plantation was home to James Chesnut Sr., one of the wealthiest men in South Carolina, and James Chesnut Jr., a lawyer in nearby Columbia, as well as over five hundred enslaved men, women, and children.[28] As a result of Robinson's visit, one of the Chesnut men (possibly acting on behalf of the extended Chesnut family) contributed fifty dollars. Robinson collected a further fifty-five dollars in the course of his fundraising trip, though he did not specify where the money came from. Robinson was not the only rural agent of famine relief making the rounds of Southern plantations in the spring of 1847; at the same time Henry W. Connor was soliciting funds from as far away as Alabama. Indeed, two weeks after the country committee was established, Connor reported that, "from the country, the contributions have been proportionately liberal and with a spirit equally commendable" to those from the city."[29]

By the end of the famine, the Hibernian Society's published donor lists recorded 168 donations referencing a total of 98 individuals by name, and a collection of anonymous "poor men," "friends," "friends to Ireland," and "gentlemen." Many of the people who contributed to this relief effort gave exclusively to Ireland. These were not men who gave indiscriminately to contemporary causes; only a few could be found on the donor lists of other charitable groups. Although slightly more than 10 percent of donors gave anonymously, it was in the interest of the Hibernian Society to highlight elite donors who might draw in others, and in the interests of some donors that their charity be known. Indeed, historians and theorists of philanthropy have argued that the genre of public subscription lists was a way for the philanthropic elite to advertise their moral and economic distinction.[30] Unsurprisingly, then the donor lists that the Hibernian Society published in local papers included people of social and political prominence. Thirteen of the donors served at some point in their lives in government.[31] They included current members of the South Carolina legislature, and men who would join the Confederate government a decade later. Most of the donors were enslavers. Furthermore, donations from enslavers were disproportionately high; contributions from men who held people in bondage accounted for nearly 70 percent of all funds collected.[32]

In his letter to fellow Quakers, Richard Allen had warned that the Society of Friends must treat all donations from South Carolina as implicated in perpetuating slavery. He argued that the demography of South Carolina, where "the white population numbers about two hundred thousand, whilst there are about three hundred thousand slaves," meant that it was "inevitable" that "all the whites who have any ambition are constantly endeavouring to raise themselves so far as to be able to employ slaves to do their work."[33] Even those who would never muster enough resources to hold other people in bondage, Allen argued, made inappropriate donors. The "large class of low white men, generally idle, drunken, and dissolute, who are ever ready for all kinds of turbulent and wicked conduct" also contributed to the violence of slavery by participating in "the *lynching* of abolitionists."[34] Allen concluded that his colleagues must acknowledge that "the greater portion of money that comes from South Carolina in particular *must* come from slaveholders" or people who benefit from and perpetuate slavery.[35] In short, as Allen contended in the nineteenth century, and as Stephanie McCurry would later systematically demonstrate, every white South Carolinian was complicit in the system of enslavement, either by being an active enslaver or seeking to become one.[36]

Defending Enslaver Morality

One of the reasons that enslavers might have been drawn to famine philanthropy was because abolitionists in the nineteenth century had been successful, as Allen noted, in broadcasting the "anti-Christian enormity" of slavery to the wider world.[37] Abolitionists, many Quakers among them, described ending of slavery as the central humanitarian cause of the nineteenth century.[38] For them, to abhor slavery was the principal evidence of a person's humanity. For example, one abolitionist speaker argued in 1835 that knowledge of the sufferings of enslaved people should break down "every unnatural restraint, and calling forth the simplest and deepest of all human emotions, the feeling of man for his fellow man, and bringing out the strongest intellectual and moral powers to his rescue."[39] Frederick Douglass used similar language in his *Narrative of the Life of Frederick Douglass, an American Slave* to describe how learning of enslavers' violence would "shock the humanity of his nonslaveholding neighbors," and that "few [enslavers] are willing to incur the odium attaching to the reputation of being a cruel master."[40] Throughout the nineteenth century, abolitionists worked, and largely succeeded, to associate abolition with humane instincts, and slavery with inhumanity.

Consequently, enslavers took any opportunity to broadcast evidence of their own humane impulses and morality. These arguments took different forms in the years preceding the famine. Some slaveholders argued that slavery in the United States was humane in contrast to the cruelly unrealizable promise of freedom because Black people were incapable of the self-determination that freedom required.[41] Others contended that the institution of slavery was the only way for people of different inclinations to live together.[42] Still other enslavers celebrated individual paternalistic decisions not to enact the full cruelty of slavery to justify the benevolence of the whole system.[43] Famine philanthropy offered yet another opportunity to for enslavers to advertise their humanity and benevolent instincts. This impulse was not unique to donors to the Charleston Hibernian Society; however, enslavers and the publications that supported slavery took great pains to argue that famine philanthropy was an unparalleled example in the history of charitable giving, because doing so gave them an opportunity to challenge abolitionists' frequent and damning accusations of inhumanity. These donations thus served as much as a public performance as efforts to aid the starving Irish.[44]

Southern newspapers were crucial to this effort. The *Charleston Mercury* was one among several major newspapers that worked to shape public opinion, and it worked to tie national or international news stories to local or regional concerns.[45] The *Charleston Courier*—Charleston's other major newspaper—was a moderate commercial periodical, which tended, when pushed on national political issues, to support the federal government's positions. It served as a voice for merchants and agriculturalists living and profiting in Charleston. These papers, along with the *Southern Patriot*, which also represented broader regional interests, broadcast celebrations of enslavers' philanthropy.

In 1847, the *Mercury* claimed that efforts to relieve Ireland proved that South Carolina was a "state that cannot be surpassed in hospitality and kindness to the distressed and isolated stranger anywhere in the world."[46] For the *Mercury*'s editors, supporting local and regional concerns meant aligning with the politics exemplified by John C. Calhoun, the former vice president and South Carolina politician who vehemently espoused states' rights and, eventually, Southern secession.[47] Throughout the 1840s and 1850s, the *Mercury* often railed against antislavery campaigns and attempts by the federal government to make slavery illegal in newly admitted states, both of which its editors cast as forms of Northern aggression.[48] For the *Mercury*, focusing on the unique morality of South Carolina supported enslavers' claims that slavery was not inhumane and centered the state as the most appropriate political unit through which to celebrate that humanity.

Enslavers often argued that they had been blessed by God and had a responsibility to be charitable to those less fortunate than themselves. In a letter printed in the *Charleston Courier* a few days after the Charleston Irish relief committee was formed, the planter William Elliott, writing under the pseudonym "Agricola," called for "some of our wealthy rice and cotton planters [to] make a donation, if not in money, of small rice or their surplus corn, and sent by the earliest opportunity to that unfortunate people."[49] As New York City papers had done to encourage donations from among their readers, Elliott argued that rural elites in particular should share the "unexampled prosperity" and "abundance" that had "blessed the labors of the year," because the value of their produce had "advanced far above former years."[50] For Elliott and his contemporaries, the fact that the abundance of their produce was due to the exploitation of enslaved labor did not bear mentioning. To overproduce was evidence of planters' sagacity and divine blessing, which should, Elliott argued, be shared with the starving Irish. This overproduction was even more evidence of the fundamentally humane impulses of enslavers.

In one issue of the *Southern Patriot* from February 1847 alone, there appeared four articles commending Southern beneficence. The *Patriot's* editors wrote that they found it "truly gratifying to remark the liberality which has thus far marked most of the donations made in behalf of the poor of unhappy Ireland" and particularly singled out collections "taken up for the relief of the destitute of Ireland" at the dedication of a Charleston synagogue.[51]

In March 1847, the *Courier* described the money collected by the Hibernian Society as "evidence of the deep sympathy that prevails all over the country at this present moment, for the distressed condition of Ireland" and reminded readers "that the Committee of Relief, in this city, are daily receiving remittances from almost every part of the State besides the very liberal donations recently noticed within the city."[52] In early March, a reader wrote to the *Mercury* that he had "been not a little gratified at the numerous expressions of sympathy for suffering Ireland, and [was] proud of this benevolent feature in our national character. The history of the world cannot find a parallel instance of national generosity."[53] Across the North Atlantic, commentary on the famine often celebrated the generosity of donors. However, in Charleston, these laudatory pieces were unique because they were in direct conversation with abolitionist claims concerning the inhumanity of its donors and the system that provided their wealth.

Charleston papers were not alone in their celebration of donations from enslavers and people who benefited from slavery. In Alabama, the *Weekly Flag & Advertiser* wrote that "the feeling exhibited throughout this country is highly creditable to the character of our people, one reflecting more real glory upon our name, than a thousand victories gained by the prowess of our soldiers in war."[54] Another Alabama paper, the *Southern Advocate*, made a similar claim, commenting that the effect of the circulation of "the appalling facts, that thousands of Irish are actually starving," was "the pervading feeling of generous sympathy by which the whole country, throughout the length and breadth of our land, are acquainted at this crisis." It further stated that Alabama donors were to be particularly praised because "'he gives twice, who quickly gives.' It is life—human life—the life of your brother, that is at stake."[55] The *New Orleans Picayune*, the first penny paper in the South, famous for its boosterism on behalf of the city of New Orleans, embracing temperance and other local reform causes, supporting westward expansion and opposing abolition in the strongest possible terms, described donations made by enslavers as evidence of "nobly expressed feeling[s] of generosity and sympathy."[56] The *Picayune's* mission was to undermine the prevalence of privileged political voices, in favor of the voice of "the people."[57] It reflected not party politics, but an aggressively regional perspective. Newspapers across the South agreed that for the people accused by abolitionists of having failed to meet their moral obligations, donating to famine relief provided an opportunity to offer evidence of morality.

The Humanity of Slavery

In addition to using their participation in famine relief to prove their superior morality, enslavers also used the fact that relief was required at all as a foil for defenses of the comparative humanity of slavery. These advocates relied on a set of paternalistic arguments; they claimed that plantations protected enslaved peoples' well-being, and that enslavement was evidence of affection.[58] Enslavers favorably contrasted this system with the impoverished condition of factory workers in Northern cities, and the famine in Ireland offered another and more extreme comparative example. In contrast to enslaved people, who, enslavers contended, were fed, clothed, and cared for, the nominally free Irish were suffering horribly, ignored and exploited by Britain.

The fact that donations were required, enslavers argued, meant that Irish suffering was unique in its magnitude. In turn, the extent of Irish suffering revealed the benevolence of the US system of enslavement. Even before the famine began, a writer in the *Daily Picayune* had used Ireland as a benchmark for misery across the British empire, contending that "the condition of the most abject slave in the Colonies is, in my opinion, better far than that of the unfortunate Irish peasant."[59] In July 1847, the *Charleston Mercury* argued that slavery could not be inhumane or unchristian, because the population of Black people enslaved in the South "are increasing in much greater ratio than the Whites," and that this increase disproved "the assumed Divine Mission of the Abolitionist, unless we come to the conclusion that Heaven permits their increase as slaves, in order to render more wonderful and impressive their future

destruction or doom." This argument disregarded, of course, the brutal "scientific" management of plantations that intentionally increased
the population of enslaved people for enslavers' profit.[60] At the end of
1847, the *Mercury* asserted that the experiences of the Irish were like
those of formerly enslaved people in the Caribbean, but that emancipation, rather than their former enslavement, was the cause of the latter's
distress. An article about the West Indies argued that "next to Irish
distress, that of Jamaica stares us in the face. It is indisputable that the
emancipation of the Negroes" caused more harm than their previous
enslavement and had "reduced Jamaica and many other islands to the
verge of ruin."[61] Explicitly connecting this claim to Ireland, in 1848 the
paper reported on a letter that it claimed had been written to Daniel
O'Connell by John England, an Irish American and the first Catholic
bishop of the Diocese of Charleston. According to the *Mercury*, England told O'Connell that if he "could succeed in securing the Irish as
good a physical state as the negroes," the bishop "would be agreeably
surprised."[62] A few days later, the *Mercury* wrote that "impartial travel-
ers tell us that the physical condition of our negroes is much better than
that of the peasantry of Europe."[63] Throughout the early nineteenth
century, slaveholders continuously asserted that enslaved people were
better off than the Irish, or than other impoverished people in Europe.
It was such a ubiquitous claim that Frederick Douglass had to consistently refute it in his tour of Ireland in 1845. Comparing enslavers to
wolves, he asked, "Was it not to be presumed that the wolf would say
that the lamb loved to be eaten up by him?"[64] The argument that the
enslaved were better off than Irish peasants worked in tandem with
claims that donations to Ireland were evidence of enslaver benevolence.

Co-opting Irish Misery

Finally, the slaveholding class of the South used the issue of famine
relief to construct parallels between poor British governance during the
famine to what they claimed was overreach by the federal government
in the United States. Newspapers and commentators made this argument by highlighting shared experiences of resistance. Like New York
City newspapers, they emphasized the importance of Irish soldiers
in the American Revolution and the War of 1812, reminding readers

of a shared resistance to British rule and, consequently, to tyranny.[65] These papers argued that just as Irishmen had historically fought British imperialism in Ireland, just as they had fought alongside the American colonies and against Britain in the American Revolution, and just as they were continuing to fight Britain by proxy in the war with Mexico, so, too, were white Southerners resisting the unjust imposition of the will of the American government.

In 1847, the *Jeffersonian Republican*, a party-political newspaper published in New Orleans that supported states' rights and the independence of yeomen farmers, commented: "Long before the commencement of the American Revolution that generous [Irish] people were heart and soul with the patriots of this country."[66] The white men running Irish relief meetings in the South echoed this language and, in doing so sought to link Irish and Southern experiences of government overreach. One day before the *Republican* rhetorically placed Irish people in the United States' deep historical past, the *Charleston Mercury* printed an article about a relief meeting at which one speaker "eloquently alluded to the great services rendered to America by the Irish, in the Revolution."[67] In April, the *Charleston Courier* reported the proceedings at another relief meeting, at which the chair "appealed to the patriotism and gratitude of his hearers, [since] every field of battle which illustrated our revolution was moistened by the blood of Irishmen shed in our cause." The speech ended: "The Sons of St. Patrick deserved the aid of the countrymen of Washington."[68] These appeals worked on multiple levels. They inserted the Irish into American history and played on American sympathy by reminding listeners and readers of the debt of revolutionary gratitude owed to the Irish people, while at the same time, they established the Irish as long-time participants in struggles against tyranny on both sides of the Atlantic.

This was a political imaginary, promulgated through both politicians and the press, that put the British treatment of Ireland and the United States' treatment of the Southern slaveocracy in the same conceptual frame. Proslavery pundits appropriated Irish distress to underscore what they saw as the South's own marginalization and to critique US federal policies, particularly attempts to limit the expansion of slavery. They also used Britain's treatment of Ireland to draw attention to British involvement in North America. In October 1845, the *Charleston Mercury* quipped that "'we shall never make anything of Canada' observed an English colonist, 'until we Anglicise and Protestantise it.' To which a French seigneur rejoined, with bitterness, 'Had you not better finish Ireland first!'"[69] This kind of language indicated that the people reading and writing for the *Mercury* were thinking about Ireland in imperial, as well as extractive, terms. In early 1846, the *Jeffersonian Republican* supported a congressional resolution for America to annex Ireland, calling for "success to Ireland! The iron hoof of England has too long trodden her down."[70] These kinds of articles cast Ireland as the victim of rapacious imperialism, and an exemplar of poor imperial governance.

This framing dovetailed with popular conceptions of the dangers that Britain posed to slavery in the American South. As white Southerners practiced seeing Britain as an imperial threat on both sides of the Atlantic, they began to draw connections between the British and US governments. Many white Southerners were uneasy about the threat that Britain—a formidable global power—presented to the commercial and political interests of the United States. Enslavers were particularly anxious about the spread of British evangelical abolitionism, which had caused emancipation in the British Caribbean in the 1830s. They feared that these abolitionists had identified the United States as their next crusade.[71] Some went so far as to suggest that Northern efforts to arrest the spread of slave states were the result of British political intrigues.[72]

The more immediate danger, however, came from the federal government and the industrial interests of the North. In the 1840s, Congress was working to diffuse growing tensions between states in which slavery was legal and those in which it was illegal. One component of the suggested compromise was a proposal known as the Wilmot Proviso, by the Pennsylvania congressman David Wilmot, which sought to prohibit the expansion of slavery into new territories and allow extant territories to decide the issue of slavery by a popular vote.

For slavery's apologists, the Wilmot Proviso seemed like evidence of federal overreach in the spirit of the British Empire. The proviso was intended to give the federal government control over the spread of slavery, to address Northern anxieties about slavery in the rapidly expanding United States, and to assuage states where slavery was legal. The 1820 Missouri compromise had established a precedent for maintaining equal numbers of slave and non–slave states, prohibiting slavery north of the 36°30' line of latitude, at the northern border of Arkansas territory. However, the annexation of Texas, the Mexican American War, and the subsequent admission of Texas as a state where slavery was legal raised Northern hackles, since Texas was a vast territory and unchecked by a newly admitted free state. Antislavery Democrats saw the proviso as a defensive strategy to satisfy antislavery constituents in the North, and as a means to curtail the power of the Southern oligarchy.[73] In contrast, Southerners and western Democrats saw moves like the Wilmot Proviso as an attack on the political and economic autonomy of slaveholders imposed by a central federal power.[74] Although the proposed legislation attempted to balance Northern interests (admitting California as a free state and abolishing the slave trade in the District of Columbia) with those of the South (denying congressional authority over the interstate slave trade and establishing a harsher fugitive slave act), Southerners read the bills as an assault on the slave economy by way of prohibiting the expansion of slavery into some newly admitted states.[75]

In an ironic turn of phrase, Southerners used the language of "slavery" to describe Irish subjugation to Britain, and, by proxy, the South to the North. When they invoked the language of slavery in their reporting on Ireland and the Wilmot Proviso, Southern commentators were not referring to racial chattel slavery (which they did not consider to be abhorrent) but, rather, to economic political slavery. This was a common theme in Southern commentary of the period, beyond discourse about the famine. For example, in his study of the Civil War in American memory, David Blight recounts the postbellum testimony of a Southern planter who was asked whether he would like to see the "'old feeling' to resume between the sections." The planter replied, "No Sir, never. The people of the South feel they have been . . . most tyrannically oppressed by the North. All our rights have been trampled upon. We knew that we had a perfect right to go and leave you, we were only carrying out the principles of the Revolution.'"[76] These ideas were made manifest in Southern reports of the famine and appeals for aid, where understandings about revolutionary sentiment and the ideology of slavery were intertwined.

Those who supported the expansion of slavery warned that Ireland, whose economy was stymied by Britain, was a harbinger of what was to come in the South. They were particularly concerned about the

economic consequences of limiting slavery to the states in which slavery was currently legal. In August 1847, the *Mercury* noted that while
proponents of the Wilmot Proviso wanted to limit the spread of slavery,
and therefore of enslaved people, to new states, any limit on "the extent
of arable land" would be destructive to white Southern prosperity. This
argument turned on the idea that for enslavers to be economically successful, they must necessarily be able to expand their landholdings. That
expansion would only be profitable if they were guaranteed enslaved
labor to work newly acquired land. Further, new territories in which
slavery was legal would provide a continuously open market for the
sale of enslaved people, in direct contravention of claims that enslaved
people and their families were cared for by the people who held them
in bondage. The *Mercury* opined that "as it has been with [the Irish],
so must it be with us, but with this additional disadvantage to us, that
in Ireland a partial relief is found in migration, while to us this is prohibited by the Wilmot Proviso." Ireland, in this case, foreshadowed a
future in which, the *Mercury* predicted Southern states "are to be kept
in a political state of blockade, until existence itself shall have been consumed."[77] As both the famine and the debate over the Wilmot Proviso
continued, the *Mercury* became more explicit still, asking whether "the
people of the South are content to assume the relation to the North
that Ireland now sustains towards England."[78] Other parallels were
drawn between Ireland and America as well. A lecture advertised in the
Mercury of January 31, 1846, purported to speak to "the relative con-
nexions of these three nations," summarizing "the growth of England
and her decay—the rising power of Ireland—the youth of America and
her destiny."[79]

Congress took until 1850 to work out the terms of a compromise
that might assuage both slave and free states. A few weeks before the
August 22 vote on the compromise bills, a meeting opposing any kind
of Southern capitulation was held in Macon, Georgia. At this meeting,
Southerners voiced their objections through a public reading of a letter from the former president of Texas, General Mirabeau Buonaparte
Lamar.[80] Lamar expressed his vehement opposition to any further
limitations on slavery and cast the US government, which he believed
was driven by Northern interests, as merely "another great dynasty

erected upon its ruins—a Russian empire which makes Hungary of the South."[81] News of Lamar's letter, and the political metaphors it relied on, circulated throughout Georgia and South Carolina. One month after the Macon meeting, an anonymous letter to the *Charleston Mercury* suggested that it would "oblige a large number of subscribers by giving this letter a place in your columns" because "the name of Mirabeau B. Lamar is associated with all that is chivalrous and daring, and because Lamar was "ready to peril all in defense of Southern Liberty." Despite this praise, the anonymous letter writer somewhat amended Lamar's critique. He made no mention of linking the South's fate to that of Hungary, instead cautioning that "the Southern States, I fear are fast becoming the Ireland of the North American continent, inhabited by a people generous, brave and magnanimous, and yet bound down by heartless and ambitious traitors."[82] This rewritten letter signified the culmination of a long history of appropriating Ireland in the American South. It was evidence of a rhetorical relationship —supported by a monetary bond in the form of donations—that proposed a broad structure of oppression linking slaveholders and the starving Irish and casting federal limitations on the South's slave economy as tantamount to death by starvation.

Narratives about Ireland and Irish relief that circulated in the US South during the famine presented an image of Irish suffering deeply entwined with Southern politics. Irish soldiers populated narratives of the American Revolution. Irish distress was described as equivalent to the political pain caused by the Wilmot Proviso. Irish starvation was judged to be immeasurably worse than any oppression that enslaved people suffered. Donations to Ireland from enslavers were acts of solidarity toward people who suffered under a similar yoke of tyranny.

Enslavers' rhetorical use of famine relief was just what Richard Allen feared when he encouraged the Society of Friends to reject the donations coming from the Charleston Hibernian Society. The majority of donations to the Hibernian Society relief operation were direct profits of slavery and were, in consequence, "blood-stained contributions to the sacred cause of suffering humanity."[83] Enslavers also, as Allen predicted, used their charity to stamp themselves "with the seal of Christian fellowship."[84] So, too, did they appeal to the public "to recognize" them as benefactors "to our countrymen."[85] Whether the Dublin members of the Society of Friends meant to or not, famine relief did offer enslavers an avenue to argue for their own humanity. As the next chapter shows, however, they were not the only Americans in the South to put famine relief to this kind of rhetorical use.

Claiming Humanity

Nancy Brown joined the First African Baptist Church in Richmond, Virginia on July 11, 1846.[1] Seven months later, she, along with her husband and other members of Richmond's oldest Black congregation, raised twenty-six dollars and thirty-four cents "for the suffering of Ireland."[2] This was a considerable sum. The church had never before raised these kinds of funds to aid sufferers outside of their own community.[3] After the collection was taken up, the church leadership sent the money to Richmond's Famine Relief Committee, which in turn passed it on to the Quakers—including Richard Allen—who were providing relief and aid on the ground in Ireland. In a matter of months, money collected among Black Richmonders was being used to feed Irish victims of famine.

This was not Nancy Brown's only experience of fundraising and benevolence. The First African Baptist Church routinely took up donations from among congregants to fund its workings. Nancy also lived and worked in proximity to white Richmonders who were steeped in the norms and expectations of white Southern charity. Before she joined the church, Nancy was enslaved by Joseph H. Colquitt, a member of Richmond's First Presbyterian Church, which hosted "numerously attended" meetings to raise money for Irish famine relief.[4] He also fundraised closer to home; as a prominent member of the Henrico Agricultural and Horticultural Society, he solicited donations to improve agriculture and to advocate for white farmers in Virginia.[5] Colquitt sold Nancy to Philip E. Tabb Jr., whose family contributed one hundred dollars to the Richmond famine fund.[6] The Tabb family, too, was involved in charitable efforts in Richmond. Philip's father was a member of a committee tasked with raising funds to bring "Popular Education" to white Virginians.[7] Four months later, Tabb sold Nancy back to Colquitt, who sold her once again to a man named Samuel Cottrell. The charitable impulses that these men evinced toward fellow white Virginians did not extend to Nancy. Eighteen months after she participated in the First African Baptist Church's famine fundraising, Nancy and her children were sold again, this time to a man from North Carolina.[8] She was never reunited with her Richmond community, nor did she ever see her husband again.[9]

Most congregants of the First African Baptist Church were enslaved and subject to the same kind of cruelty that Nancy experienced. This made the church's famine collection all the more extraordinary. However, theirs was not simply a valedictory story of exceptional generosity in the face of enslavement. These men and women had no connection to Ireland; they had no reason to feel solidarity with the Irish. In fact, newspapers that circulated in Richmond—both those that supported and those that opposed slavery—argued against solidarity between Irish and enslaved people. Despite these disjunctures, donations from Black congregants in Richmond can be read as a deliberate use of white charitable norms to challenge white claims of Black inhumanity.

Enslaved and Free Donors

The First African Baptist Church began as part of the First Baptist Church, which had been founded in the late eighteenth century to provide for better "spiritual oversight" of both white and enslaved congregants in Richmond. In the years that followed its founding, church membership expanded. By the early nineteenth century, Black congregants—enslaved and free—outnumbered whites. In the 1830s, a group of white parishioners objected to attending church with Black people.[10] In response, Black congregants argued that they should have a separate church and raised funds to purchase the building in which the First Baptist Church met.[11] The white congregation moved to new premises, and a white pastor named Robert Ryland, who was himself an enslaver, was appointed to provide white spiritual oversight for the newly formed Black congregation. The rest of the church's leadership was drawn from Richmond's free Black community.[12] This lay leadership administered meetings, made financial decisions, managed membership, and oversaw congregants' social and charitable activities.[13] By the time that famine funds were collected in winter of 1847, the church was an established center of Black life in Richmond.

Unlike white famine donors in Charleston, whose names were published in newspapers and pamphlets distributed by relief associations, the contributions made by members of the First African Baptist Church were sparsely documented. Any motivations that donors might have had for their contribution have not been preserved. No one recorded the names of individual donors; the only records remaining are the names of people who were members of the church at the time that the donation was taken up.[14] In the summer of 1846, that membership numbered over two thousand.[15] Most did not attend regular meetings, however. The majority of congregants were enslaved and subject to the whims of the white people who controlled their labor.[16] Their experiences varied. Some congregants were held in bondage by local tobacco merchants; the labor of others was rented to local ironworks, factories, and mills.[17] Some, like Nancy Brown's husband Henry, engaged in self-hire, where enslavers sent them to Richmond in exchange for a set fee. If they were able to make more than that, they were often permitted to keep the difference.[18] Women frequently undertook work outside of enslavers' households and were able to negotiate the terms of their employment. The First African Baptist Church's white pastor, Robert Ryland, reported that the people he enslaved, "when we were about to furnish their fall or spring clothing, would often say that, by patching their old garments, they could do without *new* ones, and would ask us for the *money* instead."[19] Regardless of this, however, remuneration was paltry. In Southern cities in the 1840s, an enslaved person's labor could be rented for four dollars per month.[20] The twenty-six dollars raised by First African Baptist Church, then, might have represented the better part of one enslaved person's labor for a year.

In other parts of the South, the situation was even worse. While in Richmond it was common for enslaved people to engage in practices of self-hire, elsewhere it was forbidden. In Alabama, where donors from Lowndes County chose to send money instead of giving up food, for instance, it was illegal to "buy, sell, or receive, of, to or from a slave, any commodity whatsoever, without the leave or consent of the master, owner or overseer of such slave."[21] Lest enslavers be tempted to allow enslaved people to work on their own, the law stipulated that an enslaver was prohibited from "permit[ting] his or her slave to go at large or hire him or herself out."[22] While these laws were primarily intended to limit the mobility of enslaved people, and thus their ability to escape, they also recognized that money was power and sought to limit the capacity of enslaved people to amass capital. Fundamentally, these laws meant that possessing money—a sure sign of illicit work—would likely be read by some white Southerners as the commission of a crime.

In Richmond, the men and women who were able to exercise some control over the circumstances of their labor could attend church more often. The institution of slavery in cities was, as Clifton Ellis and Rebecca Ginsburg note, "more precarious and fragile" than on plantations, making it possible for enslaved people to establish community networks and develop mutual aid societies.[23] Many settled in burgeoning Black neighborhoods. Some lived in shared tenement housing, while others illegally rented rooms from free Black Richmonders at the edges of the city. People who shared these domestic spaces were often related, through birth, marriage, or other less formal kinship structures. Other social communities developed as well, in regular gambling games, at grocery stores, and in snack houses and cookshops.[24] As Midori Takagi has noted, collectively these spaces made possible a degree of self-sufficiency and social life, serving as sites of information exchange, gossip, and deliberation. However, congregants outside of these structures—especially those who accompanied enslavers to Richmond on business—had little control over when they arrived, departed the city, or attended church. The First African Baptist Church was a mobile and fluctuating community that was enmeshed in networks that crossed antebellum Virginia.[25] Some had access to capital; many did not. Collectively, however, they gave.

Uses of Black Charity

Enslaved and free Black people in the South had ample reasons not to give their hard-earned money to strangers an ocean away. At a time when access to capital was limited, Black charitable practices were most frequently directed toward members of their own communities. Cash, however small an amount, could quite literally mean the difference between life and death, or between freedom and bondage, for congregants and those whom they loved.

Despite restrictions on their labor, enslaved people did grow crops, sell goods, work extra hours, and raise funds. Through licit and illicit means, they accrued capital, and that capital was often a mechanism to assert autonomy and resist oppression.[26] With it, they began to establish chains of property ownership that had the potential to transcend generations. Though this acquisition of property was frequently disrupted, it was one small way that they challenged the heritability of slavery. They purchased foods, goods or medicines for themselves or their families; several reported using money earned from hired out labor to purchase clothes for Sunday services that allowed them to celebrate moments of accomplishment.[27] Some saved for manumission.

Most enslavers were more likely to promise manumission than deliver it, but it was nonetheless a hope that many kept alive. In this period, some enslaved people collectively raised money to purchase the freedom of family members or appealed to local free people to purchase that freedom for them.[28] Nancy Brown's husband, Henry, for example, agreed to give Samuel Cottrell fifty dollars in exchange for the promise that "he would prevent her [Nancy] from being sold away."[29] Cottrell took the money and did not keep this promise. It was he who sold Nancy to North Carolina, away from her husband, congregation, and Richmond community. Although twenty-seven dollars was only a fraction of the cost of manumission, the money raised by the First African Baptist Church for Ireland could have been used to contribute to the freedom of an enslaved person in Richmond, to the freedom of one of the donors' friends or relatives, or, as in Henry Brown's case, to extract a promise.[30] Choosing to send money to Ireland, then, was not a simple philanthropic calculus; it was an explicit decision not to spend funds on other, potentially more personal, causes.

Unsurprisingly, when enslaved and free Black people did practice formal charity, most frequently it took the form of giving within their communities. This was another factor militating against donations to Ireland: Black philanthropy in the nineteenth century was usually designed to spread resources locally and to support local institutions. For example, the First African Baptist Church requested contributions from congregants to cover Ryland's salary. Describing the church finances, Ryland reported that "each attendant gave at least one cent at every meeting."[31] Because it funded the white pastor, this payment was an indirect condition of the congregation's continued existence. Church members also raised funds to help free Black congregants inmigrate to Liberia.[32] This kind of giving preserved and defended a religious space that provided community alongside spiritual succor.

In some cases, religious groups like the First African Baptist Church supported ancillary fraternal organizations that helped the sick, elderly, or grief-stricken.[33] In December 1848, for example, the church tasked a committee with making "some plan for the relief of the poor" within their congregation. This committee solicited funds from "public meetings or private donations" and dispersed relief based on its assessments of the wants and needs of applicants.[34] Black congregations and other groups also distributed funds to the locally impoverished and to schools. The meetings of these charitable associations were typically clandestine, both because they were not licensed by state governments and because the groups often included enslaved people, who were prohibited from congregating outside of religious services.[35] Unlike those of their white counterparts, donations to these funds were generally on the order of cents rather than dollars.[36] In other ways, these charitable forms did not directly match those practiced in white spaces. For instance, instead of passing a collection plate around a church, Black churches would announce a collection and invite congregants to the front of the church en masse.[37] Rather than focus on each person as the collection plate passed them, this kind of giving deemphasized the public performance of individualized charity. Both contribution and distribution were manifestations of communal egalitarianism.[38] In the 1840s, Black Richmonders, especially those affiliated with the First African Baptist Church, were expert practitioners of in-group charity.

Although Black communities did on occasion give to outsiders, and even sometimes globally, these funds were typically directed to distant brethren—for example, to Black missionaries at work in Africa.[39] In other words, while Black collectives rarely dispensed aid outside of the direct community, when they did, it was in solidarity with those with whom they could directly identify. This communal focus might suggest that the First African Baptist Church sent money to Ireland because congregants felt a sense of solidarity with the Irish; after all, their charitable work to this point had been focused on community members.

However, this interpretation is contravened by narratives about Ireland in both the white Southern and Northern Black press that cast Irish and enslaved people in opposition to each other. For groups of people who tended not to give to causes outside of their own sphere, the Irish famine was not likely to be a compelling exception.

Black News Networks

Although it is impossible to know how specific enslaved or free Black people in Richmond would have interpreted the Irish famine, news and commentary from the North and from across the Atlantic reached Black Richmonders, often through networks that abolitionists had established decades before. Joanna Brooks has argued that the few explicit descriptions of enslaved peoples' news-consuming practices in this period should be read not as extraordinary exceptions, but as part of a "black counterpublic" made up of producers and consumers of information that fostered collective identities in opposition to dominant white economic and political interests.[40] Interest in the famine was certainly a part of this counterpublic. Famine donations from the First African Baptist Church might also be read as part of that same constellation of resistive acts.

In the 1820s, newspapers printed in Northern states and intended for Black audiences had been common throughout the South. They were distributed by agents who worked secretly to get reading material to Black news consumers.[41] These newspapers were read by free and enslaved people alike, and those who could not read listened to news that was read aloud.[42] In the 1830s, state statutes across the South criminalized teaching enslaved people to read, because white Southerners feared that literacy would lead to rebellion.[43] In a letter written in 1830, the governor of Virginia, William Giles, reported on covert attempts to circulate antislavery literature in Richmond. He warned that "I have many reasons for believing; that during the last year; and up to the present time, there has been an encreasing activity in circulating amongst the people of color insurrectionary pamphlets and speeches."[44] Despite laws that sought to prevent literacy, enslaved people living in cities were significantly more likely to be able to read than their rural counterparts.[45] However, white efforts to limit abolitionist literature meant that both free and enslaved Black people's access to news was circumscribed. By the start of the famine, explicitly Black newspapers did not circulate in cities like Richmond, and readers were forced to seek out printed material furtively, for fear of being recognized and harshly punished.[46]

White efforts to suppress these networks increased in the middle decades of the nineteenth century, but there is some evidence that individual distributors persisted, and that antislavery societies in the North routinely sent abolitionist literature to Southern states.[47] Biographies and oral histories produced after the Civil War contain stories of enslaved men and women who acquired, read, and, in some cases, retained pages from white newspapers.[48] In his autobiography, Frederick Douglass commented that "nothing seemed to make" the woman who enslaved him "more angry than to see me with a newspaper. . . . I have seen her rush at me with a face made all up of fury, and snatch from me a newspaper, in a manner that fully revealed her apprehension."[49]

Churches like First African Baptist were nodes in networks that carried news surreptitiously throughout the South. Booker T. Washington described this circulation of news as part of a "grapevine telegraph" that helped enslaved communities keep abreast of national events.[50] Recounting his experience a decade after the famine, Washington noted that "the slaves on our far-off plantation, miles from any railroad or large city or daily newspaper, knew what the issues involved were," and that this news was often ferried by enslaved people who were "sent to the post-office for the mail" and who "would linger about the place long enough to get the drift of the conversation from the group of white people who naturally congregated there, after receiving the mail to discuss the latest news."[51] Touring Black preachers who ran Sabbath schools or delivered sermons on plantations or in the homes of enslaved people were known to travel from plantation to plantation, carrying news that might not otherwise have crossed the distance.[52] In the year preceding the Richmond donation, congregants came to the First African Baptist Church from across the South, and from different sites of news access: from Warsaw (50 miles northeast toward the Chesapeake Bay); Augusta (120 miles west, in the Blue Ridge Mountains near Charlottesville); and Williamsburg (50 miles to the southeast, near the mouth of the James River), among others. Traveling from these places to Richmond rendered congregants as part of this "grapevine telegraph," in contact with other people on the move and with access to different news sources.

Some of the famine news that came through these networks originated in white abolitionist newspapers published in the North. These newspapers proliferated in the middle decades of the nineteenth century. William Lloyd Garrison founded one of the most famous of these, *The Liberator*, in Boston in 1831. The *National Era* was founded in early 1847 in Washington, DC. It would go on to serially publish *Uncle Tom's Cabin* in the 1850s.[53] The editors of these papers incorporated Ireland into their reporting but were careful to foreground their abolitionist message. For example, throughout the famine, *The Liberator* published accounts of Irish distress, but often paired them with reminders that many Irish people opposed slavery. A December 1845 article enjoined "Southern slaveholders!" to "read the following proceedings, if you wish to know what are the feelings of the people of Ireland, in relation to your nefarious slave system!" What followed was an account from the *Cork Examiner* detailing an antislavery meeting that held of a vote of thanks in celebration of abolitionists in the United States.[54] The abolitionist views of these Irish, *The Liberator* intimated, made them especially fine recipients of relief.

The *National Era* also printed several accounts of Irish suffering and starvation, drawn from newspapers in both Ireland and the United States. Instead of celebrating abolitionist Irish people as ideal recipients of aid, the *National Era* called attention to examples of "exalted charity" from the United States, "reaching forth her hand to rescue unhappy Ireland."[55] It lauded instances of generosity from both Black and white Americans. In March 1847, the editors observed "with pleasure" donations from "the laboring classes throughout the country for the suffering poor of Ireland."[56] Included among these were the "mostly female" workers "of the Richmond cotton factory," which in this period employed enslaved and free Black women alongside white workers.[57] These white abolitionist newspapers used the famine to celebrate the reach of antislavery sentiments and call attention to the humane efforts of enslaved and free people.

Free and enslaved Black people in Richmond may have gotten Irish news from material printed in Black newspapers as well, traveling via the same networks that brought antislavery literature to the South. Although there were no Southern Black newspapers, there was a robust Black print culture in the North. Many were short lived, like *Freedom's Journal*, which ran from 1827 to 1829, or the *Ram's Horn*, which ran from 1847 to 1848.[58] The editors of *Freedom's Journal* made their focus and audience clear on the front page, writing that, in founding the paper, "we wish to plead our own cause. Too long have others spoken for us. Too long has the publick been deceived by misrepresentations."[59] In late 1847, Frederick Douglass founded another Black newspaper, the *North Star*, in Rochester, New York. The *North Star* would run, under a variety of names, until the 1850s.[60] It circulated widely throughout the Atlantic, sharing antislavery news and opinion from the United States with Britain, Canada, and the Caribbean.[61] Black editors intended these papers to foster the development of a Black middle class and to celebrate community values of education, industriousness, and moderation.[62] In addition to this local focus, the papers published on world events, including the famine in Ireland.

The *North Star*'s Irish reporting was particularly notable because Douglass, already famous for his *Narrative of the Life of Frederick Douglass, an American Slave*, had been traveling and lecturing in the United Kingdom, including Ireland, before returning to New York to begin publishing his new newspaper. News of Douglass's lecture tour, and of his new paper circulated widely among the white press, including in the South. A December 1845 article in the *Charleston Mercury* called Douglass "a runaway slave" who was "creating a sensation in Ireland."[63] Through the Black abolitionist or white press, it seems that news of Douglass's tour reached Richmond.

Douglass observed firsthand the extent of Irish distress. In a letter written to fellow abolitionist William Lloyd Garrison after visiting Ireland in February 1846 and subsequently reprinted in *The Liberator*, Douglass lamented that "the limits of a single letter are insufficient to allow any thing like a faithful description of those painful exhibitions of human misery, which meet the eye of a stranger at almost every step." Although he described "an Irish hut" that seemed "constructed to promote the very reverse of anything like domestic comfort" and was populated by people "in much the same degradation as the American slaves," he was famously, even at the time, cautious about Irish support.[64] Many Irish emigrants in the United States actively supported slavery, and, notwithstanding *The Liberator*'s reporting on Cork antislavery meetings, many people in Ireland were unwilling to speak against it. Douglass was also wary of drawing connections between the experiences of enslaved people and those of the Irish because of how those comparisons were weaponized by enslavers. Speaking to a crowd in Limerick, he asserted that "there was nothing like American slavery on the soil on which he now stood. Negro-slavery consisted not in taking away a man's property, but in making property of him."[65] He often minimized the sufferings of the poor in Ireland, as part of a broader argument that even the most destitute Irish person was not subject to the indignity of enslavement.[66]

This active rejection of the framework of solidarity between the Irish and enslaved people was made manifest in the *North Star*. An article in January 1848 celebrated the benevolence of Irish Quakers, who had "made one and the same operation the means of serving the starving Irishman and the imbruted American slave." However, it pointed out, this success relied on the fact that destitute Irish people owned their own labor and were therefore able to work for wages "in the manufacture of elegant little works of taste and fancy" that could be sold at antislavery bazaars.[67] When Douglass referenced Ireland both privately and in speeches, and when the *North Star* commented on Irish affairs, it was almost always in the context of a broad obligation to "human freedom" and frequently included appeals that Irish people first attend to the cause of "the African slave."[68] Like other Black papers that emphasized middle-class respectability, Douglass's *North Star* was concerned with challenging white narratives of Black inferiority. When white Americans turned to Ireland as an example of authentic suffering, Douglass worked to decenter the plight of famine victims in Ireland and recenter the horrors of enslavement. Black consumers of this commentary in the South would not have learned to see themselves in solidarity with the Irish, but, rather, would have learned that claims of common experience were often used to undermine abolitionist messages.

Interpreting the Famine through the White Southern Press

Members of the First African Baptist Church would also have learned of the famine and discourse around famine relief through white news networks. Like Nancy Brown, many congregants of the First African Baptist Church were enslaved by people who participated in famine relief projects. For instance, Lucy Powell and Mary Robinson were both held in bondage by William McFarland, who was responsible for sending the money raised by the church to the Richmond Famine Committee.[69] Lucy Lovey, Jane Lewis, Games Gwathmey, Watson Taylor, Thomas Sidney, Jesse Brown, and George Brekenridge were all enslaved by members of the Gwathmey family, and they were likely to have heard that James L. Gwathmey, who worked at the Virginia Seminary in Roanoke, was raising funds on behalf of Ireland.[70] Others were connected to established Richmond families for whom the famine would have been a frequent topic of discussion. Matilda Banks and Mary Gunor were both enslaved by the white minister of the First African Baptist Church, Robert Ryland. Enslaved people who worked in households were in an ideal position to overhear the discussions of the news of the day and would have conveyed such news to people elsewhere.

What they likely would have learned was that white Southerners considered the Irish to be suffering from unique misery. Although no records exist of enslaved or free peoples' reactions to famine news, it is difficult to imagine that that news, circulating in white Richmond, would have convinced Black donors of shared community with the Irish. Throughout the famine, the white press emphasized the incomparability of Irish suffering. Like the Charleston and New Orleans papers discussed in the previous chapter, Richmond papers described Irish suffering as far worse than any other plight. Scenes from rural Ireland were "a picture more heart touching than perhaps misery ever before presented to the eye of philanthropy," and Irish famine victims were "suffering and beloved (and the more beloved because of their greatly suffering)."[71] Other papers did the same. One article, reporting on the donation from the enslaved people laboring in Lowndesboro, Alabama, argued that "slavery, as it is among us would be a blessing compared to the galling bitterness of the chain that eats into the very bones of the

Irish people, a chain rusted for centuries with the blood of brave people, and which carries with it in each alternate link, fever and famine!"[72]

For more specific reasons, as well, congregants of the First African Baptist Church would not have experienced solidarity with the Irish. For instance, they would likely not have found the experience of "[Irish] wretches, millions of them, who work 16 or 18 hours in the 24" to be uniquely horrible.[73] In the 1840s and 1850s, enslaved workers in Richmond's tobacco factories were expected to work similarly long days and to process a minimum of forty-five pounds of tobacco each day.[74] Irish experiences of overwork did not rival their own. They might also have balked at another theme in white famine reporting: that Irish people were forced to eat foodstuffs not even suitable for animals. The *Richmond Commercial Compiler* wrote that "the very swine [of Ireland] will not eat the diseased potatoes and yet the poor people are compelled to eat them or starve." At the same time, it was a common practice to give enslaved people food that was near or past spoiling, and Southern Black people, both enslaved and free, generally survived on a subsistence diet.[75] While the *Richmond Whig* lamented that Irish people were forced to eat yams, which were "a poor substitute, in respect to luxury at least, for the Irish potato," enslaved people would have found yams a common part of their rations. White assumptions about the desirability of food made clear that distant Irish bodies were valued very differently from enslaved ones by the white press.

The *Richmond Whig* specifically rejected similarities between the experiences of enslaved and Irish people and enjoined abolitionists to "turn their attention to the great Irish charnel houses," where they "might behold scenes of misery and hear cries of agony, such as never were or will be heard in any rice or cotton-field or negro cabin."[76] Articles like these made it clear that white commentators could muster sympathy for distantly starving Irish men and women in ways that they could not for Black Richmonders. This kind of reporting would have been unlikely to provoke sympathy for the Irish among the congregants of the First African Baptist Church.

Moreover, Black donors would likely have had trouble seeing themselves in solidarity with Irish revolutionaries, whose violent revolt in response to famine conditions the white Southern press celebrated and supported, often co-opting the language of emancipation. In late March

1846, the *Richmond Enquirer* noted that Irish "struggles for deliverance from oppression, must enlist in its behalf the encouragement and approbation of all friends of liberty throughout the world."[77] The *Richmond Whig* suggested that those struggles were a direct consequence of a lack of food, reporting "a large number of 'deaths from starvation' are chronicled in almost every paper from that ill-fated country—and murders and horrid outrages are constantly occurring—there had been several bread riots in Dublin."[78] For these newspapers, Irish people who were subject to restrictions on their food or freedom were celebrated when they responded with violence.

The white press also associated these celebrations of Irish revolutionary spirit with the coercion of Irish labor. At a public dinner in Richmond in October 1847 to celebrate Seneca M. Conway, a noted advocate for yeoman farmers, one toast published in the *Richmond Enquirer* proclaimed that the Irish crisis was "not a visitation of Providence but the result of the workings of an infernal aristocracy. It is high time to look to ourselves and cry, beware!"[79] This speaker credited Irish distress with an oppressive aristocracy and warned that, left unchecked, aristocratic impulses in the United States might lead to similar woe. These accounts were paired with reports about the coercion of Irish men and women "to be employed extensively on the public works." Indeed, physical labor in exchange for food did not seem to sit well with Irish workers. The *Richmond Commercial Courier* reported in late 1847 that "the state of Ireland is truly frightful. A system of agrarian resistance is everywhere manifested; landlords daily falling before the vengeance of the people."[80]

Naturally, white Southerners did not seem to see the irony in these statements. The congregants of the First African Baptist Church, however, were acutely aware of the fact that their experiences of suffering did not generate the kind of sympathy that Irish distress did. Many Black Richmonders were, too, filled with "reckless despair." They, too, labored in unchosen work in exchange for the food needed to maintain their lives; they, too, were governed by an oppressive aristocracy that engaged in unfair, extractive labor practices and experienced starvation and worse. In fact, in the 1840s, white Virginians harbored deep anxieties about the possibility that enslaved people might rebel. Nancy Brown's husband, Henry, recalled years later that, when he first "came to the city of Richmond, an extraordinary occurrence took place which caused great excited all over the town. I did not then know precisely what was the cause of this excitement, for I could get no satisfactory information from my master, only he said that some of the slaves had plotted to kill their owners. I have since learned that it was the famous Nat Turner's insurrection" that killed over fifty white men and women.[81] Richmonders in 1847, both Black and white, were aware of the potential for enslaved rebellion. They were also familiar with texts that seemed to incite resistance, and that had been brought to Richmond in the 1830s via the same abolitionist networks that carried Black newspapers in the 1840s. David Walker's *Appeal to the Coloured Citizens of the World*, for example, included a reminder that "they want us for their slaves, and think nothing of murdering us . . . therefore, if there is an *attempt* made by us, kill or be killed. . . . And believe this, that it is no more harm for you to kill a man who is trying to kill you, than it is for you to take a drink of water when thirsty."[82] These events reverberated throughout the 1840s, causing white Southerners to suspect a rebellion in nearly every action that enslaved people took.[83] Those same white Southerners celebrated Irish revolutionary impulses.

In myriad ways, news of the famine reached enslaved and free Black people in the American South. The news about Ireland that would have circulated in Richmond's Black communities presented a complicated view of the crisis. Enslaved people knew that white Richmonders participated in famine relief and, like other white Southerners, cast their donations as evidence of humanity in the face of abolitionists' claims to the contrary. White newspapers like the *Richmond Enquirer*, *Richmond Whig*, and *Richmond Commercial Compiler* all carried news of Irish suffering intended for white readers like those circulating in other Southern papers. Black and abolitionist papers memorialized Irish starvation but refused to countenance comparisons between Irish and enslaved people. These various narratives collectively cast the Irish as in need of help, despite their free status, while at the same time failing to establish any sense of solidarity between the Irish and prospective Black donors in Richmond.

Famine Philanthropy and Black Humanity

Although there is scant evidence for feelings of solidarity between the congregants of the First African Baptist Church and the Irish recipients of their aid, the fact of the donation itself points to other possible uses for famine relief. One use for Black Richmonders might have been to point out white Richmonders' hypocrisy in supporting the starving in Ireland while enslaved people suffered in their city. The abolitionist newspaper the *National Era* raised the question of whether funds for Ireland might be put to a good use domestically. After Congress debated whether to pass the Irish Relief Act in 1847, the paper noted that if Congress "may appropriate money to relieve the poor in Ireland," then why could it not also "set apart a fund to be used by the States in aid of the relief of our two and a half million of slaves?"[84] Similarly, in May 1847, the *National Era* reprinted a speech given by the reverend Joshua Leavitt at the American and Foreign Anti-Slavery Society in which he posited that, had enslaved people been given access to bibles, it would have brought them "within the compass of human sympathy, so that the world would have cared for them as much as it cares for the starving Irish."[85] If pointing out this hypocrisy was the intention of the First African Baptist Church donors, it was entirely lost on the writers and editors of white newspapers.

In Richmond's Black communities, charity was a way to spread wealth, build community, and raise everyone up. White Southerners thought of philanthropy very differently. In addition to the political benefits that they believed they gained from associating themselves with Ireland, white Southerners saw their own participation in famine relief as part of a long tradition of benevolent superiority. This raises another possibility about the uses to which famine philanthropy was put: congregants of the First African Baptist Church might have been adopting white vernaculars of giving to make a claim about their own humanity and morality.

White philanthropic traditions spanned Southern geographies. In the rural South, large plantation owners held considerable social power. Part of that power was an obligation to help the poor in their immediate district and, in select and often capricious cases, to help the people they enslaved.[86] However, in comparison to elite Northerners, wealthy, enslaving Southerners were far more reluctant to support charitable endeavors. In part, this was to preserve the dominance of white enslavers. Southern elites limited the expansion of institutions of civil society, like voluntary associations, lest they become alternative sources of social power.[87] Southern ladies used charity as a gesture of condescension, and as a marker of superiority over the people they helped.[88] In cities, members of voluntary associations tended to be people with some property, but not significant wealth.[89] In Richmond, elites responsible for dispensing aid to paupers in the 1840s and 1850s increasingly believed that pauperism was traceable to "those departures from the code of morality" and, consequently, that Richmond's tax base should not be required to spend their money on reforming the unreformable poor.[90] Relief in these cities was confined to the "worthy poor."[91] In this period, to be worthy was almost always to be white. Enslaved people were banned from public relief in Richmond.[92] The First African Baptist Church's establishment of a poor relief fund confirms that the needs of congregants were not being met through other means.

In short, for white Southerners, to receive charity was to have failed, while to give charity was evidence of superior resource management as well as morality. As Stephanie McCurry has documented, requests for charitable assistance by poor whites were often seen as one of the "most distasteful" encounters between elites and non-elites.[93] Asking for help signified a failure of independence.[94] By the middle years of the famine, white Southerners had developed a philanthropic ethos that made clear that poor whites had access to elite charity because their skin was white, and because their social status would never encroach on that of their benefactors.[95] If members of the First African Baptist Church were familiar with this framework—and there is every indication that enslaved and free Black people in Richmond were familiar with what white Richmonders thought—then the decision to raise money to send to Ireland begins to look like a claim of morality and humanity.

The Irish were ideal candidates for this project. They were distant symbols of impoverished whiteness and were not embedded in the systems of violence that could pose a real danger to enslaved people's lives. Distance meant that the recipients of the First African Baptist Church's aid could never respond to the donation. While raising these funds was symbolically significant, it did not come with the same risks that donations to proximate poor whites would have. White Southerners in need were deeply familiar with the power relationships implied in aid; taking help from enslaved people would have been unthinkable. But the Irish—unnamed and undifferentiated—were an ocean away. Furthermore, since the First African Baptist Church donation was aggregated with other contributions from Richmond, Irish sufferers would never know that the source of their aid was Black donors.

White Richmonders, on the other hand, would have had to read of this contribution in the *Richmond Whig* and *Richmond Enquirer*, alongside the names of their white peers.[96] Some of the donors whose names were published alongside the "1st African Church," like E. H. Frayser and Samuel Putney, enslaved members of the congregation. Beyond these short records, the donation made by the congregants of the First African Baptist Church went unremarked in the white Richmond press and, indeed, in the white press across the United States. For the white Southern press, donations made by enslaved people seemed only to be worthy of comment when they validated arguments about the benevolence of slavery. Reports of the donation that opened this book, made by enslaved people laboring on Morgan Smith's plantation and published across the United States, emphasized that news of the event "ought to convince the abolitionists that Southern slavery is not the stern and cruel system in its practical effects."[97] In contrast, the donation from the First African Baptist Church received the briefest mention. It is impossible to say why white newspaper editors and writers did not comment, but one likely explanation is that this instance of charity did not fit into their expectations of benevolence. Especially in spaces where giving to the needy was a mark of superiority, donations from an autonomous Black collective incompatible with white interpretations of charity.

Though the archive is silent on their motivations, the most likely explanation for Black donors' decisions to send funds to Ireland lay in the space between white and Black vernaculars of giving in the Antebellum South. For many donors to Irish famine relief—and for white Southerners—solidarity with the starving Irish was a powerful reason to give because of the rhetorical uses it enabled. While Black charitable practices in this period tended to foster community, there is no evidence that these donors, or people like them, sought to use famine philanthropy to build solidarity with the Irish. Indeed, enslaved and free Black people had little to gain in such claims of community with Irish sufferers. They likely had experience with abolitionists' arguments that a focus on Irish suffering undermined claims to the inhumanity of slavery in the United States. They were also likely familiar with white writers' and commentators' use of Irish starvation and Black charity to argue for the relative humanity of slavery. For the congregants of the First African Baptist Church, famine philanthropy's use was in its appropriation of the white charitable model (seen weaponized by enslavers in the previous chapter) that cast givers as exceptionally humane. Among the many strategies that Black people used in this period to challenge the violent unfreedom of slavery, being seen to act benevolently toward a group of nearly universally recognized distant sufferers had the potential to undermine white assumptions about Black humanity.

A little over a month after the First African Baptist Church raised funds, Indigenous donors in the Cherokee and Choctaw nations gathered for a similar purpose. Like Black donors in Richmond, they were subject to the violent assumptions of white supremacy in the United States. They were also familiar with white understandings of philanthropy, and particularly the relationship between philanthropy and the "civilizing mission." Their donations might also be read acts of resistance, in ways that echoed and diverged from the First African Baptist Church's uses of famine philanthropy.

Resistance

In the 1840s Skullyville was a bustling town on the eastern edge of the Choctaw Nation, in what is now the US State of Oklahoma. It had been established as part of the United States' efforts to control and expropriate Indigenous people, and it persisted as a place where Choctaws and their Indigenous neighbors rebuilt lives that had been disjointed by these colonial ambitions. In the spring of 1847, Skullyville also became another site of Irish famine philanthropy.

The town that became Skullyville began as a Choctaw Agency. Agencies were administrative centers staffed by "Indian Agents," representatives of the US federal government who worked to exert influence over the Indigenous nations within whose borders they were located.[1] White settlers initially called the area "Pebble Springs."[2] The name "Skullyville," which quickly supplanted the English toponym, derived from *Iskvli*, the Choctaw word for money.[3] This name described the ways that local Choctaws used the agency: it was from the agency building that the federal government disbursed the annuities that had been promised to the Choctaw Nation in successive nineteenth-century treaties.[4] This distribution of annuities meant that Skullyville also became a place of commerce. Choctaws who had been coerced or forced from their ancestral lands in the southeast in the 1830s established farms and plantations nearby. Indigenous and white traders also set up shop, hoping to capitalize on visitors to the agency building and on the town's proximity to the Arkansas river trade route. Their customers included Chickasaws and Seminoles who, like the Choctaws, had been "removed" west by the federal government. US soldiers garrisoned at Fort Smith, fifteen miles away, also frequented the town.[5] By the late 1840s, Skullyville had become a site of Indigenous business and negotiation.

These various financial exchanges made Skullyville an ideal site for famine fundraising. On March 23, 1847, the agency building hosted an Irish relief meeting much like the others that had been held across

North America that spring.[6] William Armstrong, who was then serving as the federal government's agent to the Choctaws, opened the proceedings.[7] He read a pamphlet that had been printed and distributed by a relief committee in Memphis, Tennessee.[8] Having described Irish distress, Armstrong then called for members of the crowd to make donations. Reporting on the incident, the *Arkansas Intelligencer*, published a few miles from Skullyville, across the US border, wrote that "the meeting contributed $170," and that "all subscribed, Agents, Missionaries, Traders, and Indians" and "a considerable portion of funds was made up by the latter."[9] In a separate letter to the editor, a person who attended the meeting wrote that on the list of donors "you will perceive the names of many full-blooded Choctaw Indians, who knew nothing more, cared nothing more, than the fact, that across the Big Water, there were thousands of human beings starving to death."[10] Two weeks later, the *Intelligencer* printed a letter from Memphis acknowledging receipt of the donation.[11]

This donation is one of the most often remembered and celebrated instances of famine relief. At the time, it was remarked upon in white newspapers across the United States. Some wrote that $170 had been collected. Others reported that it had been $710.[12] All marveled at "the poor Indian sending his mite to the poor Irish."[13] More recently, this donation has been commemorated in famine ceremonies, public events, artwork, and even children's books.[14] In 2017, the artist Alex Pentek installed a sculpture in its honor in Midleton, a small town in County Cork. At the sculpture's dedication ceremony, Gary Batton, Chief of the Choctaw Nation, remarked to the Irish press that the sculpture was significant because "your story is our story."[15] Of course, this event and the rosy picture that has been painted of it is an incomplete story. In fact, Indigenous scholars have called for attention to the role that narratives about Irish and Indigenous historical relationships have played in obscuring the violence of settler colonialism.[16] These ongoing negotiations of the meaning of the Choctaw donation demonstrate that this act of famine philanthropy was significant at the time, and its significance continues to reverberate today.

The Skullyville meeting was not the only instance of famine philanthropy among Indigenous nations west of the Mississippi. Ten days earlier a similarly constituted group had gathered at the US Army outpost of Fort Gibson in the Cherokee Nation to hear news of the famine and take up donations.[17] On May 14, several months after the meetings in Fort Gibson and Skullyville, the down of Doaksville, home both to a Choctaw Agency and to the first Choctaw-language newspaper, hosted yet another famine relief meeting.[18] These gatherings took place only a decade after many Cherokees and Choctaws had been forced by the US government from their lands in the Southeast. Few members of either nation had substantial financial or emotional resources to share with distant sufferers in the 1840s; indeed, many were still experiencing their own financial and emotional traumas.[19] Nevertheless, as other unlikely donors across the North Atlantic had done, Cherokees and Choctaws agreed to send funds to Ireland.

Like the examples that preceded it, these instances of Indigenous engagement with famine relief should be read as political as well as charitable acts. These acts were conditioned by Cherokees' and Choctaws' experiences living in and around Fort Gibson, Skullyville, and Doaksville, and the information environments of the Cherokee and Choctaw Nations in the 1840s. The meanings of the donations, however, were not fixed. Missionaries and Indigenous commentators used them to debate the success of "civilizing" and Christianizing missions. Like the Richmond donors, some Indigenous leaders employed white vernaculars of charity and culture to solidify political power and authority in Indian Territory. For others the donations reflected a sense of solidarity with the oppressed and dispossessed Irish, which helped Cherokees and Choctaws, in limited and pragmatic ways, to critique the US colonial project.

Indigenous people in the era following the Trail of Tears did not act as a monolith; they undertook many—sometimes competing—acts of self-determination. However, despite their different approaches and understandings, Cherokees and Choctaws engaged in this unprecedented act of transnational giving because doing so bought valuable moral and political capital in the wake of removal, and at a time when many other avenues of protest were closed to them.

The Cherokee and Choctaw Nations after Removal

The years preceding the famine had been marked by violence and dislocation that would shape Cherokees' and Choctaws' collective and individual responses to Irish famine relief. In the late eighteenth century, federal policies toward Indigenous nations had been designed to influence and make treaties with established Indigenous communities.[20] However, as white settlers in the Southeast (many of them Irish or Irish American) became increasingly covetous of Indigenous lands in the early decades of the nineteenth century, that policy changed.[21] The US federal government, in support of the state governments of Georgia and Mississippi, began to abrogate treaties and deny Cherokee and Choctaw claims to tribal lands in the Southeast. Federal officials encouraged, often with violence and threats, Cherokee and Choctaw leaders to sign treaties that exchanged their ancestral homelands for land west of the Mississippi.

In the three decades before the famine, US officials successfully dispossessed Cherokees and Choctaws of a significant portion of their tribal lands in Georgia, Alabama, North Carolina, Mississippi, and Tennessee. In 1820 a small group of Choctaws signed the Treaty of Doak's Stand, which ceded six million acres of Choctaw lands in Mississippi and accepted thirteen million acres of "unimproved" land in Arkansas.[22] Some Choctaws moved West, hoping that doing so would limit future dispossession. However, white settlers had already established homesteads in the eastern portion of this cession and petitioned the federal government to take back some of the territory ceded to the Choctaw Nation. In 1825, after negotiations fraught with corruption, Choctaw representatives agreed to cede back the eastern portion of their western territory in exchange for six thousand dollars paid annually by the federal government for sixteen years.[23] The remaining lands, too, were occupied, but by people the government did not feel bound to protect. The Caddos, Wichitas, Comanches, Kiowas, Apaches, Arapahos, Cheyennes, and Osages living west of the Mississippi did not receive the same considerations as white settlers.[24]

Cherokees' experiences of treaty-making mirrored those of the Choctaws. Despite Cherokee alliances with the United States in the War of 1812, the federal government forced treaties in the aftermath of the war that exacted land cessions of over two million acres.[25] Just as some Choctaws had moved west because of cessions, so, too, did some Cherokees. Tribal leaders feared that this migration would undermine common Cherokee title to land and worked to consolidate tribal governments and enact laws that would protect communal landholdings.[26]

In 1830, in response to white dissatisfaction, President Andrew Jackson proposed a national plan of "Indian removal." Factions within the Cherokee and Choctaw nations strategized various—and often divergent—ways to resist dispossession.[27] Some sought to claim the inherent right to remain on their ancestral homelands. Others leveraged alliances with missionaries who feared that removal would undermine their proselytization efforts.[28] Still others opposed removal in principle but believed that moving west was the best way to protect the integrity of the Cherokee and Choctaw nations as political entities.[29] In 1831, five thousand Choctaws attended a treaty council with federal representatives. After proceedings reached a standstill, the US government agents sent the assembled Choctaws home. A small group, many of whom were known to be sympathetic to the government's removal plan, remained and signed the removal Treaty of Dancing Rabbit Creek on behalf of the entire Choctaw Nation.[30]

A similar story played out in the Cherokee Nation. In the 1830s, the Principal Cherokee Chief, John Ross, and the majority of the Cherokee Nation had publicly and adamantly opposed removal. However, a minority of Cherokee elites believed that neither US federal nor state authorities could be trusted to treat the Cherokee Nation in the Southeast justly. For these leaders, giving up their ancestral homelands was preferable to continuing to be assaulted by violent white Georgians.[31] In 1835, this smaller group signed a removal treaty on behalf of the entire Cherokee Nation.

In the aftermath of treaties that most Cherokees and Choctaws had not agreed to, the federal government claimed authority to violently expel men and women who refused to leave their lands in the Southeast. Cherokees and Choctaws were forced to march hundreds of miles along what would come to be known as the "Trail of Tears" to Indian Territory, in what is now the state of Oklahoma.[32] Records of the dispossession and forced march west are scant, but scholars estimate that one in four Cherokees died, and that every family lost at least one relative.[33] Choctaws suffered similarly. Thousands died of disease and starvation on their march west.[34]

Tensions in the Cherokee Nation between those who had supported the removal treaty and those who had opposed it traveled west with them. Hostilities escalated throughout the 1840s.[35] Legal and political structures, disrupted by removal, were not sufficient to prevent a series of coordinated assassinations of treaty signers.[36] In late 1846, the US agent to the Cherokees. Colonel James McKissick, sent a letter to the Office of Indian Affairs in Washington, DC, reporting "cases of outrage" in the Cherokee Nation, the same terminology used to describe tenants' attacks on landlords in Ireland and central New York. The federal official who responded to McKissick's letter lamented that it was troubling to hear that "every member of the Cherokee Community" was not "obviously impressed with the many advantages secured to them by the late treaty."[37] Life in the Cherokee Nation in the 1840s was marked by unrest and disagreement, which made paying attention to distant sufferers all the more unlikely.

In the decades after removal, Choctaws were also struggling to rebuild. The Choctaw Nation was organized in three districts, each of which was ruled by a Chief who had led before removal and who served in a national legislature.[38] Whereas some of these Chiefs had supported the adoption of white cultural and religious practices before removal, after their dispossession west they argued that Choctaws should resist the assimilationist impulses of white settlers. The Chief of the Moshulatubbee district, where Skullyville was located, for example, was especially hostile to missionaries, whom he blamed for aiding in Choctaw dispossession. Missionaries who attempted to establish schools in his district in the aftermath of removal met with hostility.[39]

Choctaws were also plagued by floods and rampant sickness, which killed one out of every five Choctaws living west of the Mississippi after removal.[40] In 1847, a decade after the federal government's Indian Removal policies began, white missionaries reported that many Choctaws were still houseless, and that "several hundred" remained "encamped about the Agency" with little permanent support. Residents of this encampment appeared to missionaries as "very much degraded and extremely filthy."[41] One army officer reported "much sickness" among the recently removed Choctaws, made worse because the government had provided "no provision for medical attention or for simple remedies to be given them."[42]

Although Cherokees and Choctaws in the 1840s disagreed about many things, both within and beyond their respective nations, for most, political stability, shelter, and medicine were priorities. Like the Richmond donors in the previous chapter, they had little obvious reason to send money to Ireland.

Famine News in Indigenous Newspapers

Cherokees and Choctaws learned about the famine through both the white and Indigenous press. Not only did multiple white newspapers circulate in Indian Territory, but the Nations themselves also had vibrant print cultures that pre-dated removal. The primary non-Native newspaper in the area was the *Arkansas Intelligencer*, which was published twenty-five miles from the Choctaw capital and six miles from the border of Indian Territory. This was a Democratic party paper intended to spread news "from a point further west than was ever before paper published in the United States."[43] Native agents for the paper distributed it widely within the Cherokee and Choctaw Nations.[44]

Newspapers written both by and for Cherokees and Choctaws were also published in Indian Territory. Indigenous publishing began before the Cherokees and Choctaws were dispossessed of their lands in the Southeast. In 1828, Elias Boudinot had established the first Indigenous-language newspaper, the *Cherokee Phoenix*, in Georgia. He used the paper to foster a Cherokee reading public and to interject Cherokee experiences into a public sphere that was largely dominated by white culture and writing.[45] While the *Cherokee Phoenix* did not move west with the Cherokee Nation, the desire for a Cherokee newspaper did. In 1844, as one of its first official acts after removal, the Cherokee Nation government established the *Cherokee Advocate* with aims similar to the *Phoenix*, exemplified by the slogan "Our Rights, Our Country, Our Race." Four years later, missionaries in the Choctaw nation founded the *Choctaw Telegraph*. Despite its evangelist origins, this paper was written and edited by Choctaws and was intended to serve Choctaws' secular as well as religious needs.

These papers were published in English as well as in Native syllabaries and sought to reach as wide range of readers as possible, both within and beyond Indian Territory. In fact, the *Cherokee Advocate* positioned itself as a paper that crossed tribal boundaries. Its prospectus noted that "our location, and station we occupy relative to the Creeks, Chickasaws, Choctaws, Osages, Senecas, Delawares and other Indians, are such as will enable us at all times to furnish the readers of the paper with the latest and most correct border news."[46]

As was common at the time, both Indigenous and regional newspapers reprinted stories from further afield. Although reprinting from overseas papers declined in much of the United States in the 1830s as foreign correspondents became more common, newspapers in Indian Territory relied on faraway periodicals for much of their nonlocal news.[47] In the course of reporting on the famine, Indigenous newspapers cited the *New York Globe, New York Tribune, Scientific America* (New York), the *Reveille* (Matamoros, Mexico), both the *New Orleans Picayune* and *Delta*, the *New Era* (Jackson, Tennessee), the *Missouri Republican* (St. Louis), the *Louisville* (Kentucky) *Democrat*, the *Dollar Times* (Boston), the *Cincinnati* (Ohio) *Times*, and the *Albany* (New York) *Cultivator*. In addition, the *Cherokee Advocate* and *Arkansas Intelligencer* quoted occasionally from the *London Times*, the *Cork Examiner*, the *Cork Reporter*, *The Nation*, and the *Liverpool Times*. Reprinted articles from these periodicals, as well as editorial commentary in the *Cherokee Advocate, Choctaw Telegraph*, and *Arkansas Intelligencer*, introduced people in Indian Territory to Irish suffering.

These newspapers deployed writing—often used against Indigenous people by settler colonists—as a tool to promulgate Indigenous rhetoric and perspectives.[48] As Hillary Wyss has argued, missionaries often taught Indigenous people to read in the hopes that they would become passive consumers of their information—in Wyss's words, a "Readerly Indian."[49] What missionaries feared was "Writerly Indians," who used both English and Indigenous writing technologies to articulate political autonomy, and personal identity.[50] Both the *Cherokee Advocate* and the *Choctaw Telegraph* illustrated how Indigenous people living in Indian Territory used text to articulate sovereignty that did not derive from the US federal government.

The fact that news about Ireland was published in these newspapers does not itself explain why Indigenous individuals, themselves often scraping by after their dispossession, would have donated money to sufferers thousands of miles away. The newspapers that circulated within

Indian Territory provide evidence of how the meaning of these donations was appropriated and contested. The first point of contestation was over whether the donations should be attributed to Christian proselytizing efforts or to intrinsic Indigenous humanity; the second concerned whether they served as evidence of moral superiority or as a bridge between people similarly subject to colonial abuses. These multiple and disputed meanings offer possible explanations for why Cherokees and Choctaws might have chosen to send funds to Ireland as they were recovering from disastrous circumstances close to home. They also point to yet more ways in which engagement with famine relief could be politically useful.

Missionary Propaganda

As soon as the famine donations were reported, articles in white newspapers argued that Cherokee and Choctaw famine philanthropy was evidence of internalized Christian values. This explanation turned on the assumption that Cherokees and Choctaws were assimilable, and that inferior Indigenous traditions and beliefs fell away when confronted with proselytizing messages.[51] For missionaries, the success of Christianizing projects was evidence that they should be allowed to continue to operate in Indian Territory. For example, the author of an article in *Arkansas Intelligencer* describing the Choctaw donation celebrated it as a "voice of benevolence from the western wilderness" and championed "the 'poor Indian' sending his mite to the poor Irish!" The writer continued to develop this theme, enjoining readers to note "what an agreeable reflection it must give to the Christian and the philanthropist, to witness this evidence of civilisation and Christian spirit existing among our red neighbors. They are repaying the Christian world a consideration for bringing them out from benighted ignorance and heathen barbarism. Not only by contributing a few dollars but by affording evidence that the labours of the Christian missionary have not been in vain."[52] In one clause, the *Arkansas Intelligencer* praised Choctaw donors for their generosity but, in the next, gave actual credit to missionaries. Then, it further reminded readers that despite this act of startling generosity their "red neighbors" were still only a few steps away from "benighted ignorance and heathen barbarism." A letter to the editor of the *Intelligencer* expressed similar sentiments, marveling, "Is this not a sublime spectacle? The Red man of the new, bestowing alms upon the people of the Old world? With them, it be literally complying with that golden rule of Christianity, of returning good for evil."[53]

Commentators across the United States shared the *Intelligencer's* perspective. For instance, in late April 1847, Thomas Pim Cope, a Philadelphia Quaker merchant who coordinated both Quaker famine relief projects as well as proselytizing missions, wrote that "among the novel & interesting occurrences of the times, not the least extraordinary & gratifying is the circumstance of the Choctaw Indians having held a meeting at their agency for the relief of the starving poor of Ireland, at which $710 were contributed, the agent, the missionaries & the Indians subscribing."[54] Newspapers as far away as Maine used the *Intelligencer's* language to echo Pim Cope's sentiments celebrating the Choctaw donation. Each emphasized the surprising fact that "poor Indian[s]" would send their "mite" to the "poor Irish."[55]

Missionaries operating in the Cherokee and Choctaw Nations would have been particularly pleased with this interpretation. Many had been explicitly excluded from treaty negotiations because federal officials feared they would oppose removal.[56] In Indian Territory, many missionaries were faced with hostility on the part of Indigenous leaders and citizens.[57] Claiming credit for Cherokees' and Choctaws' philanthropic impulses offered an opportunity for missionaries to assert their ongoing influence among Indigenous communities.

Indigenous commentators challenged interpretations that cast their donations merely as evidence of acculturation. While public charity was certainly among the tools that Indigenous people used to make claims to "civility," and therefore, political autonomy, in the aftermath of removal, the *Cherokee Advocate* framed famine philanthropy as an outgrowth of their own culture and worldview, not adoption of a white, Christian one. In July 1847, the *Cherokee Advocate* reprinted an article from the Philadelphia-based *United States Gazette* that proclaimed, "Among the many noble deeds of disinterested benevolence which the present famine in Europe has called forth, none can be more gratifying to enlightened men than the liberality of our red brethren . . . displayed at a late meeting in the Cherokee nation." The writer went on to note that Indigenous philanthropy was "the more acceptable that it comes from those upon whom the white man has but little claim. It teaches us that the Indian, made like as we are, has a humanity common among us."[58] The editors of the *Cherokee Advocate* chose not to reprint examples of the most common trope in white reporting on the Choctaw and Cherokee donations: that the donations were evidence of the superiority of white morality. Instead, they reproduced an article that explicitly argued for Indigenous humanity. In choosing to publish commentary from a white newspaper that contravened missionaries' claim, the editors of the *Cherokee Advocate* challenged prevailing white interpretations of Indigenous philanthropy.

The reprinted *United States Gazette* article referenced Indigenous giving practices that preceded missionary's assimilation efforts. Giving and receiving gifts were parts of everyday life in both the Cherokee and Choctaw nations, as reflected in the multiplicity of local charitable projects undertaken by Cherokees and Choctaws in eighteenth and early nineteenth centuries. Many were infrastructural: constructing a new church, funding a female seminary, or purchasing materials for an industrial school.[59] In a few, politically useful, cases gift-giving extended beyond Indigenous communities, as a means of building relationships between otherwise unrelated groups.[60] For example, the early eighteenth-century Choctaws, who were formally allied with the French, agreed to supply surplus corn when French supplies were depleted. This corn was likely given with the expectation of reciprocity. LeAnne Howe suggests that we think about this donation as foreign aid—in other words, giving with a political purpose, and between political allies.[61] Cherokees and Choctaws in the nineteenth century were familiar with aiding others and considered giving a necessary part of community and political life.

These practices meant that Cherokees and Choctaws were familiar with both local and distant relief on the eve of the famine. In May 1847, the *Cherokee Advocate* published an article explicitly calling for readers to give to Ireland. It drew attention to "all the large cities, in the towns and villages, and throughout the country public [where] meetings have been held and speedy and energetic measures adopted." It particularly celebrated the fact that "our neighbors, the Choctaws, have lent a helping hand, and so have the Cherokees." While this article did not cast these donations as evidence of missionaries' success, it did make an explicit link between shared experiences of Irish sufferers and Native donors and asked that readers "not hesitate" to give, even though "the sufferers are separated from us by hundreds of miles. It should be enough for us to know that those who are dying for bread are our fellow beings."[62] For the *Cherokee Advocate*, Indigenous donations to famine relief were not merely the expression of generosity, but the natural and appropriate behavior of one group of "fellow beings" to another.[63]

This language reflected Indigenous expectations about giving practices. Scholars of Native giving practices argue that, in contrast to white charitable norms, Cherokee and Choctaw gift-giving did not reflect social power relations. Giving did not signal the giver's superiority over the recipient; rather, it was a reciprocal necessity born of the need to constantly redistribute goods to the benefit of the community, however broadly construed.[64] Giving a gift, or participating in famine relief efforts, had the potential to render previously disparate groups into "fellow beings."

The phrase "fellow beings," of course, had the potential to take on multiple meanings. An alternative to Indigenous interpretations of giving, likely favored by missionaries, was that the Irish were fellow sufferers in Christ, and that Cherokees and Choctaws were obligated by Christian doctrine to help. These alternative interpretations point to two different ways that famine philanthropy was politically useful in Indian Territory. For missionaries, it had the potential to legitimize their presence; for some Cherokees and Choctaws—particularly those who resisted missionaries' influence—it had the potential to prove that white Christianity was superfluous to Indigenous needs.

Challenging Settler Colonialism

While public expressions of charity and philanthropy had broad political uses, choosing to give to Ireland had particular potential—potential that was rooted in Ireland's colonial history, as well as parallels between Irish experiences of the famine and Indigenous experiences of the Trail of Tears.

Indigenous newspapers reported on crop failures across Europe during this period, but it emphasized Irish suffering over that of other

Europeans. Many members of the Cherokee Nation had personal ties to Scotland, making the focus on Ireland particularly notable. According to Christine Kinealy, the Scots would have been more obvious recipients of aid, because many people of Scottish descent had intermarried with Cherokees in Georgia.[65] Indeed, John Ross, the Principal Chief of the Cherokee Nation, called attention to the fact that Ireland had been the focus of relief efforts, at the expense of Scotland. After a meeting was eventually called for Scottish famine relief in May 1847, Ross praised the Cherokee famine donors, but went on to chastise those who paid too much attention to the starving Irish. He argued that it was "particularly incumbent on the Cherokee people" to afford relief to the Scottish, likely because many Cherokees, including Ross, were "themselves descended from Scottish ancestors." Despite these connections, he noted that, so far, the "the attention of the benevolent community has seemed to be directed more to Ireland."[66] Nevertheless, appeals for aid in Indian Territory newspapers continued to focus predominantly on Ireland.

If, as some Indigenous commentators insisted, donations to Irish famine relief were not a marker of acculturation, and if, as John Ross claimed, these donations did not reflect some special kinship to the Irish, then giving to Ireland must have served some other purpose. As I have argued throughout this book, I believe that the answer can be found in the semantic emptiness of the famine, and its ability to mirror multiple political causes. In her history of Cherokee diplomatic correspondence, Claudia Haake argues that people subject to colonial violence often had to choose between radical and covert acts of resistance. The former strategy had the potential to backfire, causing "political annihilation"; the latter, which involved seeking legitimacy through the logic of the dominant order, could often effect more immediate change.[67] This is similar to James Scott's lens of "hidden transcripts": actions that carry one meaning for those in power and still another "unstated" meaning for subordinate groups.[68] Through this framing, Cherokee and Choctaw donations to famine relief might be read as a way for Indigenous donors to demonstrate their relative wealth, comfort, and consequently to claim political power through success in acceding to the logic of the dominant order. They might also be read as a fictive bridge between two groups subject to the violence of colonialism.

Just as white Americans were keen to interpret the Choctaw donation as evidence of Indigenous inferiority, so, too, did some Indigenous commentators work to perpetuate the idea that they were in fact well off, perhaps better off than white citizens of the United States as well as starving Europeans an ocean away. This interpretation was common in the reporting of the *Choctaw Intelligencer*, which began publication three years after the famine collections in Indian Territory. In September 1850, it reported that "an Irishman named John Collins" had "died in Buffalo, recently from starvation. He was found dead in bed after having retired fasting that he might keep his children alive."[69] Two months later, it published an article celebrating the Choctaw "art of living." Whereas most white Americans "look upon the Choctaws as still a wandering race, wearing the tomahawk and scalping knife," the article claimed that they were in fact more prosperous than many whites. For this claim the article offered several pieces of evidence: "that in more than one state" it would be possible to "find more cabins and huts than you will find in this nation"; that "the Sabbath is better observed among the enlightened Choctaws than among many of the highly favored in many states"; that "there are more adults who learn to read, than among most whites"; and, finally, that "there is more interest in schools and religion than among country people in many states."[70] It made no mention of the famine fundraising that had taken place in the Nation three years earlier, but juxtaposed with descriptions of a white immigrant's death, it suggests an interpretative frame designed to remind readers that Choctaws were not like poor whites, either at home or abroad. None of the Indigenous newspapers ever claimed that these donations were evidence of Indigenous superiority over the Irish. However, such implicit comparisons would have been useful to Indigenous elites, like those who signed the removal treaties and who argued that if Choctaws and Cherokees could satisfactorily adopt white American lifeways the United States might relent in its attacks on Indigenous sovereignty.

Comparisons between Irish and Indigenous people also had the potential to call attention to shared experiences of settler colonialism. Although few people in the 1840s—either Indigenous or white American—were using the language of imperialism to describe US-Indigenous relations, language critical of the federal government's treatment of Indigenous nations was present in the ways that Indigenous leaders in the years prior to the removal characterized US government actions as examples of bad faith.

Articulations of Cherokee nationhood in the years before removal turned on critiques of state governments' coercion and the failure of the US government to act responsibly toward sovereign Indigenous nations.[71] A letter from the Cherokee nation addressed to Congress in 1829 and published in the *Cherokee Phoenix* deployed the language of duplicity in its characterization of US Indian policy, asking how Indigenous leaders should view "the conduct of the United States . . . in their intercourse with" Indigenous nations, when those nations "have *never ceded*, nor ever *forfeited*" the right to lands that were nevertheless being seized. According to these authors, removal "would be in the highest degree oppressive."[72] A pamphlet recounting a meeting in support of Indigenous rights held in Philadelphia in 1830 made a similar claim. A speaker asked, "Shall a government founded on that celebrated exposition of the rights of man, which accompanied our declaration of independence, grossly violate those rights in others?" Referencing the American Revolution, he went on to inquire, "If *dependent nations* have a right *to declare themselves independent*, ought not *independent nations* be permitted to *remain independent?*" Furthermore, given that Indigenous nations had long been treated as independent and sovereign, "can a people be viewed as the friends of liberty at home, who are ready to avail themselves of superior strength to exercise tyranny abroad?"[73] Speaking against removal in Boston in 1832, the Cherokee Chief John Ridge compared "his people" with Bostonians' revolutionary ancestors, whose "first resistance was made against the designs of Great Britain to enslave this people" of Britain's American colonies.[74] Ridge cast the Cherokees as allied with the United States against imperial tyranny. In each of these examples Indigenous people couched their experiences vis-à-vis the United States in the context—if not explicit terms—of settler colonialism.

After their dispossession and resettlement west of the Mississippi, Choctaws and Cherokees turned to official channels to defend their sovereignty. The Choctaw leader Peter Pitchlynn advocated for years, beginning in the 1830s, that the US government owed the Choctaw Nation for unpaid "amounts" promised by the Treaty of Dancing Rabbit Creek. Congress held hearings on the issue between 1837 and 1845, ultimately passing laws that denied Choctaws the payments.[75] At the same time, Choctaws challenged government surveyors who had deferred to white settlers' land claims, depriving Choctaws of land promised to them by treaty.[76] These formal engagements with the federal government after removal made continuing to speak out directly risky, as these appeals turned to some degree on the ongoing willingness of the federal government to engage with Indigenous leaders.

Thus, another potential political use of famine relief was as a means of expressing the harm of colonialism while maintaining plausible deniability. This was made possible by parallels between Irish and Indigenous experiences. Cherokees, Choctaws, and Irish people had experienced violent settler colonization. British colonists had begun to settle in Ireland in the sixteenth century and, like the US colonists, they seized the best farmlands from the "uncivilized" native inhabitants and pushing them to the margins. In fact, the tactics that the United States used to implement Indigenous dispossession were inherited from British experiments in Ireland. While the United States frequently repudiated its imperial predecessor, scholars have noted that the American Revolution was in many ways an attempt to enact settler colonialism without British oversight.[77] The antecedents to Andrew Jackson's Indian Removal policies can be found both in pre-Revolutionary British treaties with Indigenous nations and in the actions of British settlers in pre-Revolutionary North America.[78] In sum, the treatment of the Irish by Britain and Indigenous people by the United States came from the same body of laws and practices. Indigenous expropriation was a central strategy of both British and US settler colonialism, a strategy that the British had begun to perfect in Ireland.[79]

Perhaps because of the relevance of this historical parallel, critics of US expansion also relied British imperial failure as a cautionary tale about overreach. In a speech against the war with Mexico, Henry Clay argued that Britain exemplified failed empire, especially with respect to Ireland. Clay reminded listeners that, despite Britain's long-standing experience with Ireland, and many attempts to subdue Irish rebellions, "insurrection and rebellion have been the order of the day, and yet, up to this time, Ireland remains," and that "every Irishman hates, with a mortal hatred, his Saxon oppressor."[80] In using an imperial example, Clay illustrated that westward expansion, the doctrine of manifest destiny, Indian removal, and proselytizing missions in the trans-Mississippi West were seen, even by some white commentators, as imperial behavior, if not formal imperialism.[81]

Indigenous newspapers also took Britain to task for its treatment of Ireland. In March 1847, the *Cherokee Advocate* reprinted an account by a Catholic clergyman who blamed Ireland's crisis on "the unfortunate misgovernment of this country," on "the want of parental sympathy for the people," and on "not timely interfering and rescuing a generous, noble, and a devoted people."[82] In May the *Cherokee Advocate* wrote that it was the "oppressed condition" forced on the Irish by Britain, rather than any intrinsic failures of Irish people or soil, "that is to be deplored." The author continued: "The Irish nation is tithed and taxed and rented until the energies of the people are subdued, until there is no wonder that they suffer and die—these facts even thus succinctly stated, we believe will be of interest to our readers."[83] In the *Cherokee Advocate*, as in many other contemporary periodicals, the Irish famine served as an opportunity to critique British governance, particularly Britain's arbitrary power over colonial spaces.

Like the Cherokee and Choctaws, the Irish had experienced first-hand what it meant to be a disposable population within an expanding polity. In the wake of the 1840s crop failures, thousands of Irish were forcibly evicted from their lands, either to be virtually imprisoned in poorhouses or shipped overseas.[84] Experiences of dispossession and forced removal suffered by the southeastern tribes were equally—if not more—horrific. Scholars estimate that, in total, over 13,000 Indigenous people died as a result of the United States' Indian Removal policies, and still more suffered before it. James Mooney, an amateur ethnographer, recounted the process of removal as told to him "from the lips of the actors in the tragedy": "Stockade forts were erected for gathering and holding the Indians preparatory to removal. From these, squads of troops were sent out to search with rifle and bayonet every small cabin hidden away in the coves or by the sides of mountain streams, to seize and bring in as prisoners all of the occupants, however or wherever they might be found. Families at dinner were startled by the sudden gleam of bayonets in the doorway and rose up to be driven with blows and oaths along the weary miles of trail that lead to the stockades. . . . In many cases, on turning for one last look as they crossed the ridge, they saw their homes in flames."[85] The men and women who suffered on the Trail of Tears would have seen parallels in an article in the *Cherokee Advocate* from June 1846 reporting that "the quays at Cork, as we read, are crowded to inconvenience with passengers and their luggage. Already one vessel has sailed with a full complement of passengers, and twenty three others with nearly four thousand emigrants are preparing at that port for sea."[86] A few months later, the same paper reprinted an article from the *Liverpool Times* arguing that "the number of persons in the most utter destitution, arriving from Ireland" in British cities "still continues." The article closed by observing, "It is clear, however, that this evil cannot be allowed to proceed without the most ruinous consequences."[87] For both Irish and Indigenous peoples, the experience of dislocation was fresh in memory.

Also like the Irish, eviction for the Cherokee and Choctaw meant starvation and disease. The Choctaw district chief Greenwood Leflore reported in 1830 that "a considerable portion of them [the Choctaw emigrants] are poor and leaving with means hardly sufficient to sustain them on their journey, will reach the place of their future residence in a very destitute condition."[88] Similarly, the missionary Alexander Talley stated that emigrants had "perished with cold and hunger" and had been forced to sleep in "a deep and extensive forest . . . in a linen tent covered with ice and snow for a week, with but two blankets to cover a bed of grass."[89] Eviction led, unequivocally, to death.

When Indigenous writers described the experience of the Irish, this suffering was far from a distant memory. In April 1846, the *Cherokee Advocate* reported, "In Roscrea, an important and populous district, the poor are living in the refuse of diseased potatoes and crowds may be seen from morning till night in the fields, grubbing the stray potatoes that may have remained on the ground after digging. . . . Wherever one looks, the misery of the poor is really heart rending." The article closed by editorializing that these conditions constituted "a new and an awful phase in the type of Irish misery and woe."[90] When, one year later, the same paper wrote of the "famine lands" of Ireland in which "old and the young, the feeble and the stout hearted, have been stricken down and hurried to another world," the descriptions were so terrible that the unnamed author posited that readers might "hardly credit the reports of the sufferings, disease and death which have reached us."[91] In writing this, the Indigenous authors were perhaps hoping that their own experience might be as heartrending to readers as that of the Irish.

For Cherokees, Choctaws, and the Irish, the traumas of removal, eviction, and expropriation were bound up not only in the physical experience of being uprooted but also in exile from ancestral lands. The 1829 testimony of one Cherokee elder illustrated this attachment to the Nation's spiritual home. In a speech resisting removal, he declared, "My aged bones will soon be laid under ground, and I wish them laid in the bosom of this earth we have received from our fathers who had it from the Great Being above. When I shall sleep in forgetfulness, I hope my bones will not be deserted by you."[92] Colonel George S. Gaines, who was tasked with overseeing Choctaw removal, recounted the same ties to the land: "The feeling which many of them evince in separating, never to return again, from their own long cherished hills, poor as they are in this section of the country, is truly painful to witness."[93] A traveler who passed groups of Cherokees on the Trail of Tears en route to Indian Territory remarked, "We learn from the inhabitants on the road where the Indians passed that they buried fourteen or fifteen at every stopping place, and they made a journey of ten miles per day only on an average."[94]

In the spring of 1847, just before the famine relief meeting in Skullyville, the *Cherokee Advocate* printed a litany of accounts of Irish deaths. Many of these articles featured people who died far from home, or who could not be buried with appropriate rites or ceremony. One described men forced to labor on public roads who had "not energy enough to keep their blood in circulation, and they drop down from the united effects of cold and hunger, never to rise again."[95] Another recounted "a whole family . . . ill with fever, having lost two of its number within two days," and who were evicted from their home by an "unfeeling landlord [who] had unhinged the door, took off their blankets, and left them to die without shelter, clothing or food." The same article described a scene in which "four corpses lay in" the streets of Skibereen, in County Cork, "as they had died, without preparation of any kind."[96] These descriptions of dislocation and death at the hands of Britain mirrored the Cherokee and Choctaw experiences at the hands of the United States.

Interspersed with these accounts, the *Cherokee Advocate* published articles pointing to the US government's failures to attend to the needs of Cherokees and Choctaws. One, from March 4, 1847, opined that government representatives "must know what we have been subjected to, during and prior to, our forcible removal west," including being deprived of "the comforts and enjoyments of domestic life" and left with "absolute poverty."[97] Two weeks later, in an article following numerous accounts of horrific Irish deaths, an anonymous author asked, "Why has there not been a disposition of Cherokee affairs? It can be answered in but one way—because there was not a will."[98] Lack of political will to attend to the needs of marginalized people had real consequences. For the Irish it meant degrading deaths, often far from home. For Cherokees and Choctaws, it had meant starvation and roadside burials in the 1830s and continued poverty in the 1840s. For Cherokees and Choctaws who buried their relatives by the roadside on the Trail of Tears, or who wished they could have buried their children among their ancestral kin on tribal lands in the American Southeast, stories of Irish distress would have evoked both memories and profound sympathy.

Writing about the early American republic, Jeffrey L. Pasley, Andrew W. Robertson, and David Waldstreicher note that "ordinary people may have seized popular politics—and cultural politics—precisely because real power and real economic resources were not so easily to be had."[99] Cherokee and Choctaw decisions to give hundreds of dollars to people "separated from [them] by hundreds of miles" took place at the time when famine relief was being put to multiple and occasionally conflicting uses.[100] Some white commentators, like Henry Clay, treated the famine as a harbinger of what was to come if the United States emulated imperial Britain. However, few white Americans were willing to turn the same lens on their own treatment of the Indigenous population, and few Cherokees and Choctaws were in a position to do so. Nonetheless, Indigenous commentators and editors put famine relief to political use in service of claims to sovereignty and political autonomy. Some invoked their own famine philanthropy to contest the colonizing and civilizing efforts of missionaries in the trans-Mississippi west. Others used reports of the famine and of famine philanthropy to highlight Indigenous morality and capacity for fellow-feeling in contrast to prevailing American ideas that Indigenous people required white guidance to act humanely. By critiquing British treatment of the Irish, they spoke to their fellow citizens of the tragic injustice of their own removal. At a moment when philanthropic practices were changing from immediate help for the proximate to institutionalized help for the generalized masses, when Indigenous people were being pushed to the literal and figurative edges of American space, and when access to the political power required to critique US policy was still out of reach, writers in Indian Territory used famine relief to embrace their own generosity and critique the danger of imperial rule.

Conclusion

Reverberations

When the community of enslaved people in Lowndes, Alabama, gathered in April 1847 to donate fifty dollars to Ireland, they might not have known how connected they were to the thousands of other people who were simultaneously participating in Irish famine relief. However, donations like theirs and those of their compatriots persist in the public imagination, illustrating the political power of relief more than a century after Irish potato crops had failed.

In May 2020, hundreds of Irish people came together virtually to raise and send funds to people in the Navajo Nation and on the Hopi Reservation in Arizona, Utah, and New Mexico. Although COVID was a global event, it was particularly deadly for Indigenous people in the United States, who, in comparison to white people, were more than three times as likely to contract the illness, more than four times as likely to be hospitalized, and significantly more likely to die.[1] Between 2020 and 2022, nearly thirty thousand people from Ireland collectively donated over one million dollars to the Navajo & Hopi Families COVID-19 Relief fund.[2]

Irish donors reported that they were compelled by the story of the Choctaw Nation during the famine. One man, quoted in the *New York Times*, said that he had "already known what the Choctaw did in the famine, so short a time after they'd been through the Trail of Tears," and that it had always struck him "for its kindness and generosity and I see that too in the Irish people."[3] In response to the donation, the Navajo Nation's Attorney General, Doreen McPaul said that she hoped "that the Navajo Nation will be able to pay it forward in honor of Ireland someday."[4] When Larry Mullen Jr., the drummer for the Irish band U2, made a $100,000 donation, the Relief Fund's founder Ethel Brand reflected that "we feel a real kinship with the Irish, who have a shared legacy of colonization."[5]

Other donations to famine relief also hold a place in public memory. Organizations like CAIT (Celts & American Indians Together) and AFrI (Action from Ireland) have worked to further commemorate the donations made by the Cherokees and Choctaws.[6] In 2010, the Irish president Mary McAleese publicly thanked New York's Jewish community for the donation of $1000 made by the congregation Shearith Israel in 1847. Even those donations that have not been formally memorialized are remembered. As one Irish-American commented to me at an Irish history talk recently, "Of course we gave to the Irish. We're Americans. It's what we do." In short, the famine and famine relief continue to reverberate.

As these episodes indicate, more than 150 years after Irish newspapers first raised the possibility of a "failure of the potato crop," the Irish famine still holds a central place in the historical and popular imagination, and the utility of famine relief is still palpable. In some cases, these memories reflect celebrations of extraordinary generosity. In others, including Ethel Brand's exhortation to remember shared legacies of colonization, they reflect experiences of power and exploitation. Like the relief itself, the *memory* of Irish famine relief is both malleable and political.

In *Aiding Ireland*, I have sought to explain the multiple and overlapping meanings given to the famine and famine relief in the mid-nineteenth century. To borrow from modern descriptions of media events, I wanted to tell the story of why famine relief "went viral." In doing so, I have situated this extraordinary instance of relief in broader histories of nineteenth-century philanthropy and politics. Responses to the famine across the North Atlantic world represented a shift away from local and communal charity and toward the normalization of relief at a distance. This was made possible, I contend, by the ease with which commentators and donors could project local political concerns onto discussions of and contributions to Ireland.

Many (but certainly not all) of the communities surveyed in this book would likely have understood their interest in Irish relief in terms of humanitarianism or Christian charity. At the same time, they might have been perplexed by the myriad other reasons that compelled their compatriots to become interested in mechanisms of Irish aid, or, indeed, to give funds. It is difficult to imagine enslaved people in Richmond being of one mind with Dubliners that famine philanthropy helped to define the Irish nation, or that Dubliners would have understood their interest in famine relief policy in the context of claims of racialized humanity. It is equally difficult to imagine Cherokees and Choctaws agreeing with some London writers that international philanthropy cemented relationships within imperial communities or that empire could be a benevolent institution. Even though they had a shared understanding that government overreach was a cause of Ireland's misery, enslavers in the American South and free trade evangelists in Britain would have differed over whether the Corn Laws were the most extreme example of that overreach. Even commentators in different parts of New York State framed the famine differently. These various understandings are not a paradox to be solved, however. Instead, I argue that Irish famine relief was popular precisely because it was politically useful and served so many different causes.

Although different communities, politicians, and commentators had their own distinct reasons for their framings of famine relief, some characteristics of the crisis made it conducive to empty signification. For one, the famine was conditioned and exacerbated by British colonialism, which by the nineteenth century had similarly impacted sites and communities around the world in a wide range of ways. For another, information technology made it possible for news of a crisis to spread faster and farther than had been the case even a decade before. Furthermore, the reason for the blight itself was not obvious, opening it up to a variety of interpretations. Moreover, political concerns around the North Atlantic made it possible for people to feel, rightly or wrongly, that they had something to gain by associating themselves with Ireland. Finally, many of those who became interested in famine relief were distant from the sites of suffering and did not have personal connections to Irish people in distress, making it all the more possible for them to project their own political concerns and difficulties onto the starving Irish.

I do not mean to suggest, however, that this early instance of coincident—if not coordinated—international philanthropy was, or could have been, prompted only by an Irish food crisis. Rather, it is my contention that the famine was the right catastrophe at the right time: it took place within a confluence of technological, cultural, political, and economic forces that made it, and the relief that it occasioned, a cause célèbre that facilitated many and sometimes competing political uses. Additionally, in framing interest in Irish relief as part of a set of political strategies available to people in the nineteenth century, I am also arguing that we should see the famine, famine relief, and philanthropy more broadly, in new ways.

The famine is often written about as an event with global consequences, linked to the development of an Irish diaspora. The movement of hundreds of thousands of people out of Ireland, and their settlement around the world, is rightly heralded as a turning point, both for Ireland and for the places where the Irish people went. However, as I hope to have demonstrated, the movement of news out of Ireland, the discussion of relief policy abroad, and the movement of funds back is equally important. These processes shaped ideas about Ireland for generations to come. Irish Americans in the late nineteenth and early twentieth centuries often suppressed famine memories, both because they were sources of trauma, and because they invoked images of Ireland inexorably linked with poverty.[7] More recently, memories of the famine and relief efforts have resulted in numerous public monuments, including famine memorials in Skibbereen, Mayo, Dublin, Toronto, Grosse Île, New York City, Boston, Philadelphia, and Sydney.[8] While these were driven in part by diasporic communities, they also reflect the impact of widespread famine news on sites around the world. Finally, as was the case with the Cherokees and Choctaws, and later the Navajos and Hopis, famine relief forged connections that transcended ethnicity as well as space, and that persisted well beyond the crisis.

Widespread interest in famine relief was neither inevitable nor simply a reflection of humanitarian fervor. It was not simply that when people learned of the famine, they opened their wallets. Shapers of public opinion—whether through the press, rhetoric, or personal connections—worked to fit Ireland into their own politics and to map their own concerns onto Ireland. Transnational Irish famine relief established international philanthropy as a way of critiquing structures of governance both at home and abroad. This was an especially valuable tool for marginalized peoples who had the resources to act philanthropically but were excluded from formal political structures. Through famine relief they could demonstrate virtue and civility while at the same time making claims of shared suffering and solidarity with the

Irish. In sum, distant philanthropy allowed them to critique the very societies that marginalized them. This interpretation does not make the relief efforts any less extraordinary; neither does it undermine the very real compassion that people felt for the starving Irish.

Finally, the stories told in this book act as a bridge between the kind of local charity that characterized the eighteenth century and the institutional philanthropy that emerged at the end of the nineteenth century. *Aiding Ireland* brings forward in time arguments made by scholars who study philanthropy in the late nineteenth and early twentieth centuries about the political utility of aid and relief efforts. For example, Heather Curtis, Helen Hatton and Oonagh Walsh—among others—have demonstrated the ways in which charitable associations used philanthropy to grow or empower themselves, while remaining true to their founding, and, in many cases, religious ideals.[9] Histories of twentieth-century institutional philanthropy feature extragovernmental groups and individuals who identified social problems that governments did not address, and, like "dissatisfied consumers," sought private-sector solutions to public ills.[10] The classic international philanthropic entities that characterized this period included the American Red Cross, which spearheaded campaigns to aid war wounded, prisoners, refugees, and victims of war around the world; Andrew Carnegie's campaigns for free public libraries; and the Rockefeller Foundation's fundraising for international public health and the arts.

Scholars studying this institutional philanthropy have explored the ways in which it operated as a kind of "soft power" that generated goodwill among suffering populations and built multilateral cooperation in the face of disaster. For example, in *Philanthropy in America*, Oliver Zunz argues that foundation philanthropy, with its roots in the Gilded Age, was fundamentally important in expanding American civil society and promulgating American ideals (though he notes that it was also complicit in the promulgation of racism and xenophobia under the auspices of scientific charity).[11] In *Foundations of the American Century*, Inderjeet Parmar contends that while American foundations often failed at their espoused aims of bringing democracy to the "third world" and alleviating poverty, they were remarkably successful in extending American hegemony into developing countries.[12]

International interest in famine relief was a precursor to these uses of philanthropy. In the course of engaging with famine relief, either as policy or through donations, people around the world learned to use relief both to take direct political action and to comment on politics at a distance. Taken together, these case studies of famine relief suggest that crises that become empty signifiers can capture the global imagination. Once captured, they can be put to a range of political uses, often hidden within the rhetoric of aid.

When writers in the Irish national press used famine relief as a litmus test for participation in the Irish nation, when tenant farmers described communities of solidarity as a mechanism of relief, and when enslaved and Indigenous people publicly participated in vernaculars of charity, they were all ascribing new meaning to the famine. At the same time, they were helping to build new practices and structures of meaning around giving. These structures of meaning, like the Irish diasporic communities that formed in the wake of famine immigration, would continue to shape the world beyond Ireland for years to come.

ACKNOWLEDGMENTS

This book began in J. J. Lee's office in Glucksman Ireland House at New York University in my second year of grad school. I'd just read about the Choctaw donation to Ireland in Christine Kinealy's *A Death Dealing Famine*. Thinking that these donations might make for a good seminar paper topic, I asked where I might begin reading about how news of the famine spread across the Atlantic and informed donations from Britain and North America. To the best of my recollection, Joe replied, "Congratulations, you have a dissertation topic." Fifteen years, many trips back and forth across the Atlantic, and innumerable instances of generous help and support – from librarians, archivists, colleagues, and friends – later, that germ of an idea has grown into this book. A botanical metaphor might not be entirely appropriate for a book about the aftermath of a catastrophic crop failure, but, like a plant, this book would not exist without myriad sources of support, sustenance, light, and some targeted pruning.

I have been lucky to be a part of communities which encouraged and sustained my work. At NYU, I learned from scholars who urged me to simultaneously think with and against the archive. Joe Lee's counsel to always consider how sources might tell incomplete stories, Nicole Eustace's reminder to take seriously historical subjects' emotional lives, and Martha Hodes's encouragement to explore "leaps of grounded imagination" all helped me to understand how diverse groups of people around the world came to be invested in Irish famine relief. I am also grateful to have been welcomed into the Atlantic History program, which fostered a kind of interdisciplinary and transnational thinking that has shaped the rest of my career. Karen Kupperman and Lauren Benton both modeled a curiosity about historical actors' experiences crossing and troubling borders and helped me to formulate a research project that did the same. The NYU Atlantic Workshop introduced me to a dazzling array of scholars and allowed me space to test out my own ideas. Thank you to Zara Anishanslin, Kevin Arlyck, Karen Auman, Greg Childs, Christian Crouch, Jennie Egloff, Devin Jacobs, Dan Kanhofer, Andrew Lee, Alexander Manivitz, Max Mischler, Jeppe Mulich, Kate Mulry, Hayley Negrin, Mairin Odle, Emma Otheguy, Gabriel Rocha, Samantha Seeley, Jenny Shaw, Katy Walker, and Jerusha Westbury for providing invaluable feedback and a scholarly home. I am also grateful for the mentorship and support of Karl Appuhn, Molly Nolan, and the late Marilyn Young, who gave me much-needed advice about how to approach a career as a professional historian.

Across Washington Square Park, Glucksman Ireland House was always a generative environment where Marion Casey, Miriam Nyhan Grey, Thomas Truxes, John Waters and Nicholas Wolf demonstrated what was to be gained from an interdisciplinary approach to Irish studies. I am delighted that this book is a part of the Glucksman Irish Diaspora Series.

Research for this book was generously supported by several different institutions and grants. The Henry M. MacCracken program at NYU and the Jean Downey Scholarship for Irish Studies allowed me the time and space to write the dissertation from which this book developed. My two semesters as a Glucksman Fellow at University College Cork, funded by the Irish government, gave me access to archives necessary to understand everyday life in Ireland during the famine. The history department at UCC, and particularly Gabriel Doherty and Laurence Geary, offered an intellectual home away from home. A short-term Gest Fellowship from the Quaker Collections at Haverford College helped me to understand the vast scope of relief logistics. It was in the Quaker & Special Collections at Haverford that I encountered Richard Allen's letter to his fellow Friends—my first concrete piece of evidence marking famine philanthropy as explicitly political. Working with the newspapers that make up the archival basis for this book meant that I got to spend time in delightful reading rooms on both sides of the Atlantic. In the United States, these included the American Antiquarian Society, the New York Historical Society, the New York Public Library, the Oklahoma State Archives, the South Carolina Historical Society, the Charleston Hibernian Society, the New York State Library, and the Albany Institute of History & Art. Archivists from the Arkansas State Archives and the Alabama State Archives offered help from afar, giving me access to material I would not otherwise have been able to use. In Ireland, the National Archives of Ireland, National

Library of Ireland, Cork County Archives, Cork City Library, and the Friends Historical Library proved invaluable. So, too, did the British National Archives and the Library of the Society of Friends in London.

Over this book's long growth, I've had the privilege to present excerpts at scholarly societies and venues. Material from chapter 8 originally appeared in "A 'Voice of Benevolence From the Western Wilderness': Native Philanthropy and Political Critique in the Trans-Mississippi West" *Journal of the Early Republic* 35:4 (Winter 2015) 553–78. I also received incisive and helpful feedback from audiences at the American Historical Association, the Organization of American Historians, the Massachusetts Historical Society's Digital History and Modern American Society and Culture Seminars, the Lake Institute for Faith and Giving, the Liverpool Bluecoat, California State University Bakersfield's History Forum, Queens College Belfast, the Society for the Study of Nineteenth-Century Ireland, a workshop on "Brokers of Aid" in Sweden, and the American Conference for Irish Studies. Through the ACIS, I met Peter Grey, Christine Kinealy, Michael De Nie, Cian McMahon, and many others, whose advice and formative feedback helped make this book better.

Over the past decade, I have had the privilege to work at three institutions which supported the development and completion of this project. Writing and research support from the Dean of the Faculty at Davidson College, a Dean's Travel Grant from California State University Fullerton, and a Bates Faculty Development Fund grant have been instrumental in its completion. At Davidson, CSUF, and now at Bates, I benefited from extraordinary mentorship, professional development, and support. I thank you to Andrew Baker, Jonathan Berkey, Erik Bernardino, Wes Chaney, Margie Brown-Coronel, Kate Burlingham, Ben Cawthra, Vivien Dietz, Nancy Fitch, Natalie Fousekis, Cora Granata, Michael Guasco, Aitana Guia, Vokler Janssen, Sarah Lynch, Jane Mangan, Jonathan Markley, Rob McLain, Karen Melvin, Stephen Neufeld, Stephen O'Connor, Patrick Otim, Jasamin Rostam-Kolayi, Mark Sample, Caroline Shaw, Jess Stern, Patricia Tilburg, Mark Tizzoni, John Wertheimer, and Alison Varzally for building departments that support and foster junior and contingent colleagues. Thanks also to Lauren Ashwell, Myron Beasley, Marcus Bruce, Dale Chapman, Carrie Diaz-Eaton, Michelle Greene, Meredith Greer, Rebecca Herzig, Barry Lawson and Asha Tamirisa for easing my transition to Bates College and to Interdisciplinary Studies.

Writing in community has been a central part of my work process. At NYU, Ademide Adelusi-Adeluyi, Natalie Blum-Ross, Tom Fleischman, Laura Honsberger, Aaron Jakes, Julia Kraut, Shaul Mitelpunkt, Kate Mulry, Nathalie Pierre, Einav Rabinovitch-Fox, David Rainbow, Amy Weiss, Jerusha Westbury, and Sarah Zarrow helped me to solidify my hypotheses and hone my arguments. At Davidson Alison Bory, Bes Ceka, Dylan Fitz, Gabriel Klehr, Christine Marshall, Jeff Rose, Alice Wiemers, and Caroline Wiest helped me to practice writing for interdisciplinary audiences. In the midst of COVID, regular writing sessions with Margaret Creighton, Jonathan Kurzfeld, Francisca Lopez, Alison Melnick-Dyer, Karen Melvin, Stephanie Pridgeon, Tiffany Salter, Lauren Tilton, Caroline Wiest, and Beth Woodward helped me to move forward when global events conspired to stall all progress. At NYU Press and Glucksman Ireland House, Clara Platter, Miriam Nyhan Grey, and Kevin Kenny helped shepherd this project from book proposal to completed manuscript. The anonymous readers of earlier manuscript drafts made this book immeasurably stronger. In the final stages, Tara Dankel provided incisive developmental editing support, and in the last weeks before I completed the book Jane Hanson, Kate Mulry, Samantha Seeley and Patrick Shrout read generously and gave critical and essential feedback.

I must close by thanking the friends and family who supported me from outside of the academy. They have listened to me talk about this project on long walks, in diners, over brunch, on vacation, while playing board games, and in many other moments. They have also reminded me to take breaths and breaks at necessary moments. Thank you to Maria Cecire, Shelon Clarke, Tony Clarke, Peter D'Angelo, Heidi Drassinower, Alexa Hamilton, Emily Hayes-Walsh, Malachy Kronberg, Jordan Lopez, Altair Rasco, Mike Rossi, Jen DeSanto Rossi, Jeff Shrensel, Matt Walsh, Pete Wisnieski, and Chase Wyatt. Finally, a very special thanks to my brother Tim Shrout, who has always been my biggest cheerleader; to my parents, Jane Hanson and Pat Shrout, and to Alan Coes, Jacoba Coes and Penney Riegelman, whose love, support, and patience have been unflagging; to Max, who is a constant source of comfort and love; and to Charles Coes, who believed in the success of this book even when I had doubts. Any success is a tribute to the foregoing, and any errors are entirely mine.

NOTES

INTRODUCTION

1 *Weekly Flag & Advertiser*, April 8, 1847.

2 Edward Baptist, *The Half Has Never Been Told: Slavery and the Making of American Capitalism* (New York: Basic Books, 2014), chapter 4.

3 In her suit for divorce a few years after the Lowndesboro donation, Smith's wife, Sarah, cited his treatment of enslaved people while in a "phrenzy from drunkenness." She documented Smith's rape of an enslaved women and complained that "he will, in order to annoy and distress her, causelessly punish and ill-treat . . . and take the life and seriously injure" the people he enslaved. She detailed in particular Smith's obsession with forcibly "administering medicines to the slaves" until they died, and she reported that "no entreaty or persuasion can induce him to desist." Frank J. Smith, "Petition to the Hon. P. H. Cook Judge of Probate for Lowndes County," November 15, 1860, Records of the Probate Court, Minutes, 1859–1860, Vol. 9, 722–24, Lowndes County Courthouse, Hayneville, Alabama.

4 *Weekly Flag & Advertiser*, April 8, 1847.

5 Lawrence H. Officer and Samuel H. Williamson, "Measuring Worth—Measures of Worth, Inflation Rates, Saving Calculator, Relative Value, Worth of a Dollar, Worth of a Pound, Purchasing Power, Gold Prices, GDP, History of Wages, Average Wage," 2010, www.measuringworth.com.

6 John G. Aiken, "A Digest of the Laws of the State of Alabama" (Philadelphia, 1833), 393, Alabama Department of Archives and History.

7 Tein McDonald, "Balancing Learning and Action: When Something Must Be Done, What Is the Right 'Something'?," *Ecological Management & Restoration* 8, no. 2 (2007): 82–82.

8 Victoria Davis contends that Patrick Kavanagh coined the phrase "an gorta mór" for his book of poetry, *The Great Hunger*, in 1942. Victoria Davis, "Restating a Parochial Vision: A Reconsideration of Patrick Kavanagh, Flann O'Brien, and Brendan Behan" (PhD. diss, University of Texas, Austin, 2005), 108.

9 Many works have explored the transnational movement of Irish people and the impact of that migration on sites of arrival. See, e.g., David Fitzpatrick, *Irish Emigration, 1801–1921* (Dublin: Economic and Social History Society of Ireland, 1984); Kerby A. Miller, *Emigrants and Exiles: Ireland and the Irish Exodus to North America* (New York: Oxford University Press, 1985); Donald H. Akenson, *The Irish Diaspora: A Primer* (Belfast: P. D. Meany Co. Institute of Irish Studies, Queen's University of Belfast, 1993); and Joseph Lee and Marion R. Casey, *Making the Irish American:*

History and Heritage of the Irish in the United States (New York: New York University Press, 2006).

10 Kevin Kenny, "Diaspora and Comparison: The Global Irish as a Case Study," *Journal of American History* 90, no. 1 (2003): 134–62.

11 The first histories of the famine were produced almost before the crisis had reached its peak. British treasury secretary Charles Trevelyan's 1848 treatise *The Irish Crisis* sought to exonerate the British government and to prevent more money from the English exchequer pouring into Ireland. Similarly fervent ideological positions led Irish nationalists like John Mitchel to argue throughout the 1840s and 1850s that the British government was directly culpable for the famine, having failed for years to appropriately administer Ireland. Subsequent scholars adopted these nationalist accusations and put the question of who was to blame at the center of famine histories. In the twentieth century, Robert Dudley Edwards and Thomas Desmond Williams located the causes of the famine in mere British blundering, rather than outright malice. Cecil Woodham-Smith challenged these arguments in her 1962 book, *The Great Hunger*, contending that the Irish famine was the product of willful British neglect and exportation of food. Although recent work—in particular that of Peter Gray—has sought to more richly contextualize the political and intellectual climate that produced Britain's policies toward Ireland, the question of British culpability in "the great hunger" is, in many ways, still central in famine scholarship. C. E Trevelyan, *The Irish Crisis* (London: Longman, Brown, Green & Longmans, 1848); John Mitchel, *Jail Journal of Five Years in British Prisons* (New York: Office of the Citizen, 1854); Robert Dudley Edwards and Thomas Desmond Williams, *The Great Famine, 1845–52* (New York: New York University Press, 1957); Cecil Blanche Woodham Smith, *The Great Hunger: Ireland, 1845–1849* (New York: Harper & Row, 1962); Peter Gray, *Famine, Land, and Politics: British Government and Irish Society, 1843–1850* (Dublin: Irish Academic Press, 1999).

12 Captain Larcom, "Observations on the Census of the Population of Ireland in 1841," *Journal of the Statistical Society of London* 6, no. 4 (December 1843): 331.

13 Redcliffe N. Salaman, *The History and Social Influence of the Potato* (Cambridge: Cambridge University Press, 1985), 276–279.

14 From the *Gardener's Chronicle*, August 16, 1845, quoted in Christine Kinealy, *This Great Calamity: The Irish Famine, 1845–52* (Dublin: Gill & Macmillan, 1994), 31; D. Andrivon, "The Origin of Phytophthora Infestans Populations Present in Europe in the 1840s: A Critical Review of Historical and Scientific Evidence," *Plant Pathology* 45, no. 6 (1996): 1027–35.

15 For descriptions of the spread and extent of the rot, see Famine Relief Commission, "Famine Relief Commission Distress Reports," (1847 1845), National Archives of Ireland.

16 T. P. O'Neill, "The Scientific Investigation of the Failure of the Potato Crop in Ireland, 1845–6," *Irish Historical Studies* 5, no. 18 (1946): 123–38.

17 Robert Traill, a Protestant rector in southwestern Ireland, sent many letters to the Irish lord lieutenant in Dublin, suggesting various methods for drying the potato

crop. Files Z16246, Z16322, Z16434, Z16618, Z16870, Z17622, National Archives of Ireland.

18 Kinealy, *This Great Calamity*, 168.

19 Kinealy, 168–69.

20 Cormac Ó Gráda and Phelim P. Boyle, "Fertility Trends, Excess Mortality, and the Great Irish Famine," *Demography* 23, no. 4 (November 1986): 543–62; Melinda Grimsley-Smith, "Revisiting a 'Demographic Freak': Irish Asylums and Hidden Hunger," *Social History of Medicine* 25, no. 2 (May 1, 2012): 307–23.

21 Aoife O'Leary McNeice, "Global Networks of Relief and the Great Irish Famine" (PhD diss., Cambridge University, 2021).

22 Iain McLean and Camilla Bustani, "Irish Potatoes and British Politics: Interests, Ideology, Heresthetic, and the Repeal of the Corn Laws," *Political Studies* 1999 (1999): 817–36; Christine Kinealy, "Peel, Rotten Potatoes, and Providence: The Repeal of the Corn Laws and the Irish Famine," in *Free Trade and Reception 1815–1960*, ed. Andrew Marrison (Boca Raton, FL: CRC, 2002), 50–62; S. J. Donnelly, "Famine and Government Response, 1845–6," in *A New History of Ireland, Volume V: Ireland Under the Union, I: 1801–70* (Oxford: Clarendon, 2000), 282.

23 Kinealy, *This Great Calamity*, 46–54, 74–82.

24 For histories of the Irish Poor Law, see Virginia Crossman, *Poverty and the Poor Law in Ireland, 1838–1948* (Liverpool: Liverpool University Press, 2013); Peter Gray, *The Making of the Irish Poor Law, 1815–43* (Manchester: Manchester University Press, 2010).

25 T. P. O'Neill, "The Society of Friends and the Great Famine," *Studies: An Irish Quarterly Review* 39, no. 154 (June 1950): 203–13; Helen E. Hatton, *The Largest Amount of Good: Quaker Relief in Ireland, 1654–1921* (Montreal: McGill-Queen's University Press, 1993), 84–105.

26 Robert A. Gross, "Giving in America: From Charity to Philanthropy," in Lawrence Jacob Friedman and Mark D. McGarvie, *Charity, Philanthropy, and Civility in American History* (Cambridge: Cambridge University Press, 2003), 31..

27 Merle Curti, *American Philanthropy Abroad* (New Brunswick, NJ: Rutgers University Press, 1963), 4–5.

28 Amanda B. Moniz, *From Empire to Humanity: The American Revolution and the Origins of Humanitarianism* (Oxford: Oxford University Press, 2016), 1.

29 Julie L. Reed, *Serving the Nation: Cherokee Sovereignty and Social Welfare, 1800–1907* (Norman: University of Oklahoma Press, 2016), chapter 1.

30 Michael Katz, *In the Shadow of the Poorhouse: A Social History of Welfare in America* (New York: Basic Books, 1996), 61.

31 Curti, *American Philanthropy Abroad*, 11–15.

32 Curti, 11–15.

33 David Owen characterizes this period as the "age of benevolence." David Owen, *English Philanthropy, 1660–1960* (Cambridge, MA: Harvard University Press, 1965). Katz, *In the Shadow of the Poorhouse*; Natan Sznaider, "The Sociology of Compassion: A Study in the Sociology of Morals," *Journal for Cultural Research* 2,

no. 1 (1998): 117; Martin Gorsky, *Patterns of Philanthropy: Charity and Society in Nineteenth-Century Bristol* (Martelsham: Boydell & Brewer, 1999); Lawrence Jacob Friedman, "Philanthropy in America: Historicism and Its Discontents," in *Charity, Philanthropy, and Civility in American History*, ed. Lawrence Jacob Friedman and Mark D. McGarvie (Cambridge: Cambridge University Press, 2003), 1–20; Gray, *Making of the Irish Poor Law*.

34 Judith Sealander, "Curing Evils at Their Source: The Arrival of Scientific Giving," *Charity, Philanthropy, and Civility in American History*, ed. Lawrence Jacob Friedman and Mark D. McGarvie (Cambridge: Cambridge University Press, 2003), 217–39; Wendy Gamber, "Antebellum Reform: Salvation, Self-Control, and Social Transformation," in *Charity, Philanthropy, and Civility in American History*, ed. Lawrence Jacob Friedman and Mark D. McGarvie, 129–53 (Cambridge: Cambridge University Press, 2003); Ben Kiernan, "From Irish Famine to Congo Reform: Nineteenth-Century Roots of International Human Rights Law and Activism," *Confronting Genocide*, (Dordrecht: Springer, 2011), 13–43.

35 The *American Flag*, published in Matamoros, Mexico, along with the *Daily American Star* and *El Monitor Republicano*, both published in Mexico City, routinely carried news of the famine. Peter Gray, "Famine and Land in Ireland and India, 1845–1880: James Caird and the Political Economy of Hunger," *Historical Journal* 49, no. 1 (2006): 193–215; Norbert Götz, Georgina Brewis, and Steffen Werther, *Humanitarianism in the Modern World: The Moral Economy of Famine Relief* (Cambridge: Cambridge University Press, 2020), 36–42.

36 James Kelly, "Harvests and Hardship: Famine and Scarcity in Ireland in the Late 1720s," *Studia Hibernica*, no. 26 (1992): 65–105.

37 E. Margaret Crawford, "William Wilde's Table of Irish Famines 900–1850," in *Famine: The Irish Experience, 900–1900: Subsistence Crises and Famines in Ireland*, ed. E. Margaret Crawford (Edinburgh: J. Donald, 1989), 1–30.

38 The crisis most likely to prompt such giving would have been the famine of 1816–17, the "Year without a Summer." This famine was immediately caused by the eruption of Mt. Tambora in Indonesia and felt across Europe and North America. John D. Post, *The Last Great Subsistence Crisis in the Western World* (Baltimore, MD: Johns Hopkins University Press, 1977); Guido Alfani and Cormac Ó Gráda, eds., *Famine in European History* (Cambridge: Cambridge University Press, 2017), 101, 110.

39 Peter Gray, "Famine Relief Policy in Comparative Perspective: Ireland, Scotland, and Northwestern Europe, 1845–1849," *Éire-Ireland* 32, no. 1 (1997): 86–108; Cormac Ó Gráda, Richard Paping, and Eric Vanhaute, eds., "The European Subsistence Crisis of 1845–1850: A Comparative Perspective," in *When the Potato Failed: Causes and Effects of the "Last" European Subsistence Crisis, 1845–50* (Turnhout, Belgium: Brepols, 2007), 15–40.

40 Tom M. Devine, *The Great Highland Famine: Hunger, Emigration, and the Scottish Highlands in the Nineteenth Century* (Edinburgh: Birlinn, 2021), 33.

41 Gray, "Famine Relief Policy in Comparative Perspective."

42 Although there were philanthropic groups committed to the parallel aid of Ireland and Scotland, most donations favored Ireland. When the British Parliament totaled "donations of Food from America for the Relief of the Poor of Ireland and Scotland" through 1847, only two of the over one hundred shipments were explicitly bound for Scotland. Of the nearly two thousand donations made to the British Relief Association, which was committed to "the relief of extreme distress in Ireland and Scotland," fewer than one hundred specifically directed their donations to only to Scotland. Of the eighteen donations that specified a distribution among funds for Ireland and Scotland, only three—from "A. Beattie Esq," a doctor in the East India Company's Service in Acra; "the Congregation of St. Margaret's Chapel in Brighton"; and "Messrs. W. R. Robinson & Co"—split their contributions equally between Ireland and Scotland. Most of those who directed a distribution of their donations to both countries asked that more money, sometimes as much as double, be sent to Ireland. The vast majority of donors, however, made no determination at all about the division between Irish and Scottish sufferers, apparently preferring to trust the British Relief Association to adjudicate need. The association seemed to choose Ireland. During 1847 and 1848, the British Relief Association remitted £77,683 to Scotland; in the same years, it sent more than three times that amount to Ireland. House of Commons, "Food from America. Return of the Freight Paid by Government on Donations of Food from America, for the Relief of the Poor of Ireland and Scotland," January 31, 1848, Paper 93, Vol. 4, 1, House of Commons Papers; *Report of the British Association for the Relief of the Extreme Distress in Ireland and Scotland; with Correspondence of the Agents, Tables &c. and a List of Subscribers* (London: Richard Clay, Bread Street Hill, 1849).

43 Joel Mokyr and Cormac Ó Gráda, "Emigration and Poverty in Prefamine Ireland," *Explorations in Economic History* 19, no. 4 (October 1, 1982): 360–84; Miller, *Emigrants and Exiles*; Donald M. MacRaild, *Irish Migrants in Modern Britain, 1750–1922* (London: Macmillan International Higher Education, 1999); David T. Gleeson, *The Irish in the South, 1815–1877* (Chapel Hill: University of North Carolina Press, 2001); David N. Doyle, "The Irish in North America, 1776–1845," in *Making the Irish American: History and Heritage of the Irish in the United States*, ed. Joseph Lee and Marion R. Casey (New York: New York University Press, 2006), 171–212; Andrew Bielenberg, *The Irish Diaspora* (New York: Routledge, 2014).

44 MacRaild, *Irish Migrants in Modern Britain*, 33.

45 Graham Davis, "The Irish in Britain, 1815–1939," in *The Irish Diaspora*, ed. Andy Bielenberg (London: Routledge, 2013), 26.

46 Hasia R. Diner, "'The Most Irish City in the Union': The Era of the Great Migration, 1844–1877," in *The New York Irish*, ed. Ronald H. Bayor and Timothy J. Meagher (Baltimore, MD: Johns Hopkins University Press, 1997), 87–106; Anelise Shrout, "The Famine and New York City," in *Atlas of the Great Irish Famine, 1845–52*, ed. John Crowley, William J. Smyth, and Mike Murphy (Cork, Ireland: Cork University Press, 2012), 536–46.

47 Miller, *Emigrants and Exiles*, 316; Matthew Gallman, *Receiving Erin's Children: Philadelphia, Liverpool, and the Irish Famine Migration, 1845–1855* (Chapel Hill: University of North Carolina Press, 2000), 2–3.

48 For a discussion of the mechanisms by which both news and funds moved between emigrant communities and Ireland, see Cian T. McMahon, *The Coffin Ship: Life and Death at Sea during the Great Irish Famine* (New York: New York University Press, 2021), chapter 5.

49 Lisa Mullikin Parcell, "Early American Newswriting Style: Who, What, When, Where, Why, and How," *Journalism History* 37, no. 1 (2011): 2–11; Kevin G. Barnhurst and John C. Nerone, *The Form of News: A History* (New York City: Guilford, 2001) chapters 2 and 3.

50 Richard Daniel Altick, *The English Common Reader* (Chicago: University of Chicago Press, 1957); Michael Schudson, *Discovering the News: A Social History of American Newspapers* (New York: Basic Books, 1978); R. A. Houston, *Scottish Literacy and the Scottish Identity: Illiteracy and Society in Scotland and Northern England, 1600–1800* (Cambridge: Cambridge University Press, 1985); David M. Henkin, *City Reading: Written Words and Public Spaces in Antebellum New York* (New York: Columbia University Press, 1998); Brendan Dooley, "From Literary Criticism to Systems Theory in Early Modern Journalism History," *Journal of the History of Ideas* 51, no. 3 (1990): 461–86; Niall Ó Ciosáin, "Gaelic Culture and Language Shift," in *Nineteenth-Century Ireland: A Guide to Recent Research*, ed. Lawrence M. Geary and Margaret Kelleher (Dublin: University College Dublin Press, 2005), 136–52; Harvey J. Graff, *The Literacy Myth: Cultural Integration and Social Structure in the Nineteenth Century* (Piscataway, NJ: Transaction, 1991).

51 Edwin Emery, Michael C. Emery, and Nancy L. Roberts, *The Press and America: An Interpretative History of the Mass Media*, 9th ed. (Boston: Allyn & Bacon, 2000), 95.

52 Schudson, *Discovering the News*, 43–50. Others contend that the penny press was more highly attuned to the public's desire for sensation and for news about ordinary people. Deborah Wynne, *The Sensation Novel and the Victorian Family Magazine* (London: Palgrave Macmillan, 2001).

53 When Dublin newspapers reprinted news from other cities, they included the number of days that had passed since the news was first printed. In 1799, the *Saunders News-Letter* reported news from Cork between six and ten days later. By the 1840s, Dublin newspapers regularly reported news only four days later.

54 Robert Kielbowicz, "Newsgathering by Printers' Exchanges before the Telegraph," *Journalism History* 9, no. 2 (Summer 1982): 43; Richard R. John, *Spreading the News: The American Postal System from Franklin to Morse* (Cambridge, MA: Harvard University Press, 1995).

55 Curti, *American Philanthropy Abroad*, 42.

56 Hasia Diner also succinctly repesents this position: "People around the world gasped at the horrors of the Famine. Relief poured in. Generous Americans collected money in order to send food to Ireland's starving millions." Hasia R. Diner, *Erin's Daughters*

in America: Irish Immigrant Women in the Nineteenth Century (Baltimore, MD: Johns Hopkins University Press, 1983), 124.

57 For a discussion of the literary cultures that enabled transnational imagination, see Shirley Samuels, ed., *The Culture of Sentiment: Race, Gender, and Sentimentality in Nineteenth-Century America* (Oxford: Oxford University Press, 1992); and June Howard, "What Is Sentimentality?," *American Literary History* 11, no. 1 (1999): 63–81. For a theoretical discussion of responses to distant suffering, see Luc Boltanski, *Distant Suffering: Morality, Media and Politics* (Cambridge: Cambridge University Press, 1999).

58 Thomas L. Haskell, "Capitalism and the Origins of the Humanitarian Sensibility, Part 1 ," *The American Historical Review* 90, no. 2 (1985): 339–61; Thomas L. Haskell, "Capitalism and the Origins of the Humanitarian Sensibility, Part 1," *American Historical Review* 90, no. 3 (1985): 547–66.

59 Margaret Abruzzo, *Polemical Pain: Slavery, Cruelty, and the Rise of Humanitarianism* (Baltimore, MD: Johns Hopkins University Press, 2011), 46.

60 Ernesto Laclau, *Emancipation(s), Phronesis* (New York: Verso, 1996).

61 The idea of famine as a crisis of government as well as a crisis of food production has appeared in a range of studies of famine, including Lillian M. Li, *Fighting Famine in North China: State, Market, and Environmental Decline, 1690s–1990s* (Stanford, CA: Stanford University Press, 2007), 2; and Amartya Kumar Sen, *Poverty and Famines: An Essay on Entitlement and Deprivation* (Oxford: Oxford University Press, 1981).

62 For examples of these opportunities in the context of American, Irish, and British politics, see David Waldstreicher, *In the Midst of Perpetual Fetes: The Making of American Nationalism, 1776–1820* (Williamsburg, VA: Omohundro Institute of Early American History and Culture, 1997); Sean Farrell, *Rituals and Riots: Sectarian Violence and Political Culture in Ulster, 1784–1886* (Louisville: University Press of Kentucky, 2000); and Kathleen Wilson, *The Sense of the People: Politics, Culture and Imperialism in England, 1715–1785* (Cambridge: Cambridge University Press, 1998).

63 My definition of politics is inspired by the work of Daniel Walker Howe, David Waldstreicher, Jeffrey L. Pasley, and Andrew W. Robertson. Howe's definition of political action includes "all struggles over power, not just those decided by elections." Jeffrey L. Pasley, Andrew W. Robertson, and David Waldstreicher have suggested that political culture should include the "set of methods or practices" that "people brought with them into the political realm," regardless of how broadly that realm is conceived. Daniel Walker Howe, "The Evangelical Movement and Political Culture in the North during the Second Party System," *Journal of American History* 77, no. 4 (1991): 1235–36; Jeffrey L. Pasley, Andrew W. Robertson, and David Waldstreicher, eds., *Beyond the Founders: New Approaches to the Political History of the Early American Republic* (Chapel Hill: University of North Carolina Press, 2004), 6.

64 Shawn Teresa Flanigan, "Charity as Resistance: Connections between Charity, Contentious Politics, and Terror," *Studies in Conflict & Terrorism* 29, no. 7 (2006): 642–43.

65 Jean E. Fairfax, "Black Philanthropy: Its Heritage and Its Future," *New Directions for Philanthropic Fundraising* 1995, no. 8 (1995): 20.

66 Stella Shao, "Asian American Giving: Issues and Challenges (A Practitioner's Perspective)," *New Directions for Philanthropic Fundraising* 1995, no. 8 (1995): 53–64.

67 Brian Hanley, "The Politics of Noraid," *Irish Political Studies* 19, no. 1 (March 1, 2004): 1–17.

68 R. M. Entman, "Framing: Toward Clarification of a Fractured Paradigm," *Journal of Communication* 43, no. 4 (1993): 52; Dietram A. Scheufele, "Framing as a Theory of Media Effects," *Journal of Communication* 49, no. 1 (1999): 103–22; W. A. Gamson and A. Modigliani, "The Changing Culture of Affirmative Action," ed. R. G. Braungart and M. M. Braungart, *Research in Political Sociology* 3 (1987): 137–77.

I. THE IRISH NATION

1 *Freeman's Journal*, August 18, 1845.

2 *The Nation*, August 23, 1845.

3 *The Nation*, September 6, 1845; *Dublin Evening Mail*, September 17, 1845.

4 "Constabulary Reports," 1845, Famine Relief Commission, Chief Secretary's Office Registered Papers, Z series, National Archives of Ireland.

5 Dublin Mansion House Committee for the Relief of Distress in Ireland, *Report of the Mansion House Committee on the Potato Disease*. Dublin: J. Browne, 1846), 1.

6 Dublin Mansion House Committee, *Report*, 1.

7 O'Connell's speech was reported in *The Nation*, November 1, 1845.

8 Dublin Mansion House Committee, *Report*, 4.

9 Dublin Mansion House Committee, 6.

10 Christine Kinealy, *This Great Calamity: The Irish Famine, 1845–52* (Dublin: Gill & Macmillan, 1994), 33.

11 *The Nation*, November 8th, 1845.

12 A. B. Scott, "Latin Learning and Literature in Ireland, 1169–1500," in *A New History of Ireland, Volume 1: Prehistoric and Early Ireland*, ed. Dáibhí Ó Cróinín (Oxford: Oxford University Press, 2005), 936.

13 Anne J. Duggan, "The Power of Documents: The Curious Case of Laudabiliter," in *Aspects of Power and Authority in the Middle Ages*, ed. Brenda M. Bolton, Christine E. Meek, and C. E. Meek (Turnhout: Brepols, 2008), 241–75.

14 J. A. Watt, "The Anglo-Irish Colony under Strain, 1327–99," in *A New History of Ireland, Volume II: Medieval Ireland, 1169–1534* (Oxford: Oxford University Press, 2008), 352–96.

15 Quoted in Watt, "Anglo-Irish Colony under Strain," 387.

16 Watt.

17 G. A. Hayes-Mccoy, "The Completion of The Tudor Conquest and the Advance of the Counter-Reformation, 1571–1603," in *A New History of Ireland, Volume III: Early Modern Ireland, 1534–1691*, ed. T. W. Moody, F. X. Martin, and F. J. Byrne (Oxford: Oxford University Press, 2009), 94–141.

18 For a discussion of the historical literature on Ireland's status as a colony or simply part of an imperial project see John Gibney, "Early Modern Ireland: A British Atlantic Colony?," *History Compass* 6, no. 1 (January 2008): 172–82.

19 Nicholas P. Canny, *Kingdom and Colony: Ireland in the Atlantic World, 1560–1800* (Baltimore, MD: Johns Hopkins University Press, 1988).

20 David Armitage, *The Ideological Origins of the British Empire* (Cambridge: Cambridge University Press, 2000).

21 Jane Ohlmeyer, "A Laboratory for Empire? Early Modern Ireland and English Imperialism," in *Ireland and the British Empire*, ed. Kevin Kenny (Oxford: Oxford University Press, 2004), 26–60.

22 Nicholas P. Canny, "The Origins of Empire: An Introduction," in *The Oxford History of the British Empire, Volume I: The Origins of Empire: British Overseas Enterprise to the Close of the Seventeenth Century*, ed. Nicholas Canny, Alaine Low, and Wm. Roger Louis (Oxford: Oxford University Press, 1998), 6.

23 Jane Ohlmeyer, *Making Ireland English, Making Ireland English* (New Haven, CT: Yale University Press, 2012).

24 J. L. McCracken, "The Conflict between the Irish Administration and Parliament, 1753–56," *Irish Historical Studies* 3, no. 10 (1942): 159–79.

25 Joanna Innes, "Legislating for Three Kingdoms: How the Westminster Parliament Legislated for England, Scotland, and Ireland," in *Parliaments, Nations and Identities in Britain and Ireland, 1660–1850*, ed. Julian Hoppit (Manchester: Manchester University Press, 2003), 15-47.

26 In the eighteenth century, some Catholics held hereditary estates, but were largely excluded from the House of Lords on the basis of their participation in the 1691 rebellion. David Cairns and Shaun Richards, *Writing Ireland: Colonialism, Nationalism, and Culture* (Manchester: Manchester University Press, 1988.), 22.

27 Louis Cullen, "Catholics under the Penal Laws," *Eighteenth-Century Ireland / Iris an Dá Chultúr* 1 (1986): 23–36.

28 David Dickson, *New Foundations: Ireland, 1660–1800* (Dublin: Irish Academic Press 1987), chapter 2.

29 Padhraig Higgins, "Consumption, Gender, and the Politics of 'Free Trade' in Eighteenth-Century Ireland," *Eighteenth-Century Studies* 41, no. 1 (2007): 87–105.

30 Padhraig Higgins, James S. Donnelly, and Thomas Archdeacon, *A Nation of Politicians: Gender, Patriotism, and Political Culture in Late Eighteenth-Century Ireland* (Madison: University of Wisconsin Press, 2010), 128–29.

31 Irish political developments between 1760 and 1780 are synthesized in Dickson, *New Foundations*, chapter 5.

32 The political contests leading up to the Act of Union are detailed in P. M, Geoghegan, *The Irish Act of Union: A Study in High Politics, 1798–1801* (New York: St. Martin's, 1999).

33 Christine Kinealy, *A Disunited Kingdom? England, Ireland, Scotland, and Wales, 1800–1949* (Cambridge: Cambridge University Press, 1999); Christine Kinealy, "At Home with Empire: The Example of Ireland," in *At Home with the Empire: Metropolitan*

Culture and the Imperial World, ed. Catherine Hall and Sonya O. Rose (Cambridge: Cambridge University Press, 2006), 87.

34 Kinealy, "At Home with Empire."

35 Gearóid Ó Tuathaigh, "O'Connell, Daniel," in *Dictionary of Irish Biography*, ed. James Quinn (Dublin: Royal Irish Academy, 2009).

36 S. J. Connolly, "The Great Famine and Irish Politics," in *The Great Irish Famine*, ed. C. Póirtéir (Dublin: Mercier, 1995), 38.

37 James Quinn, *Young Ireland and the Writing of Irish History* (Dublin: University College Dublin Press, 2015).

38 *The Nation*, February 12, 1847.

39 Sean Ryder, "Reading Lessons: Famine and the Nation, 1846–1849," in *"Fearful Realities": New Perspectives on the Famine*, ed. Chris Morash and Richard Hayes (Blackrock, Co. Dublin: Irish Academic Press, 1996), 153.

40 Cormac Ó Gráda, "Poverty, Population and Agriculture, 1801–45," in *A New History of Ireland, Volume V: Ireland Under the Union, I: 1801–70*, ed. W. E. Vaughan (Oxford: Oxford University Press, 2010), 108–36.

41 Y. Whelan, "The Construction and Destruction of a Colonial Landscape: Monuments to British Monarchs in Dublin before and after Independence," *Journal of Historical Geography* 28, no. 4 (October 1, 2002): 511.

42 David Dickson, *Dublin: The Making of a Capital City* (Cambridge, MA: Harvard University Press, 2014), 319.

43 Ryder, "Reading Lessons," 151.

44 Marie-Louise Legg, *Newspapers and Nationalism: The Irish Provincial Press, 1850–1892* (Dublin: Four Courts, 1999), 12.

45 Brian Inglis, "O'Connell and the Irish Press, 1800–42," *Irish Historical Studies* 8, no. 29 (1952): 1.

46 Mark O'Brien, "Journalism in Ireland: The Evolution of a Discipline," in *Irish Journalism Before Independence: More a Disease Than a Profession, ed. Kevin Rafter* (Manchester, UK: Manchester University Press, 2011), 9–21.

47 Charles Mitchell, *The Newspaper Press Directory* (London: Mitchell, 1846), sec. Freeman's Journal. 332.

48 Patrick Maume, "The *Dublin Evening Mail* and Pro-Landlord Conservatism in the Age of Gladstone and Parnell," *Irish Historical Studies* 37, no. 148 (2011): 551.

49 Hugh Oram, *The Newspaper Book: A History of Newspapers in Ireland, 1649–1983* (Dublin: MO, 1983), 49; J. S. North, *The Waterloo Directory of Irish Newspapers and Periodicals, 1800–1900* (Waterloo: North Waterloo Academic Press, 1986), sec. Dublin Evening Mail; Mitchell, *Newspaper Press Directory*, sec. Dublin Evening Mail, 330.

50 *The Nation*'s motto, quoted in North, *Waterloo Directory*, sec. The Nation, 370–71. The phrase "racy of the soil" was first used in a parliamentary speech by Stephen Woulfe in April 1837. It signified a strong characteristic of a country or people. In this case, the aim of *The Nation* was to foster public opinion that was intrinsic to the Irish people, so much so that it was inextricable from Irish soil.

51   Charles Gavan Duffy, quoted in Ryder, "Reading Lessons," 152.

52   Quoted in Ryder, 152.

53   Mitchell, *Newspaper Press Directory*, 330–32.

54   Malcolm Brown, *The Politics of Irish Literature: From Thomas Davis to W. B. Yeats* (Seattle: University of Washington Press, 1972); Ryder, "Reading Lessons," 154.

55   Michael J. Winstanley, *Ireland and the Land Question, 1800–1922* (London: Taylor & Francis, 1994), 3,.

56   Gray, *Famine, Land, and Politics*, introduction and chapter 1.

57   Kinealy, *This Great Calamity*, 22–28.

58   Devon Commission, *Report from Her Majesty's Commissioners of Inquiry into the State of the Law and Practice in Respect of the Occupation of Land in Ireland, with Minutes of Evidence, Supplements, Appendices, and Index* (Dublin: Alexander Thom, 1845), 21.

59   Devon Commission, *Report from Her Majesty's Commissioners of Inquiry into the State of the Law and Practice in Respect of the Occupation of Land in Ireland, with Minutes of Evidence, Supplements, Appendices, and Index* (Dublin: Alexander Thom, 1845), 11.

60   Gray, *Famine, Land, and Politics*, 70–71.

61   *Dublin Evening Mail*, February 21, 1845.

62   O'Connell, quoted in *The Nation*, May 24, 1845.

63   *The Nation*, June 7, 1845.

64   Daniel O'Connell, *Correspondence of Daniel O'Connell: The Liberator* (London: J. Murray, 1888), 352.

65   John Mitchel, *The Last Conquest of Ireland (Perhaps)* (Glasgow: Cameron & Ferguson, 1861), 82.

66   Bryan P. McGovern, *John Mitchel: Irish Nationalist, Southern Secessionist* (Knoxville: University of Tennessee Press, 2009), 43–44.

67   *Freeman's Journal*, February 21, 1845.

68   *Freeman's Journal*, November 3,1845; *Dublin Evening Mail*, September 15, 1845; *Dublin Evening Mail*, November 17, 1845.

69   Kinealy, *This Great Calamity*, 34.

70   Quoted in Kinealy, 34.

71   "Constabulary Reports," Ballyshannon, Donegal, October 21, 1845, Famine Relief Commission, Chief Secretary's Office Registered Papers, Z series, National Archives of Ireland.

72   "Constabulary Reports," Clontarf, Dublin, October 21, 1845, Famine Relief Commission, Chief Secretary's Office Registered Papers, Z series, National Archives of Ireland.

73   "Constabulary Reports," Louth, October 21, 1845, Famine Relief Commission, Chief Secretary's Office Registered Papers, Z series, National Archives of Ireland.

74   "Constabulary Reports," Cahersiveen, Kerry, October 20, 1845, Famine Relief Commission, Chief Secretary's Office Registered Papers, Z series, National Archives of Ireland.

75 "Constabulary Reports," Carlow, October 20, 1845, Famine Relief Commission, Chief Secretary's Office Registered Papers, Z series, National Archives of Ireland.

76 *Freeman's Journal*, October 11, 1845; *Freeman's Journal*, October 18, 1845; *Freeman's Journal*, November 1, 1845.

77 *The Nation*, November 8, 1845.

78 *Dublin Evening Mail*, October 15, 1845.

79 *Freeman's Journal*, November 1, 1845.

80 *Freeman's Journal*, November 11, 1845.

81 *Dublin Evening Mail*, November 17, 1845.

82 *Dublin Evening Mail*, November 21, 1845; *Dublin Evening Mail*, December 1, 1845.

83 *Freeman's Journal*, August 18, 1846.

84 *Dublin Evening Mail*, March 13, 1846.

85 *Dublin Evening Mail*, March 30, 1846.

86 *Dublin Evening Mail*, August 14, 1846.

87 *Dublin Evening Mail*, August 22, 1846.

88 Kinealy, *This Great Calamity*, 38; Gray, *Famine, Land, and Politics*, 128–32.

89 Gray, *Famine, Land, and Politics*, 127–28.

90 Quoted in Gray, 129.

91 Gray, 128–32.

92 Gray, 138.

93 *Dublin Evening Mail*, January 24, 1846.

94 *Dublin Evening Mail*, November 9, 1846.

95 *Dublin Evening Mail*, December 4, 1846.

96 *Dublin Evening Mail*, November 18, 1846.

97 *Dublin Evening Mail*, December 14, 1846.

98 *Freeman's Journal*, August 5, 1846.

99 *The Nation*, August 15, 1846.

100 Irish Relief Association, *Report of the Proceedings of the Irish Relief Association for the Destitute Peasantry* (Dublin: Philip Dixon Hardy & Sons, 1848), vi.

101 Irish Relief Association, *Report*, x.

102 Helen E. Hatton, *The Largest Amount of Good: Quaker Relief in Ireland, 1654–1921* (Montreal: McGill-Queen's University Press, 1993), 36.

103 Central Relief Committee, Society of Friends, "Minute Book No. 1," Dublin, 1847, Relief of Distress Papers, National Archives of Ireland, 1A 42 35, 1.

104 Society of Friends Central Relief Committee, *Transactions of the Central Relief Committee of the Society of Friends during the Famine in Ireland* (Dublin: Edmund Burke, 1852), 33.

105 Christine Kinealy, *Charity and the Great Hunger in Ireland: The Kindness of Strangers* (London: Bloomsbury, 2013), 63–66.

106 Central Relief Committee, *Transactions*, 38.

107 Central Relief Committee, appendix 3.

108 Central Relief Committee, 45.

109 Kinealy, *Charity and the Great Hunger in Ireland*, 56–57.

110 Christine Kinealy, "The Irish Famine 1845–52," *North Irish Roots* 2, no. 5 (1990): 158–61.

111 *Freeman's Journal*, January 15, 1847.

112 *The Nation*, December 20, 1845.

113 *The Nation*, December 20, 1845.

114 *The Nation*, November 11, 1846.

115 *Freeman's Journal*, August 7, 1846.

116 *Freeman's Journal*, September 3, 1846.

117 *The Nation*, November 14, 1846..

118 *Dublin Evening Mail*, January 22, 1846.

119 *Dublin Evening Mail*, March 8, 1847.

120 *Dublin Evening Mail*, 30 December, 1846.

121 *The Nation*, March 11, 1848.

122 *The Nation*, July 1, 1848.

2. FOOD AND FREE TRADE

1 Archibald Prentice, *A History of the Anti–Corn Law League* (London: W. & F. G. Cash, 1852), 399.

2 Paul A. Pickering and Alex Tyrell, *The People's Bread: A History of the Anti–Corn Law League* (London: Leicester University Press, 2000), 2.

3 Pickering and Tyrell, *People's Bread*, chapters 3 and 4.

4 Miles Taylor, "Cobden, Richard," in *Oxford Dictionary of National Biography*, www .oxforddnb.com.

5 Prentice, *History of the Anti-Corn Law League*, 399

6 George L. Bernstein, "Liberals, the Irish Famine, and the Role of the State," *Irish Historical Studies* 29, no. 116 (November 1995): 514; T. Jenkins, *The Liberal Ascendancy, 1830–1886* (London: Macmillan Education, 1994), chapter 1.

7 Bernstein, "Irish Famine and the Role of the State"; Peter Gray, "'Shovelling out Your Paupers': The British State and Irish Famine Migration, 1846–1850," *Patterns of Prejudice* 33, no. 4 (1999) 47–65; Christine Kinealy, "Peel, Rotten Potatoes, and Providence: The Repeal of the Corn Laws and the Irish Famine," in *Free Trade and its Reception, 1815–1960*, ed. Andrew Marrison (Boca Raton, FL: CRC, 2002); David Nally, "'That Coming Storm': The Irish Poor Law, Colonial Biopolitics, and the Great Famine," *Annals of the Association of American Geographers* 98, no. 3 (2008): 714–41.

8 Peter Gray, "The Triumph of Dogma Ideology and Famine Relief," *History Ireland* 3, no. 2 (1995): 26–34.

9 Hazel Waters, "The Great Famine and the Rise of Anti-Irish Racism," *Race & Class* 37, no. 1 (July 1, 1995): 95–108.

10 Bernard Semmel, *The Rise of Free Trade Imperialism: Classical Political Economy, the Empire of Free Trade, and Imperialism, 1750–1850* (Cambridge: Cambridge University Press, 1970), 71–72.

11 M. J. Daunton, *Progress and Poverty: An Economic and Social History of Britain, 1700–1850* (Oxford: Oxford University Press, 1995), 137.

12 Eric J. Evans, *The Great Reform Act of 1832* (New York: Routledge, 1983).

13 John A. Phillips and Charles Wetherell, "The Great Reform Act of 1832 and the Political Modernization of England," *American Historical Review* 100, no. 2 (1995): 411–36.

14 Nancy P. Lopatin, "Refining the Limits of Political Reporting: The Provincial Press, Political Unions, and the Great Reform Act," *Victorian Periodicals Review* 31, no. 4 (1998): 337–55.

15 Andrew Walker, "The Development of the Provincial Press in England ca. 1780–1914," *Journalism Studies* 7, no. 3 (2006): 373–86; Donald Read, *Press and People, 1790–1850: Opinion in Three English Cities* (London: E. Arnold, 1961).

16 Nick Foggo, "Liverpool Mercury (1811–1904)," in *Dictionary of Nineteenth-Century Journalism*, ed. Laurel Brake and Marysa Demoor (London: Academia Press, 2009).

17 Leora Bersohn, "Manchester Guardian (1821–)," in *Dictionary of Nineteenth-Century Journalism*.

18 *Manchester Guardian*, May 5, 1821.

19 HWF, "Glasgow Herald (1783–)," in *Dictionary of Nineteenth-Century Journalism*.

20 H. C. G. Matthew, "Hunter, Samuel," in *Oxford Dictionary of National Biography*, https://www.oxforddnb.com/.

21 HWF, "Glasgow Herald (1783–)."

22 Michael J. Turner, "Before the Manchester School: Economic Theory in Early Nineteenth-Century Manchester," *History* 79, no. 256 (1994): 216–41.

23 Kinealy, "Peel, Rotten Potatoes, and Providence," 114.

24 Kinealy, 113.

25 Quoted in Pickering and Tyrell, *People's Bread*, 76; *Northern Star*, May 29, 1841.

26 Richard Cobden, *Speeches on Free Trade* (London: Macmillan, 1903), 13.

27 Pickering and Tyrell, *People's Bread*, 76–77.

28 M. J. Daunton, *Progress and Poverty: An Economic and Social History of Britain, 1700–1850* (Oxford: Oxford University Press, 1995), 553–54.

29 *Liverpool Mercury*, October 17, 1845.

30 *Liverpool Mercury*, November 7, 1845.

31 *Glasgow Herald*, December 5. 1845.

32 *Glasgow Herald*, October 20, 1845.

33 *Liverpool Mercury*, October 24, 1845.

34 *Liverpool Mercury*, October 31, 1845.

35 *Manchester Guardian*, November 12, 1845.

36 *Manchester Guardian*, October 18, 1845.

37 *Manchester Guardian*, October 22, 1845.

38 *Liverpool Mercury*, October 24, 1845.

39 *Glasgow Herald*, December 1, 1845.

40 *Manchester Guardian*, November 1, 1845.

41 *Glasgow Herald*, November 10, 1845.

42 Jordan Henry Donaldson, "The Political Methods of the Anti–Corn Law League," *Political Science Quarterly* 42, no. 1 (1927): 59.

43 Quoted in Gray, *Famine, Land, and Politics: British Government and Irish Society, 1843–1850* (Dublin: Irish Academic Press, 1999) 105.

44 Quoted in Gray, *Famine, Land, and Politics*, 105–6.

45 Cheryl Schonhardt-Bailey, "Ideology, Party, and Interests in the British Parliament," *British Journal of Political Science* 33, no. 4 (2003): 581–605; Iain McLean and Camilla Bustani, "Irish Potatoes and British Politics: Interests, Ideology, Heresthetic and the Repeal of the Corn Laws," *Political Studies* (1999): 817–36.

46 *Peel's Memoirs* quoted in Iain McLean and Camilla Bustani, "Irish Potatoes and British Politics: Interests, Ideology, Heresthetic, and the Repeal of the Corn Laws," *Political Studies* (1999): 820.

47 *Peel's Memoirs*, quoted in McLean and Bustani, "Irish Potatoes and British Politics," 821.

48 T. J. McKeown, "The Politics of Corn Law Repeal and Theories of Commercial Policy," *British Journal of Political Science* 19, no. 3 (1989): 353–80; Richard A. Gaunt, *Sir Robert Peel: The Life and Legacy* (London: I. B. Tauris, 2010), 124–25.

49 John Belcham argues that attitudes towards the Irish in Liverpool "hardened" in the wake of the famine, while Michael De Nie argues that "one is still justified in arguing that throughout the famine the true source of Ireland's woes was most consistently traced to its Celtic identity, that is, its un-Britishness." John Belchem, *Irish, Catholic, and Scouse: The History of the Liverpool-Irish, 1800–1939* (Liverpool: Liverpool University Press, 2007); Michael De Nie, *The Eternal Paddy: Irish Identity and the British Press, 1798–1882* (Madison: University of Wisconsin Press, 2004).

50 Barbara M. Kerr, "Irish Seasonal Migration to Great Britain, 1800–38," *Irish Historical Studies* 3, no. 12 (1943): 365–80.

51 Lewis Darwen, Donald M. MacRaild, Brian Gurrin, and Liam Kennedy, "'Unhappy and Wretched Creatures': Charity, Poor Relief, and Pauper Removal in Britain and Ireland during the Great Famine," *English Historical Review* 134, no. 568 (August 6, 2019): 589–619.

52 Alan J. Kidd and Ian Beesley, *Manchester: A History*, 4th ed. (Lancaster: Carnegie Publishing, 2006), 37; Frank Neal, *Sectarian Violence: The Liverpool Experience, 1819–1914; an Aspect of Anglo-Irish History* (Manchester: Manchester University Press, 1988); Frank Arneil Walker, "Glasgow's New Towns," in *Glasgow: The Forming of the City*, ed. Peter Reed (Edinburgh: Edinburgh University Press, 1993), 29–37.

53 Donald M. MacRaild, *Irish Migrants in Modern Britain, 1750–1922* (London: Macmillan International Higher Education, 1999). Overall population figures drawn from Great Britain Census Office, *Census of Great Britain 1851: Tables of the Population and Houses in the Divisions, Registration Counties, and Districts of England and Wales, in the Countries, Cities, and Burghs of Scotland, and in the Islands in the British Seas* (London: W. Clowes & Sons, 1851).

54 *Liverpool Mercury*, April 23, 1847.

55 *Glasgow Herald*, June 18, 1847.
56 *Liverpool Mercury*, March 27, 1846.
57 *Manchester Guardian*, December 30, 1846.
58 *Liverpool Mercury*, March 19, 1847.
59 Mervyn Busteed, "Irish Settlement and Identity in Manchester," in *The Great Famine and Beyond: Irish Migrants in Britain in the Nineteenth and Twentieth Centuries*, ed. Donald M. MacRaild (Dublin: Irish Academic Press, 2000): 94–141; Graham Davis, *The Irish in Britain, 1815–1914* (Dublin: Gill & Macmillan, 1991), 154.
60 *Manchester Guardian*, May 9, 1846.
61 *Liverpool Mercury*, January 1, 1847.
62 *Liverpool Mercury*, January 15, 1847.
63 *Glasgow Herald*, June 7, 1847.
64 Peter Gray, *The Making of the Irish Poor Law, 1815–43* (Manchester: University of Manchester Press, 2009).
65 Timothy Besley, Stephen Coate, and Timothy Guinnane, *Understanding the Workhouse Test: Information and Poor Relief in Nineteenth-Century England.* (New Haven, CT: Economic Growth Center, Yale University, 1993).
66 Gray, *Making of the Irish Poor Law.*
67 *Manchester Guardian*, June 17, 1846.
68 *Manchester Guardian*, December 30, 1846.
69 *Liverpool Mercury*, July 16, 1847; *Liverpool Mercury*, May 4, 1847.
70 *Manchester Guardian*, December 30, 1846.
71 *Manchester Guardian*, December 30, 1846.
72 *Liverpool Mercury*, May 4, 1847.
73 *Liverpool Mercury*, July 16, 1847.
74 *Liverpool Mercury*, July 16, 1847.
75 Virginia Crossman, *Politics, Pauperism, and Power in Late Nineteenth-Century Ireland* (Manchester: Manchester University Press, 2006), 12.
76 *Manchester Guardian*, April 10, 1847.
77 *Liverpool Mercury*, May 25, 1847.
78 *Manchester Guardian*, February 13, 1847.

3. IMPERIAL OBLIGATION

1 *Times of London*, December 6, 1848.
2 C. E. Trevelyan, *The Irish Crisis* (London: Longman, Brown, Green & Longmans, 1848). This volume contains the essay reprinted from the *Edinburgh Review*, no. 175 (January 1848).
3 Peter Gray, "National Humiliation and the Great Hunger: Fast and Famine in 1847," *Irish Historical Studies* 32, no. 126 (2000): 193–216.
4 Michael De Nie, "Curing 'The Irish Moral Plague,'" *Éire-Ireland* 32 (1997): 63–85.
5 James S. Donnelly, "'Irish Property Must Pay for Irish Poverty': British Public Opinion and the Great Irish Famine," in *"Fearful Realities": New Perspectives on the*

Famine, ed. Chris Morash and Richard Hayes (Dublin: Irish Academic Press, 1996), 60–76.

6 For examples of debates about what constituted the empire, who was an imperial actor, and whether there was a coherent logic of empire, see John M. MacKenzie, *Propaganda and Empire: The Manipulation of British Public Opinion, 1880–1960* (Manchester: Manchester University Press, 1984); Bernard Porter, *The Lion's Share* (London: Longman, 2004); P. J. Cain and A. G. Hopkins, *British Imperialism: Innovation and Expansion, 1688–1914* (London: Longman, 1993); Bernard Porter, *The Absent-Minded Imperialists, Empire, Society and Culture and Britain* (Oxford: Oxford University Press, 2004); and Catherine Hall and Sonya O. Rose, *At Home with the Empire: Metropolitan Culture and the Imperial World* (Cambridge: Cambridge University Press, 2006).

7 D. Lambert and A. Lester, "Geographies of Colonial Philanthropy," *Progress in Human Geography* 28, no. 3 (2004): 320–41; Andrew Mycock, "A Very English Affair? Defining the Borders of Empire in Nineteenth-Century British Historiography," in *The Historical Imagination in Nineteenth-Century Britain and the Low Countries*, ed. Hugh Dunthorne and Michael Wintle (Leiden: Brill, 2012), 48.

8 Catherine Hall, "The Lords of Humankind Re-Visited," *Bulletin of the School of Oriental and African Studies, University of London* 66, no. 3 (2003): 474–75.

9 Michael Barnett, *Empire of Humanity: A History of Humanitarianism* (Ithaca, NY: Cornell University Press, 2011), 55.

10 Catherine Hall, *Civilising Subjects: Metropole and Colony in the English Imagination, 1830–1867* (Chicago: University of Chicago Press, 2002); Andrea Major, "British Humanitarian Political Economy and Famine in India, 1838–1842," *Journal of British Studies* 59, no. 2 (April 2020): 232.

11 Earl Grey, *The Colonial Policy of Lord John Russell's Administration* (London: R. Bentley, 1853), 13.

12 David Fitzpatrick, "Ireland and the Empire," in *The Oxford History of the British Empire: Volume III: The Nineteenth Century*, ed. Andrew Porter and Wm Roger Louis (Oxford: Oxford University Press, 1999), 494–95.

13 Andrew Porter, "Introduction: Britain and the Empire in the Nineteenth Century," in *The Oxford History of the British Empire: Volume III*, 4; Alvin Jackson, "Ireland, the Union, and the Empire, 1800–1960," in *Ireland and the British Empire*, ed. Kevin Kenny and William Roger Louis (Oxford: Oxford University Press, 2004), 125.

14 Matthew H. Edney, *Mapping an Empire: The Geographical Construction of British India, 1765–1843* (Chicago: University of Chicago Press, 1997); Jackson, "Ireland, the Union, and the Empire," 125; Gillian M. Doherty, *The Irish Ordnance Survey: History, Culture, and Memory* (Dublin: Four Courts, 2004).

15 Georgina Sinclair, "The 'Irish' Policeman and the Empire: Influencing the Policing of the British Empire–Commonwealth," *Irish Historical Studies* 36, no. 142 (2008): 175.

16 John Gilbert McCurdy, *Quarters: The Accommodation of the British Army and the Coming of the American Revolution* (Ithaca, NY: Cornell University Press, 2019), 56.

17 Michael De Nie, *The Eternal Paddy: Irish Identity and the British Press, 1798–1882* (Madison: University of Wisconsin Press, 2004); Lewis Perry Curtis, *Apes and Angels : The Irishman in Victorian Caricature* (Washington, DC: Smithsonian Institution, 1971); Edward G. Lengel, *The Irish through British Eyes: Perceptions of Ireland in the Famine Era* (Westport, CT: Praeger, 2002).

18 Quoted in De Nie, *Eternal Paddy*, 3.

19 Thomas Babington Macaulay, *The History of England from the Accession of James II* (New York: Harper & Brothers, 1849), 2.

20 For a discussion of the fundamental interconnectedness of the British political sphere, see Ellis Archer Wasson, "The House of Commons, 1660–1945: Parliamentary Families and the Political Elite," *English Historical Review* 106, no. 420 (1991): 635–51.

21 Darwin F. Bostick, "Sir John Easthope and the *Morning Chronicle*, 1834–1848," *Victorian Periodicals Review* 12, no. 2 (1979): 51–60.

22 Michael De Nie, "The Famine, Irish Identity, and the British Press," *Irish Studies Review* 6, no. 1 (1998): 27.

23 Andrew Hobbs, "The Deleterious Dominance of *The Times* in Nineteenth-Century Scholarship," *Journal of Victorian Culture* 18, no. 4 (December 1, 2013): 473.

24 Bostick, "Sir John Easthope."

25 David Roberts, "Charles Dickens and the *Daily News*: Editorials and Editorial Writers," *Victorian Periodicals Review* 22, no. 2 (1989): 51–63.

26 James, Louis, "The Era (1838–1939)," in *Dictionary of Nineteenth-Century Journalism*, ed. Laurel Brake and Marysa Demoor (London: Academia Press, 2009).

27 Peter W. Sinnema, "Reading Nation and Class in the First Decade of the *Illustrated London News*," *Victorian Periodicals Review* 28, no. 2 (1995): 136–52.

28 Edward Jacobs, "Edward Lloyd's Sunday Newspapers and the Cultural Politics of Crime News, c. 1840–43," *Victorian Periodicals Review* 50, no. 3 (2017): 619–49.

29 Leslie Williams, "Bad Press: Thomas Campbell Foster and British Reportage on the Irish Famine, 1845–1849," in *Nineteenth-Century Media and the Construction of Identities*, ed. Laurel Brake, Bill Bell and David Finkelstein (London: Palgrave Macmillan, 2016), 295–309.

30 *Times of London*, October 4, 1845.

31 *Times of London*, November 5, 1845.

32 *Times of London*, February 26, 1846.

33 *Lloyd's Weekly Newspaper*, March 1, 1846

34 *Illustrated London News*, November 8, 1845; *Illustrated London News*, November 15, 1845.

35 *Illustrated London News*, November 8, 1845.

36 Trevelyan, *Irish Crisis*, 6–7.

37 *Times of London*, October 17, 1845.

38 *Times of London*, October 22, 1845.

39 *Times of London*, October 4, 1845.

40 *Lloyd's Weekly Newspaper*, January 18th, 1846.

41 *Lloyd's Weekly Newspaper*, March 1, 1846.

42 *The Era*, December 13, 1846.

43 Lambert and Lester, "Geographies of Colonial Philanthropy," 323.

44 Donnelly, "Irish Property Must Pay."

45 *Times of London*, October 25, 1845.

46 *Chambers's Edinburgh Journal* October 21, 1848.

47 Gray, *Famine, Land, and Politics*, 6.

48 *Morning Chronicle*, October 4, 1845.

49 *Times London*, December 3, 1845.

50 *Illustrated London News*, March 28, 1845.

51 George Poulett Scrope, *How Is Ireland to Be Governed? A Question Addressed to the New Administration of Lord Melbourne in 1834, Etc* (London: J. Ridgway, 1846), 24, 26.

52 *Times of London*, April 23, 1847.

53 *The Era*, January 17, 1847.

54 *Times of London*, October 22, 1845.

55 David Fitzpatrick, "Emigration, 1801–1870," in *A New History of Ireland, Volume V: Ireland Under the Union, I: 1801–70*, ed. W. E. Vaughan (Oxford: Clarendon, 2000), 562–621.

56 *Times of London*, October 17, 1845.

57 Thomas Campbell Foster, *Letters on the Condition of the People of Ireland* (London: Chapman & Hall, 1846), 385.

58 Foster, *Letters*, 386.

59 *Times of London*, January 20, 1846.

60 *Times of London*, April 7, 1846.

61 United Kingdom, *Hansard Parliamentary Debates* 84 (1846).

62 United Kingdom, *Hansard Parliamentary Debates* 90 (1847).

63 *Illustrated London News*, April 3, 1847.

64 *Morning Chronicle*, January 12, 1847 (and many others).

65 *Times of London*, July 5, 1847.

66 Aoife O'Leary McNeice, "'A Painful and Tender Sympathy Pervaded Every Class of Society': Consensus, Class, and Coercion in Global Giving during the Great Irish Famine," *Radical History Review* 2022, no. 143 (May 1, 2022): 165–76

67 Robert J. Scholnick, "'The Fiery Cross of Knowledge': *Chambers's Edinburgh Journal*, 1832–1844," *Victorian Periodicals Review* 32, no. 4 (1999): 324–58.

68 *Chambers's Edinburgh Journal*, January 23, 1847.

69 *Chambers's Edinburgh Journal*, January 23, 1847.

70 *Manchester Guardian*, August 15, 1846.

71 *Chambers's Edinburgh Journal*, January 15, 1848.

72 *Manchester Guardian*, May 16, 1846.

73 *Manchester Guardian*, May 16, 1846; April 3, 1847.

74 *Times of London*, November 21, 1845.

75 *Morning Chronicle*, April 4, 1846.

76 Scrope, *How Is Ireland to Be Governed?*, 3–4.

77 Scrope, 4.

78 United Kingdom, *Hansard Parliamentary Debates* 72 (1844).

79 United Kingdom, *Hansard Parliamentary Debates* 72 (1844).

80 United Kingdom, *Hansard Parliamentary Debates* 89 (1847).

81 United Kingdom, *Hansard Parliamentary Debates* 89 (1847).

82 United Kingdom, *Hansard Parliamentary Debates* 90 (1847).

83 *Morning Chronicle*, July 21, 1847.

84 *Times of London*, March 23, 1846.

85 *The Nation*, July 8, 1848; Christine Kinealy, *Repeal and Revolution: 1848 in Ireland* (Manchester: Manchester University Press, 2009), 99–100; Gary Owens, "Popular Mobilisation and the Rising of 1848: The Clubs of the Irish Confederation," in *Rebellion and Remembrance in Modern Ireland*, ed. Laurence Geary (Dublin: Four Courts, 2001), 51–63.

86 Owens, "Popular Mobilisation and the Rising of 1848," 54.

87 Kinealy, *Repeal and Revolution*, 191.

88 Kinealy, 199. Historians of Ireland have long debated whether Young Irelanders—or, indeed, other Irish nationalists—conceived of their movements in explicitly anti-imperial terms. For example, see Miles Taylor, "The 1848 Revolutions and the British Empire," *Past & Present*, no. 166 (2000): 146–80; and Matthew Kelly, "Irish Nationalist Opinion and the British Empire in the 1850s and 1860s," *Past & Present* 204, no. 1 (August 1, 2009): 127–54.

89 *Times of London*, June 27, 1850.

4. AMERICAN POWER

1 *Plate 4: Map Bounded by Liberty Street, Maiden Lane, South Street, Old Slip, William Street, Exchange Place, Broad Street, Nassau Street*, Lionel Pincus and Princess Firyal Map Division, New York Public Library Digital Collections, accessed July 5, 2022, digitalcollections.nypl.org.

2 Christine Kinealy, *Charity and the Great Hunger in Ireland: The Kindness of Strangers* (London: Bloomsbury, 2013), 85–86; Robert Greenhalgh Albion, "Yankee Domination of New York Port, 1820–1865," *New England Quarterly* 5, no. 4 (October 1, 1932): 665–98.

3 Friedrich Kapp, *Immigration and the Commissioners of Emigration of the State of New York* (New York: D. Taylor, 1870).

4 General Irish Relief Committee of the City of New York, *Aid to Ireland: Report of the General Relief Committee of the City of New York; with Schedules of Their Receipts in Money, Provisions and Clothing; the Particulars of Their Shipments and Extracts from the Correspondence and Publications* (The Committee, 1848), 5.

5 Robert Kielbowicz, "Newsgathering by Printers' Exchanges before the Telegraph," *Journalism History* 9, no. 2 (Summer 1982): 43.

6 *Cork Constitution*, November 1, 1846.

7 George Rogers Taylor, *The Transportation Revolution, 1815–1860*, (New York: Rinehart, 1951), 106.

8 Ryan Cordell, "Reprinting, Circulation, and the Network Author in Antebellum Newspapers," *American Literary History* 27, no. 3 (2015): 417–45; Ryan Cordell and David Smith, "Viral Texts: Mapping Networks of Reprinting in Nineteenth-Century Newspapers and Magazines," 2022, viraltexts.org.

9 Sean Wilentz, *The Rise of American Democracy: Jefferson to Lincoln* (New York: W. W. Norton, 2006), 245; Sean Wilentz, "On Class and Politics in Jacksonian America," *Reviews in American History* 10, no. 4 (1982): 55.

10 Wilentz, "On Class and Politics in Jacksonian America," 55.

11 Wilentz; Eric Foner, *Free Soil, Free Labor, Free Men: The Ideology of the Republican Party before the Civil War: With a New Introductory Essay* (Oxford: Oxford University Press, 1995), 19.

12 Scott Appelrouth, *Envisioning America and the American Self: Republican and Democratic Party Platforms, 1840–2016* (Routledge, 2019), 81.

13 Marc W. Kruman, "The Second American Party System and the Transformation of Revolutionary Republicanism," *Journal of the Early Republic* 12, no. 4 (1992): 525.

14 Carl N. Degler, "The Locofocos: Urban 'Agrarians,'" *Journal of Economic History* 16, no. 3 (1956): 222–23; Anthony Gronowicz, *Race and Class Politics in New York City before the Civil War* (Boston: Northeastern University Press, 1998), 48.

15 Gronowicz, *Race and Class Politics*, 65–67.

16 Judah B. Ginsberg, "Barnburners, Free Soilers, and the New York Republican Party," *New York History* 57, no. 4 (1976): 475–500.

17 Yonatan Eyal, *The Young America Movement and the Transformation of the Democratic Party, 1828–1861* (Cambridge: Cambridge University Press, 2007).

18 Wilentz, "On Class and Politics in Jacksonian America," 58; Foner, *Free Soil, Free Labor*, 19, 170; Wilentz, *Rise of American Democracy*, 488; Emily J. Arendt, "'Two Dollars a Day, and Roast Beef': Whig Culinary Partisanship and the Election of 1840," *Journal of the Early Republic* 40, no. 1 (2020): 83–115.

19 For a deeply researched overview of the history of the Whig party, see Michael F. Holt, *The Rise and Fall of the American Whig Party: Jacksonian Politics and the Onset of the Civil War* (Oxford: Oxford University Press, 2003).

20 For a discussion of the politics of nativism generally, see Tyler G. Anbinder, *Nativism and Slavery: The Northern Know Nothings and the Politics of the 1850s* (Oxford: Oxford University Press, 1994). For a variety of views on antipathy toward Irish immigrants, see Richard Jensen, "'No Irish Need Apply': The Myth of Victimization," *Journal of Social History* 36, no. 2 (2002): 405–29; Kevin Kenny, "Race, Violence, and Anti-Irish Sentiment in the Nineteenth Century," in *Making the Irish American: The History And Heritage of the Irish in the United States*, ed. Joseph J. Lee and Marion R. Casey (New York: New York University Press, 2006), 364–78.

21 Holt, *Rise and Fall*, 190.

22 James L. Crouthamel, "The Newspaper Revolution in New York, 1830–1860," *New York History* 45, no. 2 (1964): 96.

23 Eyal, *Young America Movement*, 132.

24 James L. Crouthamel, "James Gordon Bennett, the *New York Herald*, and the Development of Newspaper Sensationalism," *New York History* 54, no. 3 (1973): 294–316.

25 Quoted in Adam-Max Tuchinsky, "'The Bourgeoisie Will Fall and Fall Forever': The *New-York Tribune*, the 1848 French Revolution, and American Social Democratic Discourse," *Journal of American History* 92, no. 2 (2005): 473.

26 Tuchinsky, "Bourgeoisie Will Fall," 474.

27 For an overview of the Mexican-American War, see Paul Foos, *A Short, Offhand, Killing Affair: Soldiers and Social Conflict during the Mexican-American War* (Chapel Hill: University of North Carolina Press, 2002).

28 John H. Schroeder, "Annexation or Independence: The Texas Issue in American Politics, 1836–1845," *Southwestern Historical Quarterly* 89, no. 2 (1985): 143–44.

29 David M. Pletcher, *The Diplomacy of Annexation: Texas, Oregon, and the Mexican War* (Columbia: University of Missouri Press, 1973).

30 Schroeder, "Annexation or Independence," 143.

31 Schroeder, 137.

32 Lelia M. Roeckell, "Bonds over Bondage: British Opposition to the Annexation of Texas," *Journal of the Early Republic* 19, no. 2 (1999): 257–78.

33 For a review of the political background of the Mexican-American War, see Wilentz, *Rise of American Democracy*, 559–66.

34 Quoted in William M. Fowler, "Sloop of War/Sloop of Peace: Robert Bennet Forbes and the USS *Jamestown*," in *Proceedings of the Massachusetts Historical Society* 98 (1986): 53.

35 Merle Curti, *American Philanthropy Abroad* (New Brunswick, NJ: Rutgers University Press, 1963), 44–45.

36 *New York Herald*, May 13, 1846.

37 *New York Tribune*, January 6, 1847.

38 *New York Tribune*, May 11, 1848.

39 *New York Tribune*, February 22, 1847.

40 *New York Herald*, March 9, 1847.

41 *New York Tribune*, February 20, 1847.

42 *New York Tribune*, May 1, 1848.

43 *New York Tribune*, November 1, 1848.

44 Paul A. Gilje, "The Development of an Irish American Community in New York before the Great Migration," in *The New York Irish*, ed. Ronald H. Bayor and Timothy J. Meagher (Baltimore, MD: Johns Hopkins University Press, 1997), 80.

45 Gilje, "Development of an Irish American Community," 78–79.

46 Holt, *Rise and Fall*, 83.

47 Hasia R. Diner, "'The Most Irish City in the Union': The Era of the Great Migration, 1844–1877," in *The New York Irish*, ed. Ronald H. Bayor and

Timothy J. Meagher (Baltimore, MD: Johns Hopkins University Press, 1997), 101–2.

48 David Sim, *A Union Forever: The Irish Question and U.S. Foreign Relations in the Victorian Age* (Cornell University Press, 2013), 15–18.

49 *New York Tribune*, March 1, 1847.

50 *New York Tribune*, July 3, 1847.

51 *New York Tribune*, October 20, 1847.

52 *New York Tribune*, November 7, 1848.

53 *New York Herald*, January 24, 1847.

54 *New York Herald*, October 8, 1845.

55 *New York Herald*, November 21, 1845

56 *New York Herald*, May 10, 1846.

57 *New York Tribune*, January 14, 1846.

58 Gilje, "Development of an Irish American Community."

59 *New York Herald*, May 4, 1848.

60 *New York Herald*, June 30, 1848.

61 *New York Tribune*, June 17, 1848.

62 For an example of this kind of rhetoric, see *New York Tribune*, August 4, 1848.

63 *New York Herald*, May 10, 1846.

64 *New York Herald*, February 17, 1847.

65 *New York Tribune*, December 31, 1846.

66 *New York Tribune*, February 16, 1847.

67 *New York Herald*, March 11, 1847.

68 *New York Tribune*, January 1, 1847.

69 *New York Tribune*, February 12, 1847.

70 Paraphrased in Curti, *American Philanthropy Abroad*, 55.

71 Philip Hone, *The Diary of Philip Hone, 1828–1851* (New York: Dodd, Mead, 1889), 294–95.

72 *Diary of George Templeton Strong*, 289; quoted in Curti, *American Philanthropy Abroad*, 55.

73 *New York Tribune*, December 28, 1846.

74 *New York Herald*, February 23, 1847.

75 Angela F. Murphy, "Daniel O'Connell and the 'American Eagle' in 1845: Slavery, Diplomacy, Nativism, and the Collapse of America's First Irish Nationalist Movement," *Journal of American Ethnic History* 26, no. 2 (2007): 7.

76 *New York Tribune*, February 3, 1847.

5. LAND REFORM

1 David Murray, *Delaware County, New York; History of the Century, 1797–189— Centennial Celebration, June 9 and 10, 1897* (Delhi, NY: William Clark, 1898), 245; Charles W. McCurdy, *The Anti-Rent Era in New York Law and Politics, 1839–1865* (Chapel Hill: University of North Carolina Press, 2001), 397.

2 Henry Christman, *Tin Horns and Calico: A Decisive Episode in the Emergence of Democracy* (New York: Holt, 1945), 176.

3 Rachelle H. Saltzman, "Calico Indians and Pistol Pills: Traditional Drama, Historical Symbols, and Political Actions in Upstate New York," *New York Folklore* 20, no. 3 (January 1, 1994): 2.

4 Christman, *Tin Horns and Calico*, 179.

5 Reeve Huston, *Land and Freedom: Rural Society, Popular Protest, and Party Politics in Antebellum New York* (Oxford: Oxford University Press, 2000), 161.

6 M. R. Beames, "Rural Conflict in Pre-Famine Ireland: Peasant Assassinations in Tipperary 1837–1847," *Past & Present*, no. 81 (1978): 75–91.

7 Richard McMahon, *Homicide in Pre-Famine and Famine Ireland* (Liverpool: Liverpool University Press, 2014), 110. Contemporary newspaper accounts use the spelling "Costelloe"; McMahon uses "Costello."

8 *Cork Constitution*, November 1, 1846.

9 John T. Houdek and Charles F. Heller, "Searching for Nineteenth-Century Farm Tenants: An Evaluation of Methods," *Historical Methods* 19, no. 2 (Spring 1986): 55–61.

10 Frank Lawrence Owsley, *Plain Folk of the Old South* (Baton Rouge: Louisiana State University Press, 2008); Allan G. Bogue, *From Prairie to Corn Belt: Farming on the Illinois and Iowa Prairies in the Nineteenth Century* (Chicago: University of Chicago Press, 1963); Seddie Cogswell, *Tenure, Nativity, and Age as Factors in Iowa Agriculture, 1850–1880* (Ames: Iowa State University Press, 1975); Donald L. Winters, *Farmers without Farms: Agricultural Tenancy in Nineteenth-Century Iowa* (Westport, CT: Greenwood, 1978); Frederick A. Bode, *Farm Tenancy and the Census in Antebellum Georgia / Ginter, Donald E.* (Athens: University of Georgia Press, 1986); Houdek and Heller, "Searching for Nineteenth-Century Farm Tenants," 55–61.

11 Though contemporaries described themselves as tenants and landlords in New York, the legal structures governing their relationships to the land were not leases, but, rather, "grants in fee," whereby people frequently referred to as "tenants" paid a fee to people frequently referred to as "landlords" in exchange for ownership of the soil. However, failing to pay that fee or meet other conditions of the contract would allow the land to revert to the grantor. Because people at the time used the terms "landlord" and "tenant," even though they were not strictly legally accurate, I will use them here. McCurdy, *Anti-Rent Era in New York*, 61–68.

12 Huston, *Land and Freedom*, 13.

13 Huston, 23.

14 Huston, 23; Thomas Summerhill, *Harvest of Dissent: Agrarianism in Nineteenth-Century New York* (Urbana: University of Illinois Press, 2005), 62.

15 McCurdy, *Anti-Rent Era in New York*, 44.

16 Huston, *Land and Freedom*, 17.

17 Huston, 84–105.

18 J. R. Wordie, "The Chronology of English Enclosure, 1500–1914," *Economic History Review* 36, no. 4 (1983): 483–505; Martin Bruegel, "Unrest: Manorial Society and

the Market in the Hudson Valley, 1780–1850," *Journal of American History* 82, no. 4 (1996): 1393–424; Peter Linebaugh, "Enclosures from the Bottom Up," *Radical History Review*, no. 108 (2010): 11–27.

19 S. J. Donnelly, "Landlords and Tenants," in *A New History of Ireland, Volume V: Ireland Under the Union, I: 1801–70* (Oxford: Clarendon, 1989), 332.

20 Kevin Whelan, "Settlement and Society in Eighteenth-Century Ireland," in *A History of Settlement in Ireland*, ed. Terence B. Barry (London; New York: Routledge, 2000), 203–221.

21 M. R. Beames, "Rural Conflict in Pre-Famine Ireland: Peasant Assassinations in Tipperary 1837–1847," *Past & Present*, no. 81 (1978): 75–91.

22 Thomas Ainge Devyr, *The Odd Book of the Nineteenth Century, or, "Chivalry" in Modern Days: A Personal Record of Reform—Chiefly Land Reform, for the Last Fifty Years* (The author, 1882), 39.

23 Thomas Ainge Devyr, *Our Natural Rights: A Pamphlet for the People* (Belfast: The author, 1836), 26.

24 Thomas Ainge Devyr, *The Odd Book of the Nineteenth Century, or, "Chivalry" in Modern Days: A Personal Record of Reform—Chiefly Land Reform, for the Last Fifty Years* (Belfast: The author, 1882), 108.

25 James S. Donnelly, "Captain Rock: Ideology and Organization in the Irish Agrarian Rebellion of 1821–24," *Éire-Ireland* 42, no. 3 (2007): 63.

26 M. R. Beames, "Rural Conflict in Pre-Famine Ireland," 75.

27 Jay R. Roszman, "The Curious History of Irish 'Outrages': Irish Agrarian Violence and Collective Insecurity, 1761–1852," *Historical Research* 91, no. 253 (August 1, 2018): 493.

28 Donnelly, "Captain Rock," 64.

29 Roszman, "Curious History of Irish 'Outrages,'" 498–99.

30 Devyr, *Odd Book of the Nineteenth Century*, 135.

31 Huston, *Land and Freedom*, 138.

32 Huston, 137–38.

33 John R. Bleeker, D. Vaughan, and J. E. Gavit, J. E., *A Map of the Manor Renselaerwick*, 1767, New York State Library.

34 Huston, *Land and Freedom*, 111–15.

35 Donnelly, "Captain Rock," 64.

36 Bleeker, Vaughan, and Gavit, *Map of the Manor*.

37 Summerhill, *Harvest of Dissent*, 64–66.

38 Jamie L Bronstein, *Land Reform and Working-Class Experience in Britain and the United States, 1800–1862* (Stanford, CA: Stanford University Press, 1999), 122–25.

39 Christman, *Tin Horns and Calico*, chapter 21.

40 Huston, *Land and Freedom*, 14; Edward Potts Cheyney, *The Anti-Rent Agitation in the State of New York, 1839–1846* (Philadelphia: Porter & Coates, 1887), 42.

41 Huston, *Land and Freedom*, 26, 155.

42 N. Ó Ciosáin, *Print and Popular Culture in Ireland, 1750–1850* (London: Macmillan, 1997), 159.

43 Joel Mokyr and Cormac Ó Gráda, "Famine Disease and Famine Mortality: Lessons from the Irish Experience, 1845–1850," in *Famine Demography: Perspectives from Past and Present*, ed. Tim Dyson and Cormac Ó Gráda (Oxford: Oxford University Press, 2002) ,19–43; Cormac Ó Gráda, "Mortality and the Great Famine," in *Atlas of the Great Irish Famine, 1845–52*, ed. John Crowley, William J. Smyth, and Mike Murphy (Cork: Cork University Press, 2012), 170–79.

44 *Cork Examiner*, January 12, 1848.

45 J. S. North, "Cork Examiner," in *The Waterloo Directory of Irish Newspapers and Periodicals, 1800–1900* (Waterloo: North Waterloo Academic Press, 1986).

46 *Cork Examiner*, November 19, 1845.

47 *Cork Examiner*, November 19, 1845.

48 *Cork Examiner*, September 7, 1846.

49 North, "Cork Constitution."

50 *Cork Constitution*, August 27, 1846.

51 *Cork Constitution*, January 7, 1847.

52 *Cork Examiner*, November 19, 1846.

53 *Cork Examiner*, December 7, 1846.

54 *Cork Constitution*, November 1, 1846.

55 *Cork Examiner*, January 23, 1848.

56 Vaughan, *Landlords and Tenants*.

57 John Mitchel, *Jail Journal of Five Years in British Prisons* (New York: Office of the Citizen, 1854), 18; James S. Donnelly, "The Construction of the Memory of the Famine in Ireland and the Irish Diaspora, 1850–1900," *Éire-Ireland* 31, nos. 1–2 (1996): 26–61.

58 *Cork Examiner*, September 20, 1847.

59 *Cork Examiner*, September 20, 1847.

60 *Cork Examiner*, October 27, 1847.

61 *Cork Constitution*, April 22, 1847.

62 *Cork Constitution*, November 1, 1846.

63 *Cork Examiner*, June 14, 1847.

64 Huston, *Land and Freedom*, 139.

65 Huston, 141–43.

66 *Albany Freeholder*, November 12, 1845.

67 *Albany Freeholder*, February 11, 1846.

68 *Albany Freeholder*, February 17, 1847.

69 *Albany Freeholder*, March 4, 1846.

70 *Albany Freeholder*, April 13, 1846.

71 Reeve Huston, "The Parties and 'The People': The New York Anti-Rent Wars and the Contours of Jacksonian Politics," *Journal of the Early Republic* 20, no. 2 (2000): 241–71.

72 Huston, "Parties and 'The People.'"

73 *Anti-Renter*, January 31, 1846.

74 *Anti-Renter*, February 21, 1846.

75 Devyr, *Our Natural Rights*, 53.

76 Roy Marvin Robbins, "Horace Greeley: Land Reform and Unemployment, 1837–1862," *Agricultural History* 7, no. 1 (1933): 18–41; Jeter Allen Isely, *Horace Greeley and the Republican Party, 1853–1861: A Study of the New York Tribune*, vol. 3 (Princeton, NJ: Princeton University Press, 1947).

77 S. Wilentz, *Chants Democratic: New York City and the Rise of the American Working Class, 1788–1850* (Oxford: Oxford University Press, 2004), 338.

78 *New York Tribune*, April 29, 1846.

79 *New York Tribune*, April 29, 1846.

80 *New York Tribune*, June 25, 1846.

81 *New York Tribune*, May 28, 1847.

82 *New York Tribune*, August 11, 1847.

83 *New York Tribune*, June 25, 1846.

84 *New York Tribune*, February 6, 1847.

85 *New York Tribune*, September 11, 1846.

86 *New York Tribune*, April 3, 1847.

87 *New York Tribune*, June 15, 1847.

88 *New York Tribune*, July 17, 1847.

89 *New York Tribune*, August 4, August 11, 1847.

90 *New York Tribune*, February 24, 1848.

91 James S. Donnelly, "A Famine in Irish Politics," in *A New History of Ireland, Volume V*, 369.

92 *New York Tribune*, July 18, 1848.

93 *Albany Freeholder*, August 7, 1848.

6. SLAVERY

1 Central Relief Committee, "Minute Book No. 1," Dublin, 1847, 58, Society of Friends, Relief of Distress Papers, National Archives of Ireland.

2 Richard S. Harrison, *A Biographical Dictionary of Irish Quakers*, 2nd ed. (Dublin: Four Courts, 2008).

3 Richard Allen, "Circular," Dublin, March 29, 1847, 1, Thomas P. Cope Family Papers (HC.MC.1013), Quaker & Special Collections, Haverford College, Haverford, Pennsylvania.

4 Allen, "Circular," 2.

5 Allen, 1.

6 Allen, 1.

7 Allen, 1.

8 Allen, 2.

9 Allen, 3.

10 Allen, 3.

11 Helen E. Hatton, *The Largest Amount of Good: Quaker Relief in Ireland, 1654–1921* (Montreal: McGill-Queen's University Press, 1993), 104.

12 *Charleston Mercury*, September 20, 1850.

13 J. D. B DeBow, *Statistical View of the United States, Embracing Its Territory, Population—White, Free Colored, and Slave—Moral and Social Condition, Industry, Prosperity, and Revenue; the Detailed Statistics of Cities, Towns, and Counties; Being a Compendium of the Seventh Census* (Washington, DC: Beverly Tucker, Senate Pronter, 1854), 338–94.

14 DeBow *Statistical View of the United States*, 187.

15 Carl R. Osthaus, *Partisans of the Southern Press: Editorial Spokesmen of the Nineteenth Century* (Lexington: University Press of Kentucky, 1994), 48.

16 David T. Gleeson and Brendan J. Buttimer, "'We Are Irish Everywhere': Irish Immigrant Networks in Charleston, South Carolina, and Savannah, Georgia," *Immigrants & Minorities* 23, nos. 2–3 (2005): 186.

17 Gleeson and Buttimer, "We Are Irish Everywhere," 187.

18 David T. Gleeson, *The Irish in the South, 1815–1877* (Chapel Hill: University of North Carolina Press, 2001), 60

19 Gleeson, *Irish in the South*, 61.

20 There were several Alexander Blacks living in Charleston in the 1840s. While no record remains of which Alex Black addressed the Hibernian Society, all were members of the Charleston business class, and all were enslavers.

21 Hibernian Society Extra Meeting, Hibernian Hall, Tuesday, February 18, 1847, Hibernian Society Records, 1801–1982, 432.00, South Carolina Historical Society.

22 From the announcement of the creation of the Charleston relief committee, printed in the *Charleston Courier* on February 17, 1847.

23 Hibernian Society Extra Meeting, February 18, 1847.

24 Hibernian Society Monthly Meeting, Hibernian Hall, Tuesday, March 2, 1847, Hibernian Society Records, 1801–1982, 432.00, South Carolina Historical Society.

25 The formation of these committees was also reported in the *Charleston Mercury* of February 17, 1847.

26 *Charleston Mercury*, March 1, 1847.

27 *Charleston Courier*, April 10, 1847.

28 Elisabeth Muhlenfeld, *Mary Boykin Chesnut: A Biography* (Baton Rouge: Louisiana State University Press, 1981), 40.

29 Hibernian Society Monthly Meeting, March 2, 1847.

30 See, for example, Martin Gorsky's discussion of the public subscription list in Britain in Martin Gorsky, *Patterns of Philanthropy: Charity and Society in Nineteenth-Century Bristol* (Martelsham: Boydell & Brewer, 1999), 6; and Lori Ginzberg's discussion of the gendered aspects of charitable fundraising in *Women and the Work of Benevolence: Morality, Politics, and Class in the Nineteenth-Century United States* (New Haven, CT: Yale University Press, 1992), 44.

31 Affiliations drawn from Edward McCrady, Samuel A. Ashe, and Edward McCrady, *Cyclopedia of Eminent and Representative Men of the Carolinas of the Nineteenth Century*, (Madison, WI,: Brant & Fuller, 1892); Emily Bellinger Reynolds and Joan Reynolds Faunt, *Biographical Directory of the Senate of the State of South Carolina, 1776–1964.* (Columbia, South Carolina: South Carolina Archives Department, 1964);

Jon L. Wakelyn, *Biographical Dictionary of the Confederacy* (Westport, CT: Greenwood, 1977); Richard N Côté and Patricia H Williams, *Dictionary of South Carolina Biography* (Easley, SC: Southern Historical Press, 1985).

32 The number of enslaved people held in bondage by each donor is drawn from the 1850 US census slave schedules. These figures likely underestimate the number of slaveholding famine donors, as only those donors who could be confirmed as slaveowners were counted. Some donors chose to remain anonymous, while others had names too common to track through census records.

33 Allen, "Circular," 1.

34 Allen, 1.

35 Allen, 1.

36 Stephanie McCurry, *Masters of Small Worlds: Yeoman Households, Gender Relations, and the Political Culture of the Antebellum South Carolina Low Country* (Oxford: Oxford University Press, 1997).

37 Allen, 2.

38 Margaret Abruzzo, *Polemical Pain: Slavery, Cruelty, and the Rise of Humanitarianism* (Baltimore, MD: Johns Hopkins University Press, 2011), 7; Peter Wirzbicki, *Fighting for the Higher Law: Black and White Transcendentalists Against Slavery* (Philadelphia: University of Pennsylvania Press, 2021), 72–83.

39 Quoted in Harriet Martineau, *The Martyr Age in the United States of America: An Article from the London and Westminister Review, for December, 1838* (New York: S.W. Benedict, 1839), 25.

40 Frederick Douglass, William Lloyd Garrison, and Wendell Phillips, *Narrative of the Life of Frederick Douglass: An American Slave* (Boston: Anti-Slavery Office, 1846), 35.

41 Abruzzo, *Polemical Pain*, 121.

42 Elizabeth Fox-Genovese and Eugene D. Genovese, "The Divine Sanction of Social Order: Religious Foundations of the Southern Slaveholders' World View," *Journal of the American Academy of Religion* 55, no. 2 (1987): 211–33.

43 Walter Johnson, *Soul by Soul: Life inside the Antebellum Slave Market* (Cambridge, MA: Harvard University Press, 2001), 35–36.

44 Barbara L. Bellows, *Benevolence among Slaveholders: Assisting the Poor in Charleston, 1670–1860* (Baton Rouge: Louisiana State University Press, 1993).

45 Gerald J. Baldasty, "The Charleston, South Carolina, Press and National News, 1808–47," *Journalism Quarterly* 55, no. 3 (1978): 519–26.

46 *Charleston Mercury*, February 8, 1847.

47 Osthaus, *Partisans of the Southern Press*, 69.

48 William Huntzicker, *The Popular Press, 1833–1865*, vol. 3 (Westport, CT: Greenwood, 1999), 116–17.

49 *Charleston Courier*, February 19, 1847.

50 *Charleston Courier*, February 19, 1847.

51 *Southern Patriot*, February 26, 1847.

52 *Charleston Courier*, February 26, 1847.

53 *Charleston Mercury*, March 1, 1847.

54 *Weekly Flag & Advertiser*, February 26, 1847.

55 *Southern Advocate*, March 5, 1847.

56 Osthaus, *Partisans of the Southern Press*, chapter 3, "The Rise of a Metropolitan Giant: The New Orleans Daily Picayune, 1837–1850"; *Daily Picayune*, July 4, 1847.

57 Osthaus, 48.

58 Stephanie M. H Camp, *Closer to Freedom Enslaved Women and Everyday Resistance in the Plantation South*, 2004, 17–19.

59 *Daily Picayune*, August 9, 1845.

60 Edward Baptist, *The Half Has Never Been Told: Slavery and the Making of American Capitalism* (New York: Basic Books, 2014).

61 *Charleston Mercury*, December 31, 1847.

62 *Charleston Mercury*, August 11, 1848.

63 *Charleston Mercury*, August 21, 1848.

64 Quoted in Liam Hogan, "Frederick Douglass and His Journey from Slavery to Limerick," *Old Limerick Journal* 49 (2015): 21–26.

65 The assumption of this resistance is noted in the historiography. Toby Joyce observed that "the Irish in mid-Victorian Ireland took a keen interest in foreign wars. Generally, if Britain was involved, nationalists looked to 'Ireland's opportunity.'" Toby Joyce, "The American Civil War and Irish Nationalism," *History Ireland* 4, no. 2 (1996): 36.

66 *Jeffersonian Republican*, March 30, 1847. David Doyle and J. J. Lee have described this rhetorical work as "filiopeitism," by which Irish Americans celebrated the actions of any Irish person, real or imagined, who might have made a contribution to the United States, and particularly to the American Revolution. Joseph Lee, "Introduction: Interpreting Irish America," in *Making the Irish American: History and Heritage of the Irish in the United States*, ed. Joseph Lee and Marion R. Casey (New York: New York University Press, 2006), 3.

67 *Charleston Mercury*, March 29, 1847.

68 *Charleston Courier*, April 6, 1847.

69 *Charleston Mercury*, October 11, 1845.

70 *Jeffersonian Republican*, January 17, 1846.

71 Sam W. Haynes, *Unfinished Revolution: The Early American Republic in a British World* (Charlottesville: University of Virginia Press, 2010), 12.

72 Haynes, 240.

73 Sean Wilentz, *The Rise of American Democracy: Jefferson to Lincoln* (New York: W. W. Norton, 2006), 599; Paul Quigley, *Shifting Grounds: Nationalism and the American South, 1848–1865* (New York: Oxford University Press, 2012), 90.

74 For background on the Wilmot Proviso, see Eric Foner, "The Wilmot Proviso Revisited," *Journal of American History* 56, no. 2 (September 1969): 274.

75 For a review of the political events leading to the compromise, see Wilentz, *Rise of American Democracy*, 638.

76 Quoted in David W. Blight, *Race and Reunion: The Civil War in American Memory* (Cambridge, MA: Harvard University Press, 2001), 37.

77 *Charleston Mercury*, August 16, 1847.

78 *Charleston Mercury*, August 27, 1847.

79 *Charleston Mercury*, January 31, 1846.

80 *Georgia Telegraph*, September 10, 1850. For a discussion of the meeting, see A. K. Christian, "Mirabeau Buonaparte Lamar," *Southwestern Historical Quarterly* 24, no. 4 (April 1, 1921): 320–21.

81 Mirabeau Buonaparte Lamar, *The Papers of Mirabeau Buonaparte Lamar*, ed. Charles Adams Gulick and Winnie Allen, vol. 4 (Austin, TX: Von Boeckmann-Jones, 1924), 269.

82 *Charleston Mercury*, September 20, 1850.

83 Allen, "Circular," 3.

84 Allen, 3.

85 Allen, 3.

7. CLAIMING HUMANITY

1 First African Baptist Church (Richmond, Va.), "Minute Book 1." Accession 28255, Church records collection, The Library of Virginia, Richmond, VA.

2 First African Baptist Church, 114. The *Richmond Enquirer* of February 26, 1846, also advertised that "a collection will be taken up in the African Church, next Sunday morning and afternoon, for the relief of the Irish sufferers."

3 The church's minute books, which begin in 1841, contain evidence of fundraising for local issues or to help coreligionists. Prior to 1847, they make no mention of fundraising beyond their own community.

4 Henry Brown, *Narrative of the Life of Henry Box Brown, Written by Himself*, ed. John Ernest (Chapel Hill: University of North Carolina Press, 2008), 72; *Richmond Whig*, February 26, 1847

5 Norman C. McLeod, "Free Labor in a Slave Society: Richmond, Virginia, 1820–1860" (PhD diss., Howard University, 1991), 21. Colquitt was recorded as a member of the society in the *Richmond Enquirer* of September 18, 1845.

6 Brown, *Narrative*, 72.

7 *Richmond Enquirer*, October 8, 1845. Tabb's name is recorded as a committee member in the *Richmond Enquirer* of October 21, 1845. Thomas C. Hunt, "Popular Education in Nineteenth-Century Virginia: The Efforts of Charles Fenton Mercer," *Paedagogica Historica* 21, no. 2 (January 1, 1981): 337–46.

8 Brown, *Narrative*, 77.

9 Nancy was recorded as leaving the church on October 1, 1848. First African Baptist Church, "Minute Books," 134. Her husband Henry, motivated in part by the sale of his family, went on to practice a spectacular act of "self theft," mailing himself from Virginia to Philadelphia, and to freedom. Martha Cutter, *The Many Resurrections of Henry Box Brown* (Philadelphia: University of Pennsylvania Press, 2022).

10 Robert Ryland, "Reminiscences of the First African Baptist Church," *American Baptist Memorial* 14 (1855), 262.

11 Midori Takagi, *Rearing Wolves to Our Own Destruction: Slavery in Richmond, Virginia, 1782–1865* (Charlottesville: University of Virginia Press, 1999), 103.

12 Ryland, Robert, "Reminiscences of the First African Baptist Church," *American Baptist Memorial* 14 (1855): 263.

13 Takagi, *Rearing Wolves*, 105.

14 Like other Baptist churches, the First African documented the comings, going, transgressions, and repentance of congregants. These documentary conventions of Baptist churches in slave states meant that the record books of the First African Baptist Church preserved considerable information about the lives of free and enslaved Black Richmonders. Unlike white Baptists, Black Baptists were required to document whether they were free and, if not, to provide proof of enslavers' approval of their religious activities. This makes it possible to know where, and for whom, enslaved congregants were laboring when they were attending church in Richmond. W. Harrison Daniel, "Virginia Baptists and the Negro in the Antebellum Era," *Journal of Negro History* 56, no. 1 (1971): 1.

15 First African Baptist Church, "Minute Books," 105.

16 Of the 836 men and women who entered the church from 1845 to 1847, 215 reported themselves to be free. The remaining 621 were enslaved, generally in Virginia but occasionally in other states.

17 Ryland, "Origin and History," 247; O'Brien, "Factory, Church, and Community"; John J. Zaborney, *Slaves for Hire: Renting Enslaved Laborers in Antebellum Virginia* (Baton Rouge: Louisiana State University Press, 2012).

18 Takagi, *Rearing Wolves*, 38.

19 Ryland, "Origin and History," 271.

20 Stephanie McCurry, *Masters of Small Worlds: Yeoman Households, Gender Relations, and the Political Culture of the Antebellum South Carolina Low Country* (Oxford: Oxford University Press, 1997).

21 John G. Aiken, *A Digest of the Laws of the State of Alabama* (Philadelphia, 1833), 393.

22 Aiken, 393.

23 Clifton Ellis and Rebecca Ginsburg, "Introduction: Studying the Landscapes of North American Urban Slavery," in *Slavery in the City: Architecture and Landscapes of Urban Slavery in North America*, ed. Clifton Ellis and Rebecca Ginsburg (Charlottesville: University of Virginia Press, 2017), 1, 4, 5. The field of urban slavery has largely been defined by Richard Wade and Claudia Dale Goldin, both of whom explored the apparent breakdown of urban slavery in the decades before the Civil War. Richard C. Wade, *Slavery in the Cities: The South 1820–1860* (Oxford: Oxford University Press, 1967); Claudia Dale Goldin, *Urban Slavery in the American South, 1820–1860: A Quantitative History* (Chicago: University of Chicago Press, 1976).

24 Takagi, *Rearing Wolves*, 96–103.

25 Gregg D. Kimball, *American City, Southern Place: A Cultural History of Antebellum Richmond* (Athens: University of Georgia Press, 2003), chapter 1.

26 Dylan C Penningroth, *The Claims of Kinfolk: African American Property and Community in the Nineteenth-Century South* (Chapel Hill: University of North Carolina Press, 2003), 7.

27 Albert J. Raboteau, *Slave Religion: The "Invisible Institution" in the Antebellum South* (New York: Oxford University Press, 1978), 223.

28 Sumner Eliot Matison, "Manumission by Purchase," *Journal of Negro History* 33, no. 2 (1948): 152–53.

29 Brown, *Narrative*, 74.

30 T. Whitman, *The Price of Freedom: Slavery and Manumission in Baltimore and Early National Maryland.* (Lexington: University Press of Kentucky, 1997), 93.

31 Ryland, "Origin and History," 272.

32 Elna Green, *This Business of Relief: Confronting Poverty in a Southern City, 1740–1940* (Athens: University of Georgia Press, 2003), 48.

33 Ira Berlin, *Slaves without Masters: The Free Negro in the Antebellum South* (New York: Pantheon, 1975), 309; Takagi, *Rearing Wolves*, 2.

34 First African Baptist Church, "Minute Books," 138–39.

35 Takagi, *Rearing Wolves*, 105; John Thomas O'Brien, "*From Bondage to Citizenship: The Richmond Black Community, 1865–1867*" (PhD. diss, University of Rochester, 1990), 45.

36 Penningroth, *Claims of Kinfolk*, 102.

37 Penningroth, 102.

38 Berlin, *Slaves without Masters*, 313.

39 Berlin, 309.

40 Joanna Brooks, "The Early American Public Sphere and the Emergence of a Black Print Counterpublic," *William and Mary Quarterly* 62, no. 1 (2005): 75.

41 Gordon Fraser, "Distributed Agency: David Walker's Appeal, Black Readership, and the Politics of Self-Deportation," *ESQ: A Journal of Nineteenth-Century American Literature and Culture* 65, no. 2 (2019): 221–56.

42 Fraser, "Distributed Agency," 231.

43 O'Brien, "Factory, Church, and Community," 510.

44 Quoted in Peter P. Hinks, *David Walker's Appeal to the Coloured Citizens of the World* (Philadelphia: Penn State University Press, 2010), 96.

45 Wade, *Slavery in the Cities*, 176; Janet Cornelius, "'We Slipped and Learned to Read': Slave Accounts of the Literacy Process, 1830–1865," *Phylon (1960–)* 44, no. 3 (1983): 74–75.

46 Berlin, *Slaves without Masters*, 308; Fraser, "Distributed Agency," 246.

47 Michaël Roy, "Cheap Editions, Little Books, and Handsome Duodecimos: A Book History Approach to Antebellum Slave Narratives," *melus* 40, no. 3 (September 1, 2015): 69–93.

48 Heather Andrea Williams, *Self-Taught: African American Education in Slavery and Freedom* (Chapel Hill: University of North Carolina Press, 2005), 20.

49 Frederick Douglass, *Narrative of the Life of Frederick Douglass: An American Slave* (Boston: Anti-Slavery Office, 1846), 37.

50 Booker T. Washington, *Up from Slavery: An Autobiography* (New York: Doubleday, Page, 1901), 8; Sergio A. Lussana, *My Brother Slaves: Friendship, Masculinity, and*

Resistance in the Antebellum South (Lexington: University Press of Kentucky, 2016), chapter 5.

51 Washington, *Up from Slavery*, 8–9.

52 Raboteau, *Slave Religion*, 233.

53 Jarad Krywicki, "'The Soft Answer': The *National Era*'s Network of Understanding," *American Periodicals* 23, no. 2 (2013): 125–41.

54 *Liberator*, December 12, 1845.

55 *National Era*, February 4, 1847.

56 *National Era*, March 4, 1847.

57 Takagi, *Rearing Wolves*, 31.

58 Charles A. Simmons, *The African American Press: A History of News Coverage during National Crises, with Special Reference to Four Black Newspapers, 1827–1965* (Jefferson, NC: McFarland, 2006), 10–13.

59 Quoted in Lionel C. Barrow, "'Our Own Cause': *Freedom's Journal* and the Beginnings of the Black Press," *Journalism History* 4, no. 4 (December 1, 1977): 118.

60 Frankie Hutton, *The Early Black Press in America, 1827 to 1860* (Westport, CT: Greenwood, 1993), 166.

61 Benjamin Fagan, "The *North Star* and the Atlantic 1848," *African American Review* 47, no. 1 (2014): 52–53.

62 Hutton, *Early Black Press in America*, ix–x, 158.

63 *Charleston Mercury*, December 27, 1845.

64 *Liberator*, March 27, 1846.

65 Quoted in Christine Kinealy, *Black Abolitionists in Ireland* (New York: Routledge, 2020), 114.

66 Hannah-Rose Murray and John R. McKivigan, *Frederick Douglass in Britain and Ireland, 1845–1895* (Edinburgh: Edinburgh University Press, 2022), 29.

67 *North Star*, January 28, 1848.

68 *North Star*, February 18, 1848.

69 First African Baptist Church, "Minute Books," 96, 79, 86.

70 *Richmond Daily Whig*, April 29 1847.

71 *Richmond Enquirer*, February 22, 1847; *Richmond Enquirer*, February 26, 1847.

72 *Weekly Flag & Advertiser*, April 8, 1847.

73 *Richmond Enquirer*, November 7, 1845.

74 Takagi, *Rearing Wolves*, 90–91.

75 Jerome K. Dotson, "Consuming Bodies, Producing Race: Slavery and Diet in the Antebellum South, 1830–1865" (PhD diss., University of Wisconsin–Madison, 2016), 141.

76 *Richmond Whig*, June 4, 1847.

77 *Richmond Enquirer*, March 27, 1846.

78 *Richmond Whig*, February 16, 1847.

79 *Richmond Enquirer*, October 12, 1847.

80 *Richmond Commercial Compiler*, December 11, 1847.

81 Brown, *Narrative*, 62–63. Herbert Aptheker remains the classic work on slave revolts. Herbert Aptheker, *American Negro Slave Revolts* (New York: International, 1963).

82 Quoted in Peter P. Hinks, *To Awaken My Afflicted Brethren: David Walker and the Problem of Antebellum Slave Resistance* (State College: Penn State University Press, 2010), 134–35.

83 Aptheker, *American Negro Slave Revolts*, 328; James Sidbury, *Ploughshares into Swords: Race, Rebellion, and Identity in Gabriel's Virginia, 1730–1810* (Cambridge: Cambridge University Press, 1997), 264–75.

84 *National Era*, March 4, 1847.

85 *National Era*, May 27, 1847.

86 McCurry, *Masters of Small Worlds*, 111.

87 Kathleen D. McCarthy, *American Creed: Philanthropy and the Rise of Civil Society, 1700–1865* (Chicago: University of Chicago Press, 2003), 142.

88 Elizabeth Fox-Genovese, *Within the Plantation Household: Black and White Women of the Old South* (Chapel Hill: University of North Carolina Press, 1988), 232–33.

89 John G. Deal, "Middle-Class Benevolent Societies in Antebellum Norfolk, Virginia," in *The Southern Middle Class in the Long Nineteenth Century*, ed. Jonathan Daniel Wells and Jennifer R. Green (Baton Rouge: Louisiana State University Press, 2011), 85.

90 Quoted in Green, *This Business of Relief*, 53.

91 Deal, "Middle-Class Benevolent Societies," 88.

92 Green, *This Business of Relief*, 55.

93 McCurry, *Masters of Small Worlds*, 123.

94 McCurry, 123.

95 Timothy Lockley, *Welfare and Charity in the Antebellum South* (Gainesville: University Press of Florida, 2009), 216; Green, *This Business of Relief*, 47.

96 *Richmond Whig*, March 26, 1847; *Richmond Enquirer*. March 30, 1847.

97 *Raleigh Register*, May 11, 1847.

8. RESISTANCE

1 For an overview of the role of agents from the perspective of the United States, see R. S. Cotterill, "Federal Indian Management in the South, 1789–1825," *Mississippi Valley Historical Review* 20, no. 3 (1933): 333–52.

2 Edwin C. Bearss, "Fort Smith as the Agency for the Western Choctaws," *Arkansas Historical Quarterly* 27, no. 1 (1968): 54.

3 Muriel H. Wright, "Organization of Counties in the Choctaw and Chickasaw Nations," *Chronicles of Oklahoma* 8, no. 3 (1930): 318; Phillip Carroll Morgan, "Love Can Build a Bridge: The Choctaws' Gift to the Irish in 1847," in *Famine Pots: The Choctaw-Irish Gift Exchange, 1847–Present*, ed. LeAnne Howe and Padraig Kirwan (East Lansing: Michigan State University Press, 2020), 46; Bethany Hughes, "Beautifully Uncontainable: Of Honeysuckle and Choctaw Walking," *Mobilities* 17, no. 2 (March 4, 2022): 5.

4 Francis Paul Prucha, *American Indian Treaties: The History of a Political Anomaly* (Berkeley: University of California Press, 1994), 110, 148, 168.

5 W. B. Morris, "The Saga of Skullyville," *Chronicles of Oklahoma* 16, no. 2 (June 1938): 235–37.

6 The meeting was reported in the *Arkansas Intelligencer* of April 3, 1847.

7 Carolyn Thomas Foreman, "The Armstrongs of Indian Territory," *Chronicles of Oklahoma* 30 (Winter 1952): 420–53.

8 Neither this pamphlet nor the records of any famine relief associations in Memphis persist in the archive.

9 *Arkansas Intelligencer*, April 3, 1847.

10 *Arkansas Intelligencer*, April 3, 1847.

11 *Arkansas Intelligencer*, April 17, 1847.

12 Copies of the *Arkansas Intelligencer* article of April 3 were printed in the *New-York Commercial* of April 23; the New York *Evening Post* and New York *Spectator* of April 24; the Washington, DC, *Daily National Intelligencer* of April 27; the Baltimore *Sun*, Boston *Weekly Messenger*, *Worcester Palladium*, and *Trenton Gazette* of April 28; the *Boston Recorder* of April 29; the *Richmond Whig* and *Albany Argus* of April 30; the *Louisville Weekly Journal* of May 4; the *Christian Mirror* of Portland, Maine, *Ohio Democrat*, and *The Sun* of Pittsfield Vermont of May 6; and the *Schenectady Reflector* of May 7. Of the sixteen reprinted reports that I was able to locate, eleven reported the donation as $710. One reported it as $410, and the remaining four reported it as $170. Scholarship on the famine has tended to use the lower donation, though recent work, like the essays included in *Famine Pots*, have tended to use the higher one.

13 Padraig Kirwan, "Recognition, Resiliance, and Relief: The Meaning of Gift," in *Famine Pots*, 3–38. LeeAnne Howe and Padraig Kirwan have noted that, regardless of which amount was correct, reporting on the donation in white newspapers reflected a colonial gaze, within which inaccuracies about Indigenous people and the impoverished Irish were tolerated and, in some cases, promulgated. "Introduction," in *Famine Pots* 20.

14 Mary Louise Fitzpatrick, *The Long March: The Choctaw's Gift to Irish Famine Relief* (Hillsboro, OR: Beyond Words, 1998); "Lessons of Giving: The Choctaw and Cherokee Nations and the Famine," RTÉ, September 9, 2020, https://www.rte.ie /history/post-famine/2020/0909/1164161-lessons-of-givingthe-choctaw-and-cherokee -nations-and-the-famine/

15 "Sculpture in Ireland Honors Choctaw Nation | Choctaw Nation," www .choctawnation.com.

16 See the collected volume *Famine Pots*, particularly Jacki Thompson Rand, "Reconciliation," 165–78.

17 *Arkansas Intelligencer*, March 20, 1847.

18 *Picayune*, May 20, 1847; John Wesley Morris, "Doaksville," in *Ghost Towns of Oklahoma* (Norman: University of Oklahoma Press, 1977), 67–68.

19 Russell Thornton, *The Cherokees: A Population History* (Lincoln: University of Nebraska Press, 1992); Matthew T. Gregg and David M. Wishart, "The Price of Cherokee Removal," *Explorations in Economic History* 49, no. 4 (2012): 423–42.

20 Cotterill, "Federal Indian Management," 339.

21 Grant Foreman, *Indian Removal: The Emigration of the Five Civilized Tribes of Indians* (Norman: University of Oklahoma Press, 1972); Anthony F. C. Wallace, *Jefferson and the Indians: The Tragic Fate of the First Americans* (Cambridge, MA: Belknap Press of Harvard University Press, 1999).

22 Donna L. Akers, *Living in the Land of Death: The Choctaw Nation, 1830–1860* (East Lansing: Michigan State University Press, 2004), 32.

23 Akers, 72.

24 Akers, 73.

25 Reed, *Serving the Nation*, 62.

26 Reed, 62; Theda Perdue, "Race and Culture: Writing the Ethnohistory of the Early South," *Ethnohistory* 51, no. 4 (2004): 710.

27 Akers, *Living in the Land of Death*, 87.

28 Clara Sue Kidwell, *The Choctaws in Oklahoma: From Tribe to Nation, 1855–1970* (Norman: University of Oklahoma Press, 2008), 4.

29 Kidwell, *Choctaws in Oklahoma*, 4.

30 Akers, *Living in the Land of Death*, 89–90; Kidwell, 4.

31 Andrew Denson, *Demanding the Cherokee Nation: Indian Autonomy and American Culture, 1830–1900* (Lincoln: University of Nebraska Press, 2004), 42–49.

32 Foreman, *Indian Removal*; William G. McLoughlin, *Cherokee Renascence in the New Republic* (Princeton, NJ: Princeton University Press, 1986), 411; Theda Perdue, "The Conflict Within: The Cherokee Power Structure and Removal," *Georgia Historical Quarterly* 73, no. 3 (1989): 467–91; Akers, *Living in the Land of Death*, 112.

33 Reed, *Serving the Nation*, 76.

34 Arthur H. DeRosier, *The Removal of the Choctaw Indians* (Knoxville: University of Tennessee Press, 1970), 154–58.

35 Denson, *Demanding the Cherokee Nation*, 42–49.

36 Reed, *Serving the Nation*, 78.

37 Office of Indian Affairs to James McKissick, January 14, 1847, Letters Sent by the Office of Indian Affairs, National Archives Microfilm Publication M21, Roll 39, Records of the Bureau of Indian Affairs, NARA—Northeast Region (New York City)

38 Duane Champagne, *Social Order and Political Change: Constitutional Governments among the Cherokee, the Choctaw, the Chickasaw, and the Creek* (Stanford, CA: Stanford University Press, 1992), 78; Kidwell, *Choctaws in Oklahoma*, 5–6.

39 Akers, *Living in the Land of Death*, 104.

40 Akers, 112.

41 John C. Strong to Rev. David Green, March 31, 1847, American Board of Commissioners for Foreign Missions, 18.3.4. Choctaw Mission, 1844–1859, v. 6. Pt. 1., (Microfilm Reel 759).

42 Commissioner of Indian Affairs to Colonel James McKissick, Mar. 5, 1847, Letters Sent by the Bureau of Indian Affairs, National Archives, Microfilm Publication M21, Roll 39, Records of the Bureau of Indian Affairs, NARA—Northeast Region (New York City).

43 William F. Pope and Dunbar H. Pope, *Early Days in Arkansas: Being for the Most Part the Personal Recollections of an Old Settler* (Little Rock, AR: F. W. Allsopp, 1895), 127.

44 These agents were listed in the February 15, 1845, issue of the *Arkansas Intelligencer*. They included Peter Pitchlynn, a notable Choctaw political leader, and Daniel Folsom, the editor of the *Choctaw Telegraph*.

45 Meta G. Carstarphen, "To Sway Public Opinion: Early Persuasive Appeals in the Cherokee Phoenix and Cherokee Advocate," in *American Indians and the Mass Media*, ed. Meta G. Carstarphen and John P. Sanchez (Norman: University of Oklahoma Press, 2012), 66.

46 Quoted in Carstarphen, "To Sway Public Opinion," 66.

47 Robert Kielbowicz, "Newsgathering by Printers' Exchanges before the Telegraph," *Journalism History* 9, no. 2 (Summer 1982): 42–48.

48 Claudia B. Haake, *Modernity through Letter Writing: Cherokee and Seneca Political Representations in Response to Removal, 1830–1857* (Lincoln: University of Nebraska Press, 2020), 8.

49 Hilary E. Wyss, *English Letters and Indian Literacies: Reading, Writing, and New England Missionary Schools, 1750–1830* (Philadelphia: University of Pennsylvania Press, 2012), 6.

50 Wyss, *English Letters and Indian Literacies*, 6–7.

51 Lee Irwin, "Freedom, Law, and Prophecy: A Brief History of Native American Religious Resistance," *American Indian Quarterly* 21, no. 1 (January 1, 1997): 35–55; Circe Sturm, *Blood Politics: Race, Culture, and Identity in the Cherokee Nation of Oklahoma* (Berkeley: University of California Press, 2002), 17.

52 *Arkansas Intelligencer*, April 3, 1847.

53 *Arkansas Intelligencer*, April 3, 1847.

54 Thomas P. Cope, Diary, vol. 9, Philadelphia, 1847, 23, Friends Historical Library, Haverford College Special Collections, Haverford, Pennsylvania.

55 These far-flung reports included the *Alexandria Gazette*, April 28, 1847; *Worcester Palladium*, April 28, 1847; *Boston Recorder*, April 29, 1847; *Trenton State Gazette*, April 29, 1847; *Green Mountain Freeman*, May 6, 1847; and *Kennebec Journal*, May 7, 1847, among others.

56 Akers, *Living in the Land of Death*, 104.

57 Akers, 104–5.

58 *Cherokee Advocate*, July 15, 1847.

59 Reed, *Serving the Nation*, chapter 1.

60 Akers, *Living in the Land of Death*, 44.

61 LeAnne Howe, "Ima, Give," in *Famine Pots*, 135–38.

62 *Cherokee Advocate*, May 13, 1847

63 *Cherokee Advocate*, May 13, 1847.

64 Ronald Austin Wells, *The Honor of Giving: Philanthropy in Native America* (Bloomington: Indiana University Center on Philanthropy, 1998), 75; Laura W. Wittstock, "American Indian Giving and Philanthropy: The Overlaid Relationship," Hubert H. Humphrey Institute of Public Affairs, University of Minnesota .

65 Christine Kinealy, *The Great Irish Famine: Impact, Ideology, and Rebellion* (New York: Palgrave Macmillan, 2002), 80.

66 *Cherokee Advocate*, May 6, 1847.

67 Haake, *Modernity through Letter Writing*, 6.

68 James C. Scott, *Domination and the Arts of Resistance: Hidden Transcripts* (New Haven, CT: Yale University Press, 1990).

69 *Choctaw Intelligencer*, September 18, 1850.

70 *Choctaw Intelligencer*, November 20, 1850.

71 Denson, *Demanding the Cherokee Nation*, 25.

72 *Cherokee Phoenix*, January 20, 1830.

73 *A Vindication of the Cherokee Claims: Addressed to the Town Meeting in Philadelphia, on the 11th of January, 1830*, Philadelphia: n.p. 4.

74 *Liberator*, March 17, 1832.

75 Kidwell, *Choctaws in Oklahoma*, 15–18.

76 W. David Baird, "Arkansas's Choctaw Boundary: A Study of Justice Delayed," *Arkansas Historical Quarterly* 28, no. 3 (1969): 210.

77 Eliga H. Gould, *Among the Powers of the Earth: The American Revolution and the Making of a New World Empire* (Cambridge, MA: Harvard University Press, 2012), 3.

78 Fred Anderson and Andrew Cayton, *The Dominion of War: Empire and Liberty in North America, 1500–2000* (New York: Penguin, 2005), 66.

79 Patrick Wolfe, "After the Frontier: Separation and Absorption in US Indian Policy," *Settler Colonial Studies* 1, no. 1 (2011): 13–51.

80 *Memphis Daily Appeal*, November 24, 1847.

81 Amy Kaplan and Donald E. Pease, *Cultures of United States Imperialism* (Durham, NC: Duke University Press, 1994).

82 *Cherokee Advocate*, March 18, 1847.

83 *Cherokee Advocate*, May 6, 1847.

84 Cian T. McMahon, *The Coffin Ship: Life and Death at Sea during the Great Irish Famine*, (New York: New York University Press, 2021), 27–33.

85 James Mooney, *Myths of the Cherokee* (Washington, DC: Courier Dover, 1996), 128.

86 *Cherokee Advocate*, June 4, 1846.

87 *Cherokee Advocate*, March 18, 1847.

88 Quoted in Foreman, *Indian Removal*, 39.

89 Quoted in Foreman, 41.

90 *Cherokee Advocate*, April 23, 1846.

91 *Cherokee Advocate*, May 13, 1847.
92 *Cherokee Phoenix*, October 24, 1829.
93 (Mobile, AL) *Commercial Register*, November 12, 1831.
94 (New York) *Observer*, January 26, 1839.
95 *Cherokee Advocate*, March 18, 1847.
96 *Cherokee Advocate*, March 18, 1847.
97 *Cherokee Advocate*, March 4, 1847.
98 *Cherokee Advocate*, March 18, 1847.
99 Jeffrey L. Pasley, Andrew W. Robertson, and David Waldstreicher eds., "Introduction: Beyond the Founders," in *Beyond the Founders: New Approaches to the Political History of the Early American Republic* (Chapel Hill: University of North Carolina Press, 2004).
100 *Cherokee Advocate*, May 13, 1847.

CONCLUSION

1 "Coronavirus | Indian Health Service (IHS)," Coronavirus, accessed September 30, 2022, www.ihs.gov.
2 "Navajo & Hopi Families COVID-19 Relief Fund, Organized by Ethel Branch," gofundme.com, accessed September 30, 2022, https://www.gofundme.com/f/nhfcrf.
3 Ed O'Loughlin and Mihir Zaveri, "Irish Return an Old Favor, Helping Native Americans Battling the Virus," *New York Times*, May 5, 2020, www.nytimes.com.
4 "Ahéhee to Ireland for Supporting the Navajo Nation!," YouTube video, 3:41, May 11, 2020, www.youtube.com.
5 "U2 Drummer Donates $100,000 for Indigenous COVID-19 Relief Fund," Navajo & Hopi Families COVID-19 Relief Fund, accessed September 30, 2022, navajohopisolidarity.org.
6 "Walking with Spirit," Afri, September 22, 2016, www.afri.ie.
7 Mary Kelly, *Ireland's Great Famine in Irish-American History: Enshrining a Fateful Memory* (Washington, DC: Rowman & Littlefield, 2013).
8 For a discussion of some of these sites, see John Crowley, "Sites of Memory," in *Atlas of the Great Irish Famine, 1845–52*, ed. John Crowley, William J. Smyth, and Mike Murphy (Cork, Ireland: Cork University Press, 2012), 614–20; and Emily Mark-FitzGerald, *Commemorating the Irish Famine: Memory and the Monument* (Oxford: Oxford University Press, 2015).
9 Heather D. Curtis, *Holy Humanitarians: American Evangelicals and Global Aid* (Cambridge, MA: Harvard University Press, 2018); Helen E. Hatton, *The Largest Amount of Good: Quaker Relief in Ireland, 1654–1921* (Montreal: McGill-Queen's University Press, 1993); Oonagh Walsh, *Anglican Women in Dublin: Philanthropy, Politics, and Education in the Early Twentieth Century* (Dublin: University College Dublin Press, 2005).
10 Burton A. Weisbrod, "Towards a Theory of the Voluntary Non-Profit Sector in a Three-Sector Economy," in *Altruism, Morality, and Economic Theory*, ed. Edmund S. Phelps (New York: Russell Sage Foundation, 1975), 171–96.

11 Olivier Zunz, *Philanthropy in America: A History* (Princeton, NJ: Princeton University Press, 2012).

12 Inderjeet Parmar, *Foundations of the American Century: The Ford, Carnegie, and Rockefeller Foundations in the Rise of American Power* (New York: Columbia University Press, 2012).

BIBLIOGRAPHY

Abruzzo, Margaret. *Polemical Pain: Slavery, Cruelty, and the Rise of Humanitarianism.* Baltimore, MD: Johns Hopkins University Press, 2011.

"Ahéhee to Ireland for Supporting the Navajo Nation!" YouTube video, 3:41, May 11, 2020. www.youtube.com.

Aiken, John G. "A Digest of the Laws of the State of Alabama." Philadelphia, 1833. Alabama Department of Archives and History.

Akenson, Donald H. *The Irish Diaspora: A Primer.* Belfast: P. D. Meany Co. Institute of Irish Studies, Queen's University of Belfast, 1993.

Akers, Donna L. *Living in the Land of Death: The Choctaw Nation, 1830–1860.* East Lansing: Michigan State University Press, 2004.

Albion, Robert Greenhalgh. "Yankee Domination of New York Port, 1820–1865." *New England Quarterly* 5, no. 4 (October 1, 1932): 665–98.

Alfani, Guido, and Cormac Ó Gráda, eds. *Famine in European History.* Cambridge: Cambridge University Press, 2017.

Allen, Richard. "Circular." Dublin, 3/29 .47. Thomas P. Cope Family Papers (HC. MC.1013). Quaker & Special Collections, Haverford College, Haverford, PA.

Altick, Richard Daniel. *The English Common Reader.* Chicago: University of Chicago Press, 1957.

Anbinder, Tyler G. *Nativism and Slavery: The Northern Know Nothings and the Politics of the 1850s.* Oxford: Oxford University Press, 1994.

Anderson, Fred, and Andrew Cayton. *The Dominion of War: Empire and Liberty in North America, 1500–2000.* New York: Penguin, 2005.

Andrivon, D. "The Origin of Phytophthora Infestans Populations Present in Europe in the 1840s: A Critical Review of Historical and Scientific Evidence." *Plant Pathology* 45, no. 6 (1996): 1027–35.

Appelrouth, Scott. *Envisioning America and the American Self: Republican and Democratic Party Platforms, 1840–2016.* New York: Routledge, 2019.

Aptheker, Herbert. *American Negro Slave Revolts.* New York: International Publishers, 1963.

Arendt, Emily J. "'Two Dollars a Day, And Roast Beef': Whig Culinary Partisanship and the Election of 1840." *Journal of the Early Republic* 40, no. 1 (2020): 83–115.

Armitage, David. *The Ideological Origins of the British Empire.* Cambridge: Cambridge University Press, 2000.

Baird, W. David. "Arkansas's Choctaw Boundary: A Study of Justice Delayed." *Arkansas Historical Quarterly* 28, no. 3 (1969): 203–22.

Baldasty, Gerald J. "The Charleston, South Carolina, Press and National News, 1808–47." *Journalism Quarterly* 55, no. 3 (1978): 519-526.

Baptist, Edward. *The Half Has Never Been Told: Slavery and the Making of American Capitalism*. New York: Basic Books, 2014.

Barnett, Michael. *Empire of Humanity: A History of Humanitarianism*. Ithaca, NY: Cornell University Press, 2011.

Barnhurst, Kevin G., and John C. Nerone. *The Form of News: A History*. New York: Guilford, 2001.

Barrow, Lionel C. "'Our Own Cause': 'Freedom's Journal' and the Beginnings of the Black Press." *Journalism History* 4, no. 4 (December 1, 1977): 117–22.

Beames, M. R. "Rural Conflict in Pre-Famine Ireland: Peasant Assassinations in Tipperary 1837–1847." Past & Present, no. 81 (1978): 75–91.

Bellows, Barbara L. *Benevolence among Slaveholders: Assisting the Poor in Charleston, 1670–1860*. Baton Rouge: Louisiana State University Press, 1993.

Berlin, Ira. *Slaves without Masters: The Free Negro in the Antebellum South*. New York: Pantheon, 1975.

Bernstein, George L. "Liberals, the Irish Famine, and the Role of the State." *Irish Historical Studies* 29, no. 116 (November 1995): 513–36.

Bersohn, Leora. "Manchester Guardian (1821–)." In *Dictionary of Nineteenth-Century Journalism*, edited by Laurel Brake and Marysa Demoor. London: Academia Press, 2009.

Bielenberg, Andrew. *The Irish Diaspora*. New York: Routledge, 2014.

Bleeker, John R., Vaughan, D, and Gavit, J. E. *A Map of the Manor Renselaerwick*. 1767. New York State Library.

Blight, David W. *Race and Reunion: The Civil War in American Memory*. Cambridge, MA: Harvard University Press, 2001.

Bode, Frederick A. *Farm Tenancy and the Census in Antebellum Georgia* / Ginter, Donald E. Athens: University of Georgia Press, 1986.

Bogue, Allan G. *From Prairie to Corn Belt: Farming on the Illinois and Iowa Prairies in the Nineteenth Century*. Chicago: University of Chicago Press, 1963.

Boltanski, Luc. *Distant Suffering: Morality, Media, and Politics*. Cambridge: Cambridge University Press, 1999.

Bostick, Darwin F. "Sir John Easthope and the *Morning Chronicle*, 1834–1848." *Victorian Periodicals Review* 12, no. 2 (1979): 51–60.

Bronstein, Jamie L. *Land Reform and Working-Class Experience in Britain and the United States, 1800–1862*. Stanford, CA: Stanford University Press, 1999.

Brooks, Joanna. "The Early American Public Sphere and the Emergence of a Black Print Counterpublic." *William and Mary Quarterly* 62, no. 1 (2005): 67–92.

Brown, Henry. *Narrative of the Life of Henry Box Brown, Written by Himself*. Edited by John Ernest. Chapel Hill: University of North Carolina Press, 2008.

Brown, Malcolm. *The Politics of Irish Literature: From Thomas Davis to W. B. Yeats*. Seattle: University of Washington Press, 1972.

Bruegel, Martin. "Unrest: Manorial Society and the Market in the Hudson Valley, 1780–1850." *Journal of American History* 82, no. 4 (1996): 1393–424.

Busteed, Mervyn. "Irish Settlement and Identity in Mancester." In *The Great Famine and Beyond: Irish Migrants in Britain in the Nineteenth and Twentieth Centuries*, edited by Donald M. MacRaild, 94–141. Dublin: Irish Academic Press, 2000.

Cain, P. J., and A. G. Hopkins. *British Imperialism: Innovation and Expansion, 1688–1914*. London: Longman, 1993.

Cairns, David, and Shaun Richards. *Writing Ireland: Colonialism, Nationalism, and Culture*. Manchester: Manchester University Press, 1988.

Camp, Stephanie M. H. *Closer to Freedom: Enslaved Women and Everyday Resistance in the Plantation South*. Chapel Hill: University of North Carolina Press, 2004.

Canny, Nicholas P. *Kingdom and Colony: Ireland in the Atlantic World, 1560–1800*. Baltimore, MD: Johns Hopkins University Press, 1988.

———. "The Origins of Empire: An Introduction." In *The Oxford History of the British Empire, Volume 1, The Origins of Empire: British Overseas Enterprise to the Close of the Seventeenth Century*, edited by Nicholas Canny, Alaine Low, and Wm Roger Louis, 1–33. Oxford: Oxford University Press, 1998.

Captain Larcom. "Observations on the Census of the Population of Ireland in 1841." *Journal of the Statistical Society of London* 6, no. 4 (December 1843): 323–51.

Carstarphen, Meta G. "To Sway Public Opinion: Early Persuasive Appeals in the Cherokee Phoenix and Cherokee Advocate." In *American Indians and the Mass Media*, edited by Meta G. Carstarphen and John P. Sanchez, 56–70. Norman: University of Oklahoma Press, 2012.

Central Relief Committee, Society of Friends. "Minute Book No. 1." Dublin, 1847. Relief of Distress Papers. National Archives of Ireland. 1A 42 35.

———. *Transactions of the Central Relief Committee of the Society of Friends during the Famine in Ireland*. Dublin: Edmund Burke, 1852.

Champagne, Duane. *Social Order and Political Change: Constitutional Governments among the Cherokee, the Choctaw, the Chickasaw, and the Creek*. Stanford, CA: Stanford University Press, 1992.

Cheyney, Edward Potts. *The Anti-Rent Agitation in the State of New York, 1839–1846*. Philadelphia, PA: Porter & Coates, 1887.

Christian, A. K. "Mirabeau Buonaparte Lamar." *Southwestern Historical Quarterly* 24, no. 4 (April 1, 1921): 317–24.

Christman, Henry. *Tin Horns and Calico: A Decisive Episode in the Emergence of Democracy*. New York: Holt, 1945.

Cobden, Richard. *Speeches on Free Trade*. New York: Macmillan, 1903.

Cogswell, Seddie. *Tenure, Nativity, and Age as Factors in Iowa Agriculture, 1850–1880*. Ames: Iowa State University Press, 1975.

Connolly, S. J. "The Great Famine and Irish Politics." In *The Great Irish Famine*, edited by C. Póirtéir. Cork: Mercier, 1995.

"Constabulary Reports." 1845. Famine Relief Commission, Chief Secretary's Office Registered Papers, Z series, National Archives of Ireland.

Cordell, Ryan. "Reprinting, Circulation, and the Network Author in Antebellum Newspapers." *American Literary History* 27, no. 3 (2015): 417–45.

Cordell, Ryan, and David Smith. "Viral Texts: Mapping Networks of Reprinting in 19th-Century Newspapers and Magazines," 2022. viraltexts.org.

Cornelius, Janet. "'We Slipped and Learned to Read': Slave Accounts of the Literacy Process, 1830–1865." *Phylon (1960–)* 44, no. 3 (1983): 171–86.

Coronavirus. "Coronavirus | Indian Health Service (IHS)." www.ihs.gov.

Côté, Richard N, and Patricia H. Williams. *Dictionary of South Carolina Biography*. Easley, S.C.: Southern Historical Press, 1985.

Cotterill, R. S. "Federal Indian Management in the South 1789–1825." *Mississippi Valley Historical Review* 20, no. 3 (1933): 333–52.

Crawford, E. Margaret. "William Wilde's Table of Irish Famines 900–1850." In *Famine: The Irish Experience, 900–1900: Subsistence Crises and Famines in Ireland*, edited by E. Margaret Crawford, 1–30. Edinburgh: J. Donald, 1989.

Crossman, Virginia. *Politics, Pauperism and Power in Late Nineteenth-Century Ireland*. Manchester: Manchester University Press, 2006.

———. *Poverty and the Poor Law in Ireland 1838–1948*. Liverpool: Liverpool University Press, 2013.

Crouthamel, James L. "James Gordon Bennett, the *New York Herald*, and the Development of Newspaper Sensationalism." *New York History* 54, no. 3 (1973): 294–316.

———. "The Newspaper Revolution in New York, 1830–1860." *New York History* 45, no. 2 (1964): 91–113.

Crowley, John. "Sites of Memory." In *Atlas of the Great Irish Famine, 1845–52*, edited by John Crowley, William J. Smyth, and Mike Murphy, 614–20. Cork: Cork University Press, 2012.

Cullen, Louis. "Catholics under the Penal Laws." *Eighteenth-Century Ireland / Iris an Dá Chultúr* 1 (1986): 23–36.

Curti, Merle. *American Philanthropy Abroad*. New Brunswick, NJ: Rutgers University Press, 1963.

Curtis, Heather D. *Holy Humanitarians: American Evangelicals and Global Aid*. Cambridge, MA: Harvard University Press, 2018.

Curtis, Lewis Perry. *Apes and Angels: The Irishman in Victorian Caricature*. Washington, DC: Smithsonian Institution, 1971

Cutter, Martha. *The Many Resurrections of Henry Box Brown*. Philadelphia: University of Pennsylvania Press, 2022.

Daniel, W. Harrison. "Virginia Baptists and the Negro in the Antebellum Era." *Journal of Negro History* 56, no. 1 (1971): 1–16.

Darwen, Lewis, Donald MacRaild, Brian Gurrin, and Liam Kennedy. "'Unhappy and Wretched Creatures': Charity, Poor Relief, and Pauper Removal in Britain and Ireland during the Great Famine." *English Historical Review* 134, no. 568 (August 6, 2019): 589–619.

Daunton, M. J. *Progress and Poverty: An Economic and Social History of Britain, 1700–1850*. Oxford: Oxford University Press, 1995.

Davis, Graham. "The Irish in Britain, 1815–1939." In *The Irish Diaspora*, edited by Andy Bielenberg, 19–26. Harlow, 2000.

Davis, Victoria. "Restating a Parochial Vision: A Reconsideration of Patrick Kavanagh, Flann O'Brien, and Brendan Behan." PhD diss., University of Texas, Austin, 2005.

De Nie, Michael. "Curing 'The Irish Moral Plague.'" *Éire-Ireland* 32 (1997): 63–85.

———. *The Eternal Paddy: Irish Identity and the British Press, 1798–1882*. Madison: University of Wisconsin Press, 2004.

———. "The Famine, Irish Identity, and the British Press." *Irish Studies Review* 6, no. 1 (1998): 27–35.

Deal, John G. "Middle-Class Benevolent Societies in Antebellum Norfolk, Virginia." In *The Southern Middle Class in the Long Nineteenth Century*, edited by Jonathan Daniel Wells and Jennifer R. Green, 84–104. Baton Rouge: Louisiana State University Press, 2011.

DeBow, J. D. B. *Statistical View of the United States, Embracing Its Territory, Population— White, Free Colored, and Slave—Moral and Social Condition, Industry, Prosperity, and Revenue; the Detailed Statistics of Cities, Towns, and Counties; Being a Compendium of the Seventh Census*. Washington, DC: Beverly Tucker, Senate Pronter, 1854.

Degler, Carl N. "The Locofocos: Urban 'Agrarians.'" *Journal of Economic History* 16, no. 3 (1956): 322–33.

Denson, Andrew. *Demanding the Cherokee Nation: Indian Autonomy and American Culture, 1830–1900*. Lincoln: University of Nebraska Press, 2004.

DeRosier, Arthur H. *The Removal of the Choctaw Indians*. Knoxville: University of Tennessee Press, 1970.

Devine, Tom M. *The Great Highland Famine: Hunger, Emigration, and the Scottish Highlands in the Nineteenth Century*. Edinburgh: Birlinn, 2021.

Devon Commission. *Report from Her Majesty's Commissioners of Inquiry into the State of the Law and Practice in Respect of the Occupation of Land in Ireland, with Minutes of Evidence, Supplements, Appendices, and Index*. Dublin: Irish University Microforms, 1845.

Devyr, Thomas Ainge. *The Odd Book of the Nineteenth Century, or, "Chivalry" in Modern Days: A Personal Record of Reform—Chiefly Land Reform, for the Last Fifty Years*. Greenpoint, NY: n.p. ,1882.

———. *Our Natural Rights: A Pamphlet for the People*. Belfast: n.p., 1836.

Dickson, David. *Dublin: The Making of a Capital City. Dublin*. Cambridge, MA: Harvard University Press, 2014.

———. *New Foundations: Ireland 1660–1800*. Dublin: Irish Academic Press, 1987.

Diner, Hasia R. "'The Most Irish City in the Union': The Era of the Great Migration, 1844–1877." In *The New York Irish*, edited by Ronald H. Bayor and Timothy J. Meagher, 8–106. Balitmore, MD: John Hopkins University Press, 1997.

Doherty, Gillian M. *The Irish Ordnance Survey: History, Culture, and Memory*. Dublin: Four Courts, 2004.

Donnelly, James S. "Captain Rock: Ideology and Organization in the Irish Agrarian Rebellion of 1821–24." *Éire-Ireland* 42, no. 3 (2007): 60–103.

———. "The Construction of the Memory of the Famine in Ireland and the Irish Diaspora, 1850–1900." *Éire-Ireland* 31, nos. 1–2 (1996): 26–61.

———. "A Famine in Irish Politics." *A New History of Ireland, Volume V: Ireland under the Union, I: 1801–70*, 357–71. Oxford: Clarendon, 1989.

———. "'Irish Property Must Pay for Irish Poverty': British Public Opinion and the Great Irish Famine." In *"Fearful Realities": New Perspectives on the Famine*, edited by Chris Morash and Richard Hayes, 60–76. Dublin: Irish Academic Press, 1996.

Donnelly, James S. "Famine and Government Response, 1845–46." In *A New History of Ireland, Volume V: Ireland Under the Union, I: 1801–70*, 272–85. Oxford: Clarendon, 2000.

———. "Landlords and Tenants." In *A New History of Ireland, Volume V: Ireland Under the Union, I: 1801–70*, 332–49. Oxford: Clarendon, 1989.

Dooley, Brendan. "From Literary Criticism to Systems Theory in Early Modern Journalism History." *Journal of the History of Ideas* 51, no. 3 (1990): 461–86.

Dotson, Jerome K. "Consuming Bodies, Producing Race: Slavery and Diet in the Antebellum South, 1830–1865." PhD diss., University of Wisconsin–Madison, 2016.

Douglass, Frederick, William Lloyd Garrison, and Wendell Phillips. *Narrative of the Life of Frederick Douglass: An American Slave*. Boston: Anti-Slavery Office, 1846.

Doyle, David N. "The Irish in North America, 1776–1845." In *Making the Irish American: History and Heritage of the Irish in the United States*, edited by Joseph Lee and Marion R. Casey, 171–212. New York: New York University Press, 2006.

Dublin Mansion House Committee for the Relief of Distress in. *Report of the Mansion House Committee on the Potato Disease*. Dublin: J. Browne, 1846.

Duggan, Anne J. "The Power of Documents: The Curious Case of Laudabiliter." In *Aspects of Power and Authority in the Middle Ages*, edited by Brenda M. Bolton, Christine E. Meek, and C. E. Meek, 241–75. Turnhout: Brepols, 2008.

Earl Grey. *The Colonial Policy of Lord John Russell's Administration*. London: R. Bentley, 1853.

Edney, Matthew H. *Mapping an Empire: The Geographical Construction of British India, 1765–1843*. Chicago: University of Chicago Press, 1997.

Edwards, Robert Dudley, and Thomas Desmond Williams. *The Great Famine, 1845–52*. New York: New York University Press, 1957.

Ellis, Clifton, and Rebecca Ginsburg. "Introduction: Studying the Landscapes of North American Urban Slavery." In *Slavery in the City: Architecture and Landscapes of Urban Slavery in North America*, edited by Clifton Ellis and Rebecca Ginsburg, 1–18. Charlottesville: University of Virginia Press, 2017.

Emery, Edwin, Michael C. Emery, and Nancy L. Roberts. *The Press and America: An Interpretive History of the Mass Media*. 9th ed. Boston: Allyn & Bacon, 2000.

Entman, R. M. "Framing: Toward Clarification of a Fractured Paradigm." *Journal of Communication* 43, no. 4 (1993): 51–58.

Eyal, Yonatan. *The Young America Movement and the Transformation of the Democratic Party, 1828–1861*. Cambridge: Cambridge University Press, 2007.

Fagan, Benjamin. "'The North Star' and the Atlantic 1848." *African American Review* 47, no. 1 (2014): 51–67.

Fairfax, Jean E. "Black Philanthropy: Its Heritage and Its Future." *New Directions for Philanthropic Fundraising* 1995, no. 8 (1995): 9–21.

Famine Relief Commission. "Famine Relief Commission Distress Reports." 1845–46. National Archives of Ireland.

Farrell, Sean. *Rituals and Riots: Sectarian Violence and Political Culture in Ulster, 1784–1886.* Louisville: University Press of Kentucky, 2000.

First African Baptist Church. "Minute Books." Richmond, Virginia, 1841–59. Church Records Collection. Library of Virginia.

Fitzpatrick, David. "Emigration, 1801–1870." In *A New History of Ireland, Volume V: Ireland Under the Union, I: 1801–70,* edited by W. E. Vaughan, 562–621. Oxford: Clarendon, 2000.

———. "Ireland and the Empire." In *The Oxford History of the British Empire, Volume III: The Nineteenth Century,* edited by Andrew Porter and Wm Roger Louis, 495–521. Oxford: Oxford University Press, 1999.

———. *Irish Emigration, 1801–1921.* Economic and Social History Society of Ireland, Dublin: Economic and Social History Society of Ireland 1984.

Fitzpatrick, Mary Louise. *The Long March: The Choctaw's Gift to Irish Famine Relief.* Berkeley, CA: Beyond Words, 1998.

Flanigan, Shawn Teresa. "Charity as Resistance: Connections between Charity, Contentious Politics, and Terror." *Studies in Conflict & Terrorism* 29, no. 7 (2006): 641–55.

Foggo, Nick. "Liverpool Mercury (1811–1904)." In *Dictionary of Nineteenth-Century Journalism,* edited by Laurel Brake and Marysa Demoor. London: Academia Press, 2009.

Foner, Eric. *Free Soil, Free Labor, Free Men: The Ideology of the Republican Party before the Civil War: With a New Introductory Essay.* Oxford: Oxford University Press, 1995.

———. "The Wilmot Proviso Revisited." *Journal of American History* 56, no. 2 (September 1969): 262–79.

Foos, Paul. *A Short, Offhand, Killing Affair: Soldiers and Social Conflict during the Mexican-American War.* Chapel Hill: University of North Carolina Press, 2002.

Foreman, Carolyn Thomas. "The Armstrongs of Indian Territory." *Chronicles of Oklahoma* 30 (Winter 1952): 420–53.

Foreman, Grant. *Indian Removal: The Emigration of the Five Civilized Tribes of Indians.* Norman: University of Oklahoma Press, 1972.

Foster, Thomas Campbell. *Letters on the Condition of the People of Ireland.* London: Chapman & Hall, 1846.

Fowler, William M. "Sloop of War / Sloop of Peace: Robert Bennet Forbes and the USS Jamestown." In *Proceedings of the Massachusetts Historical Society,* no. 98 (1986): 49–59.

Fox-Genovese, Elizabeth. *Within the Plantation Household: Black and White Women of the Old South.* Chapel Hill: University of North Carolina Press, 1988.

Fox-Genovese, Elizabeth, and Eugene D. Genovese. "The Divine Sanction of Social Order: Religious Foundations of the Southern Slaveholders' World View." *Journal of the American Academy of Religion* 55, no. 2 (1987): 211–33.

Fraser, Gordon. "Distributed Agency: David Walker's Appeal, Black Readership, and the Politics of Self-Deportation." *ESQ: A Journal of Nineteenth-Century American Literature and Culture* 65, no. 2 (2019): 221–56.

Friedman, Lawrence Jacob. "Philanthropy in America: Historicism and Its Discontents." In *Charity, Philanthropy, and Civility in American History*, edited by Lawrence Jacob Friedman and Mark D. McGarvie, 1–20. Cambridge: Cambridge University Press, 2003.

Gallman, Matthew. *Receiving Erin's Children: Philadelphia, Liverpool, and the Irish Famine Migration, 1845–1855*. Chapel Hill: University of North Carolina Press, 2000.

Gamber, Wendy. "Antebellum Reform: Salvation, Self-Control, and Social Transformation." In *Charity, Philanthropy, and Civility in American History*, edited by Lawrence Jacob Friedman and Mark D. McGarvie, 129–53. Cambridge: Cambridge University Press, 2003.

Gamson, W. A., and A. Modigliani. "The Changing Culture of Affirmative Action." Edited by R. G. Braungart and M. M. Braungart. *Research in Political Sociology* 3 (1987): 137–77.

Gaunt, Richard A. *Sir Robert Peel: The Life and Legacy*. London: I. B. Tauris, 2010.

General Irish Relief Committee of the City of New York. *Aid to Ireland: Report of the General Relief Committee of the City of New York; with Schedules of Their Receipts in Money, Provisions, and Clothing; the Particulars of Their Shipments and Extracts from the Correspondence and Publications*. 1848.

Geoghegan, P. M. *The Irish Act of Union: A Study in High Politics, 1798–1801*. New York: St. Martin's, 1999.

Gibney, John. "Early Modern Ireland: A British Atlantic Colony?" *History Compass* 6, no. 1 (January 2008): 172–82.

Gilje, Paul A. "The Development of an Irish American Community in New York before the Great Migration." In *The New York Irish*, edited by Ronald H. Bayor and Timothy J. Meagher, 70–85. Baltimore, MD: Johns Hopkins University Press, 1997.

Ginsberg, Judah B. "Barnburners, Free Soilers, and the New York Republican Party." *New York History* 57, no. 4 (1976): 475–500.

Ginzberg, Lori D. *Women and the Work of Benevolence: Morality, Politics, and Class in the Nineteenth-Century United States*. New Haven, CT: Yale University Press, 1992.

Gleeson, David T. *The Irish in the South, 1815–1877*. Chapel Hill: University of North Carolina Press, 2001.

Gleeson, David T., and Brendan J. Buttimer. "'We Are Irish Everywhere': Irish Immigrant Networks in Charleston, South Carolina, and Savannah, Georgia." *Immigrants & Minorities* 23, nos. 2–3 (2005): 183–205.

Goldin, Claudia Dale. *Urban Slavery in the American South, 1820–1860: A Quantitative History*. Chicago: University of Chicago Press, 1976.

Gorsky, Martin. *Patterns of Philanthropy: Charity and Society in Nineteenth-Century Bristol*. Martlesham: Boydell & Brewer, 1999.

Götz, Norbert, Georgina Brewis, and Steffen Werther. *Humanitarianism in the Modern World: The Moral Economy of Famine Relief*. Cambridge: Cambridge University Press, 2020.

Gould, Eliga H. *Among the Powers of the Earth: The American Revolution and the Making of a New World Empire*. Cambridge, MA: Harvard University Press, 2012.

Graff, Harvey J. *The Literacy Myth: Cultural Integration and Social Structure in the Nineteenth Century*. New Brunswick, NJ: Transaction, 1991.

Gray, Peter. "Famine and Land in Ireland and India, 1845–1880: James Caird and the Political Economy of Hunger." *Historical Journal* 49, no. 1 (2006): 193–215.

———. *Famine, Land, and Politics: British Government and Irish Society, 1843–1850*. Dublin: Irish Academic Press, 1999.

———. "Famine Relief Policy in Comparative Perspective: Ireland, Scotland, and Northwestern Europe, 1845–1849." *Éire-Ireland* 32, no. 1 (1997): 86–108.

———. *The Making of the Irish Poor Law, 1815–43*. Manchester: Manchester University Press, 2010.

———. "National Humiliation and the Great Hunger: Fast and Famine in 1847." *Irish Historical Studies* 32, no. 126 (2000): 193–216.

———. "'Shovelling out Your Paulers': The British State and Irish Famine Migration, 1846–1850." *Patterns of Prejudice* 33, no. 4 (1999): 47–65.

———. "The Triumph of Dogma Ideology and Famine Relief." *History Ireland* 3, no. 2 (1995): 26–34.

Great Britain Census Office. *Census of Great Britain, 1851: Tables of the Population and Houses in the Divisions, Registration Counties, and Districts of England and Wales, in the Countries, Cities, and Burghs of Scotland, and in the Islands in the British Seas*. London: W. Clowes & Sons, 1851.

Green, Elna. *This Business of Relief: Confronting Poverty in a Southern City, 1740–1940*. Athens: University of Georgia Press, 2003.

Gregg, Matthew T., and David M. Wishart. "The Price of Cherokee Removal." *Explorations in Economic History* 49, no. 4 (2012): 423–42.

Grimsley-Smith, Melinda. "Revisiting a 'Demographic Freak': Irish Asylums and Hidden Hunger." *Social History of Medicine* 25, no. 2 (May 1, 2012): 307–23.

Gronowicz, Anthony. *Race and Class Politics in New York City before the Civil War*. Boston: Northeastern University Press, 1998.

Gross, Robert A. "Giving in America: From Charity to Philanthropy." In *Charity, Philanthropy, and Civility in American History*, edited by Lawrence Jacob Friedman and Mark D. McGarvie, 29–48. Cambridge: Cambridge University Press, 2003.

Haake, Claudia B. *Modernity through Letter Writing: Cherokee and Seneca Political Representations in Response to Removal, 1830–1857*. Lincoln: University of Nebraska Press, 2020.

Hall, Catherine. *Civilising Subjects: Metropole and Colony in the English Imagination, 1830–1867*. Chicago: University of Chicago Press, 2002.

———. "The Lords of Humankind Re-Visited." *Bulletin of the School of Oriental and African Studies* 66, no. 3 (2003): 472–85.

Hall, Catherine, and Sonya O. Rose. *At Home with the Empire: Metropolitan Culture and the Imperial World*. Cambridge: Cambridge University Press, 2006.

Hanley, Brian. "The Politics of Noraid." *Irish Political Studies* 19, no. 1 (March 1, 2004): 1–17.

A Vindication of the Cherokee Claims: Addressed to the Town Meeting in Philadelphia, on the 11th of January, 1830. n.p.

Harrison, Richard S. *A Biographical Dictionary of Irish Quakers.* 2nd ed. Dublin: Four Courts, 2008.

Haskell, Thomas L. "Capitalism and the Origins of the Humanitarian Sensibility, Part 1." *American Historical Review* 90, no. 2 (1985). 339-361.

———. "Capitalism and the Origins of the Humanitarian Sensibility, Part 2." *American Historical Review* 90, no. 3 (1985): 547–66.

Hatton, Helen E. *The Largest Amount of Good, Quaker Relief in Ireland, 1654–1921.* Montreal: McGill-Queen's University Press, 1993.

Hayes-McCoy, G. A. "The Completion of The Tudor Conquest and the Advance of the Counter-Reformation, 1571–1603." In *A New History of Ireland*, Volume III: Early Modern Ireland, 1534–1691, edited by T. W. Moody, F. X. Martin, and F. J. Byrne, 94–141. Oxford: Oxford University Press, 2009.

Haynes, Sam W. *Unfinished Revolution: The Early American Republic in a British World.* Charlottesville: University of Virginia Press, 2010.

Henkin, David M. *City Reading: Written Words and Public Spaces in Antebellum New York.* New York: Columbia University Press, 1998.

Higgins, Padhraig. "Consumption, Gender, and the Politics of 'Free Trade' in Eighteenth-Century Ireland." *Eighteenth-Century Studies* 41, no. 1 (2007): 87–105.

Higgins, Padhraig, James S. Donnelly, and Thomas Archdeacon. *A Nation of Politicians: Gender, Patriotism, and Political Culture in Late Eighteenth-Century Ireland.* Madison: University of Wisconsin Press, 2010.

Hinks, Peter P. *David Walker's Appeal to the Coloured Citizens of the World.* State College: Penn State University Press, 2010.

———. *To Awaken My Afflicted Brethren: David Walker and the Problem of Antebellum Slave Resistance.* State College: Penn State University Press, 2010.

Hobbs, Andrew. "The Deleterious Dominance of The Times in Nineteenth-Century Scholarship." *Journal of Victorian Culture* 18, no. 4 (December 1, 2013): 472–97.

Hogan, Liam. "Frederick Douglass and His Journey from Slavery to Limerick." *Old Limerick Journal* 49 (2015): 21–26.

Holt, Michael F. *The Rise and Fall of the American Whig Party: Jacksonian Politics and the Onset of the Civil War.* Oxford: Oxford University Press, 2003.

Hone, Philip. *The Diary of Philip Hone 1828–1851.* New York: Dodd, Mead, 1889.

Hood, Susan. "The Famine in the Strokestown Park House Archive." *Irish Review (1986–),* nos. 17–18 (1995): 109–17.

Houdek, John T., and Charles F. Heller. "Searching for Nineteenth-Century Farm Tenants: An Evaluation of Methods." *Historical Methods* 19, no. 2 (Spring 1986): 55–61.

House of Commons. "Food from America: Return of the Freight Paid by Government on Donations of Food from America, for the Relief of the Poor of Ireland and Scotland." January 31, 1848. Paper 93, vol. 4, 1. House of Commons Papers.

Houston, R. A. *Scottish Literacy and the Scottish Identity: Illiteracy and Society in Scotland and Northern England, 1600–1800.* Cambridge: Cambridge University Press, 1985.

Howard, June. "What Is Sentimentality?" *American Literary History* 11, no. 1 (1999): 63–81.

Howe, Daniel Walker. "The Evangelical Movement and Political Culture in the North during the Second Party System." *Journal of American History* 77, no. 4 (1991): 1216–39.

Howe, LeAnne. "Ima, Give: A Choctaw Tribalography." In *Famine Pots: The Choctaw-Irish Gift Exchange, 1847–Present*, edited by Padraig Kirwan and LeAnne Howe. 133–42. East Lansing: Michigan State University Press, 2020.

Hughes, Bethany. "Beautifully Uncontainable: Of Honeysuckle and Choctaw Walking." *Mobilities* 17, no. 2 (March 4, 2022): 238–51.

Hunt, Thomas C. "Popular Education in Nineteenth-Century Virginia: The Efforts of Charles Fenton Mercer." *Paedagogica Historica* 21, no. 2 (January 1, 1981): 337–46.

Huntzicker, William. *The Popular Press, 1833–1865*. Vol. 3. Westport, CT: Greenwood, 1999.

Huston, Reeve. *Land and Freedom: Rural Society, Popular Protest, and Party Politics in Antebellum New York*. Oxford: Oxford University Press, USA, 2000.

———. "The Parties and 'The People': The New York Anti-Rent Wars and the Contours of Jacksonian Politics." *Journal of the Early Republic* 20, no. 2 (2000): 241–71.

Hutton, Frankie. *The Early Black Press in America, 1827–1860*. Westport, CT: Greenwood, 1993.

HWF. "Glasgow Herald (1783–)." In *Dictionary of Nineteenth-Century Journalism*, edited by Laurel Brake and Marysa Demoor. London: Academia Press, 2009.

Inglis, Brian. "O'Connell and the Irish Press 1800–42." *Irish Historical Studies* 8, no. 29 (1952): 1–27.

Innes, Joanna. "Legislating for Three Kingdoms: How the Westminster Parliament Legislated for England, Scotland, and Ireland." In *Parliaments, Nations, and Identities in Britain and Ireland, 1660–1850*, edited by Julian Hoppit. 15-47. Manchester: Manchester University Press, 2003.

Irish Relief Association. *Report of the Proceedings of the Irish Relief Association for the Destitute Peasantry*. Dublin: Philip Dixon Hardy & Sons, 1848.

Irwin, Lee. "Freedom, Law, and Prophecy: A Brief History of Native American Religious Resistance." *American Indian Quarterly* 21, no. 1 (January 1, 1997): 35–55.

Isely, Jeter Allen. *Horace Greeley and the Republican Party, 1853–1861: A Study of the New York Tribune*. Vol. 3. Princeton, NJ: Princeton University Press, 1947.

Jackson, Alvin. "Ireland, the Union, and the Empire, 1800–1960." In *Ireland and the British Empire*, edited by Kevin Kenny and William Roger Louis. 123–53. Oxford: Oxford University Press, 2004.

Jacobs, Edward. "Edward Lloyd's Sunday Newspapers and the Cultural Politics of Crime News, c. 1840–43." *Victorian Periodicals Review* 50, no. 3 (2017): 619–49.

James, Louis. "The Era (1838–1939)." In *Dictionary of Nineteenth-Century Journalism*, edited by Laurel Brake and Marysa Demoor. London: Academia Press, 2009.

Jenkins, T. *The Liberal Ascendancy, 1830–1886*. London: Macmillan Education, 1994.

Jensen, Richard. "'No Irish Need Apply': A Myth of Victimization." *Journal of Social History* 36, no. 2 (2002): 405–29.

John, Richard R. *Spreading the News: The American Postal System from Franklin to Morse.* Cambridge, MA: Harvard University Press, 1995.

Johnson, Walter. *Soul by Soul: Life inside the Antebellum Slave Market.* Cambridge, MA: Harvard University Press, 2001.

Joyce, Toby. "The American Civil War and Irish Nationalism." *History Ireland* 4, no. 2 (1996): 36–41.

Kaplan, Amy, and Donald E. Pease. *Cultures of United States Imperialism.* Durham, NC: Duke University Press, 1994.

Kapp, Friedrich. *Immigration, and the Commissioners of Emigration of the State of New York.* New York: D. Taylor, 1870.

Katz, Michael. *In the Shadow of the Poorhouse: A Social History of Welfare in America.* New York: Basic Books, 1996.

Kelly, James. "Harvests and Hardship: Famine and Scarcity in Ireland in the Late 1720s." *Studia Hibernica*, no. 26 (1992): 65–105.

Kelly, Mary. *Ireland's Great Famine in Irish American History: Enshrining a Fateful Memory.* Washington, DC: Rowman & Littlefield, 2013.

Kelly, Matthew. "Irish Nationalist Opinion and the British Empire in the 1850s and 1860s." *Past & Present* 204, no. 1 (August 1, 2009): 127–54.

Kenny, Kevin. "Diaspora and Comparison: The Global Irish as a Case Study." *Journal of American History* 90, no. 1 (2003): 134–62.

———. "Race, Violence, and Anti-Irish Sentiment in the Nineteenth Century." In *Making the Irish American: The History And Heritage of the Irish in the United States*, edited by Joseph J. Lee and Marion R. Casey, 364–78. New York: New York University Press, 2006.

Kerr, Barbara M. "Irish Seasonal Migration to Great Britain, 1800–38." *Irish Historical Studies* 3, no. 12 (1943): 365–80.

Kidwell, Clara Sue. *The Choctaws in Oklahoma: From Tribe to Nation, 1855–1970.* Norman: University of Oklahoma Press, 2008.

Kielbowicz, Robert. "Newsgathering by Printers' Exchanges before the Telegraph." *Journalism History* 9, no. 2 (Summer 1982). 42-48.

Kiernan, Ben. "From Irish Famine to Congo Reform: Nineteenth-Century Roots of International Human Rights Law and Activism." In *Confronting Genocide*, 13–43. Dordrecht: Springer, 2011.

Kimball, Gregg D. *American City, Southern Place: A Cultural History of Antebellum Richmond.* Athens: University of Georgia Press, 2003.

Kinealy, Christine. *A Disunited Kingdom?: England, Ireland, Scotland, and Wales, 1800–1949.* Cambridge: Cambridge University Press, 1999.

———. "At Home with Empire: The Example of Ireland." In *At Home with the Empire: Metropolitan Culture and the Imperial World*, edited by Catherine Hall and Sonya O. Rose, 77–100. Cambridge: Cambridge University Press, 2006.

———. *Black Abolitionists in Ireland.* New York: Routledge, 2020.

———. *Charity and the Great Hunger in Ireland: The Kindness of Strangers.* London: Bloomsbury, 2013.

———. *The Great Irish Famine: Impact, Ideology, and Rebellion.* New York: Palgrave Macmillan, 2002.

———. "The Irish Famine 1845–52." *North Irish Roots* 2, no. 5 (1990): 158–61.

———. "Peel, Rotten Potatoes, and Providence: The Repeal of the Corn Laws and the Irish Famine." In *Free Trade and Reception 1815–1960*, edited by Andrew Marrison, 50–62. Boca Raton, FL: CRC, 2002.

———. *Repeal and Revolution: 1848 in Ireland.* Manchester: Manchester University Press, 2009.

———. *This Great Calamity: The Irish Famine, 1845–52.* Dublin: Gill & Macmillan, 1994.

Kirwan, Padraig. "Recognition, Resiliance and Relief: The Meaning of Gift." In *Famine Pots: The Choctaw-Irish Gift Exchange, 1847–Present*, edited by Padraig Kirwan and LeAnne Howe. 3-38. East Lansing: Michigan State University Press, 2020.

Kirwan, Padraig, and LeAnne Howe, eds. *Famine Pots: The Choctaw-Irish Gift Exchange, 1847–Present.* East Lansing: Michigan State University Press, 2020.

———. "Introduction." In *Famine Pots: The Choctaw-Irish Gift Exchange, 1847–Present*, edited by Padraig Kirwan and LeAnne Howe, xix–xiv. East Lansing: Michigan State University Press, 2020.

Kruman, Marc W. "The Second American Party System and the Transformation of Revolutionary Republicanism." *Journal of the Early Republic* 12, no. 4 (1992): 509–37.

Krywicki, Jarad. "'The Soft Answer': The 'National Era's' Network of Understanding." *American Periodicals* 23, no. 2 (2013): 125–41.

Laclau, Ernesto. *Emancipation(s).* New York: Verso, 1996.

Lamar, Mirabeau Buonaparte. *The Papers of Mirabeau Buonaparte Lamar.* Edited by Charles Adams Gulick and Winnie Allen. Vol. 4. Austin, TX: Von Boeckmann-Jones, 1924.

Lambert, D., and A. Lester. "Geographies of Colonial Philanthropy." *Progress in Human Geography* 28, no. 3 (2004): 320–41.

Lee, Joseph, and Marion R. Casey. *Making the Irish American: History and Heritage of the Irish in the United States.* New York: New York University Press, 2006.

Legg, Marie-Louise. *Newspapers and Nationalism: The Irish Provincial Press, 1850–1892.* Dublin: Four Courts, 1999.

Lengel, Edward G. *The Irish through British Eyes: Perceptions of Ireland in the Famine Era.* Westport, CT: Praeger, 2002.

"Lessons of Giving: The Choctaw and Cherokee Nations and the Famine." RTÉ, September 9, 2020. www.rte.ie.

Li, Lillian M. *Fighting Famine in North China: State, Market, and Environmental Decline, 1690s–1990s.* Stanford, CA: Stanford University Press, 2007.

Linebaugh, Peter. "Enclosures from the Bottom Up." *Radical History Review* 2010, no. 108 (2010): 11–27.

Lockley, Timothy. *Welfare and Charity in the Antebellum South.* Gainesville: University Press of Florida, 2009.

Lopatin, Nancy P. "Refining the Limits of Political Reporting: The Provincial Press, Political Unions and the Great Reform Act." *Victorian Periodicals Review* 31, no. 4 (1998): 337–55.

Lussana, Sergio A. *My Brother Slaves: Friendship, Masculinity, and Resistance in the Antebellum South*. Lexington: University Press of Kentucky, 2016.

Macaulay, Thomas Babington. *The History of England from the Accession of James II*. Vol. 1. New York, Harper & Brothers, 1849.

MacKenzie, John M. *Propaganda and Empire: The Manipulation of British Public Opinion, 1880–1960*. Manchester: Manchester University Press, 1984.

MacRaild, Donald M. *Irish Migrants in Modern Britain, 1750–1922*. New York: Macmillan International Higher Education, 1999.

Major, Andrea. "British Humanitarian Political Economy and Famine in India, 1838–1842." *Journal of British Studies* 59, no. 2 (April 2020): 221–44.

Mark-FitzGerald, Emily. *Commemorating the Irish Famine: Memory and the Monument*. Oxford: Oxford University Press, 2015.

Martineau, Harriet. *The Martyr Age in the United States of America: An Article from the* London and Westminister Review, *for December, 1838*. London: S. W. Benedict, 1839.

Matison, Sumner Eliot. "Manumission by Purchase." *Journal of Negro History* 33, no. 2 (1948): 146–67.

Matthew, H. C. G. "Hunter, Samuel." In *Oxford Dictionary of National Biography*, 2009. www.oxforddnb.com.

Maume, Patrick. "The '*Dublin Evening Mail* and Pro-Landlord Conservatism in the Age of Gladstone and Parnell." *Irish Historical Studies* 37, no. 148 (2011): 550–66.

McCarthy, Kathleen D. *American Creed: Philanthropy and the Rise of Civil Society, 1700–1865*. Chicago: University of Chicago Press, 2003.

McCracken, J. L. "The Conflict between the Irish Administration and Parliament, 1753–6." *Irish Historical Studies* 3, no. 10 (1942): 159–79.

McCrady, Edward, Samuel A. Ashe, and Edward McCrady. *Cyclopedia of Eminent and Representative Men of the Carolinas of the Nineteenth Century*. Madison, WI: Brant & Fuller, 1892.

McCurdy, Charles W. *The Anti-Rent Era in New York Law and Politics, 1839–1865*. Chapel Hill: University of North Carolina Press, 2001.

McCurdy, John Gilbert. *Quarters: The Accommodation of the British Army and the Coming of the American Revolution*. Ithaca, NY: Cornell University Press, 2019.

McCurry, Stephanie. *Masters of Small Worlds: Yeoman Households, Gender Relations, and the Political Culture of the Antebellum South Carolina Low Country*. Oxford: Oxford University Press, 1997.

McDonald, Tein. "Balancing Learning and Action: When Something Must Be Done, What Is the Right 'Something'?" *Ecological Management & Restoration* 8, no. 2 (2007): 82–82.

McGovern, Bryan P. *John Mitchel: Irish Nationalist, Southern Secessionist*. Knoxville: University of Tennessee Press, 2009.

McKeown, T. J. "The Politics of Corn Law Repeal and Theories of Commercial Policy." *British Journal of Political Science* 19, no. 3 (1989): 353–80.

McLean, Iain, and Camilla Bustani. "Irish Potatoes and British Politics: Interests, Ideology, Heresthetic, and the Repeal of the Corn Laws." *Political Studies* 1999 (1999): 817–36.

McLeod, Norman C. "Free Labor in a Slave Society: Richmond, Virginia, 1820–1860." PhD diss., Howard University, 1991.

McLoughlin, William G. *Cherokee Renascence in the New Republic*. Princeton, NJ: Princeton University Press, 1986.

McMahon, Cian T. *The Coffin Ship: Life and Death at Sea during the Great Irish Famine*. New York: New York University Press, 2021.

McMahon, Richard. *Homicide in Pre-Famine and Famine Ireland*. Liverpool: Liverpool University Press, 2014.

McNeice, Aoife O'Leary. "Global Networks of Relief and the Great Irish Famine." PhD diss., Cambridge University, 2021.

Miller, Kerby A. *Emigrants and Exiles: Ireland and the Irish Exodus to North America*. New York: Oxford University Press, 1985.

Mitchel, John. *Jail Journal of Five Years in British Prisons*. New York: Office of the Citizen, 1854.

———. *The Last Conquest of Ireland (Perhaps)*. Glasgow: Cameron & Ferguson, 1861.

Mitchell, Charles. *The Newspaper Press Directory*. London, Mitchell. 1846.

Mokyr, Joel, and Cormac Ó Gráda. "Emigration and Poverty in Prefamine Ireland." *Explorations in Economic History* 19, no. 4 (October 1, 1982): 360–84.

———. "Famine Disease and Famine Mortality: Lessons from the Irish Experience, 1845–1850." In *Famine Demography: Perspectives from Past and Present*, edited by Tim Dyson and Cormac Ó Gráda, 19–43. Oxford: Oxford University Press, 2002.

Moniz, Amanda B. *From Empire to Humanity: The American Revolution and the Origins of Humanitarianism*. Oxford: Oxford University Press, 2016.

Mooney, James. *Myths of the Cherokee*. Washington, DC.: Courier Dover, 1996.

Morgan, Phillip Carroll. "Love Can Build a Bridge: The Choctaws' Gift to the Irish in 1847." In *Famine Pots: The Choctaw-Irish Gift Exchange, 1847–Present*, edited by LeAnne Howe and Padraig Kirwan, 43–70. East Lansing: Michigan State University Press, 2020.

Morris, John Wesley. "Doaksville." In *Ghost Towns of Oklahoma*, 67–68. Norman: University of Oklahoma Press, 1977.

Morris, W. B. "The Saga of Skullyville." *Chronicles of Oklahoma* 16, no. 2 (June 1938): 234–40.

Muhlenfeld, Elisabeth. *Mary Boykin Chesnut: A Biography*. Baton Rouge: Louisiana State University Press, 1981.

Murphy, Angela F. "Daniel O'Connell and the 'American Eagle' in 1845: Slavery, Diplomacy, Nativism, and the Collapse of America's First Irish Nationalist Movement." *Journal of American Ethnic History* 26, no. 2 (2007): 3–26.

Murray, David. *Delaware County, New York; History of the Century, 1797–1897. Centennial Celebration, June 9 and 10, 1897*. New York: William Clark, 1898.

Murray, Hannah-Rose, and John R. McKivigan. *Frederick Douglass in Britain and Ireland, 1845–1895*. Edinburgh: Edinburgh University Press, 2022.

Mycock, Andrew. "A Very English Affair? Defining the Borders of Empire in Nineteenth-Century British Historiography." In *The Historical Imagination in Nineteenth-Century*

Britain and the Low Countries, edited by Hugh Dunthorne and Michael Wintle. 43-66. Leiden: Brill, 2012.

Nally, David. "'That Coming Storm': The Irish Poor Law, Colonial Biopolitics, and the Great Famine." *Annals of the Association of American Geographers* 98, no. 3 (2008). 714-741.

Navajo & Hopi Families COVID-19 Relief Fund. "U2 Drummer Donates $100,000 for Indigenous COVID-19 Relief Fund." navajohopisolidarity.org.

"Navajo & Hopi Families COVID-19 Relief Fund, Organized by Ethel Branch." www .gofundme.com.

North, J. S. "Cork Constitution." In *The Waterloo Directory of Irish Newspapers and Periodicals, 1800–1900*, 129–29. Waterloo: North Waterloo Academic Press, 1986.

———. "Cork Examiner." In *The Waterloo Directory of Irish Newspapers and Periodicals, 1800–1900*, 135–35. Waterloo: North Waterloo Academic Press, 1986.

———. *The Waterloo Directory of Irish Newspapers and Periodicals, 1800–1900*. Waterloo: North Waterloo Academic Press, 1986.

Ó Ciosáin, Niall. "Gaelic Culture and Language Shift." In *Nineteenth-Century Ireland: A Guide to Recent Research*, edited by Lawrence M. Geary and Margaret Kelleher, 136–52. Dublin: University College Dublin Press, 2005.

———. *Print and Popular Culture in Ireland, 1750-1850*. London: Macmillan, 1997.

Ó Gráda, Cormac. "Mortality and the Great Famine." In *Atlas of the Great Irish Famine, 1845–52*, edited by John Crowley, William J. Smyth, and Mike Murphy, 170–79. Cork: Cork University Press, 2012.

———. "Poverty, Population and Agriculture, 1801–45." In *A New History of Ireland, Volume V: Ireland Under the Union, I: 1801–70*, edited by W. E. Vaughan, 108–36. Oxford: Oxford University Press, 2010.

Ó Gráda, Cormac, and Phelim P. Boyle. "Fertility Trends, Excess Mortality, and the Great Irish Famine." *Demography* 23, no. 4 (November 1986): 543–62.

Ó Gráda, Cormac, Richard Paping, and Eric Vanhaute, eds. "The European Subsistence Crisis of 1845–1850: A Comparative Perspective." In *When the Potato Failed: Causes and Effects of the "Last" European Subsistence Crisis, 1845–50*, 15–40 Turnhout: Brepols, 2007.

O'Brien, John Thomas. "Factory, Church, and Community: Blacks in Antebellum Richmond." *Journal of Southern History* 44, no. 4 (November 1, 1978): 509–36.

———. "*From Bondage to Citizenship: The Richmond Black Community, 1865–1867.*" PhD diss., University of Rochester, 1990.

O'Brien, Mark, "Journalism in Ireland: The Evolution of a Discipline." In *Irish Journalism Before Independence: More a Disease than a Profession*, edited by Kevin Rafter, 9–21. Manchester: Manchester University Press, 2011.

O'Connell, Daniel. *Correspondence of Daniel O'Connell: The Liberator*. London: J. Murray, 1888.

Officer, Lawrence H., and Samuel H. Williamson. "Measuring Worth—Measures of Worth, Inflation Rates, Saving Calculator, Relative Value, Worth of a Dollar, Worth of a Pound, Purchasing Power, Gold Prices, GDP, History of Wages, Average Wage." *Measuring Worth*, 2010. http://www.measuringworth.com/.

Ohlmeyer, Jane. "A Laboratory for Empire?: Early Modern Ireland and English Imperialism." In *Ireland and the British Empire*, edited by Kevin Kenny, 26–60. Oxford: Oxford University Press, 2004.

———. *Making Ireland English. Making Ireland English.* New Haven, CT: Yale University Press, 2012.

O'Leary McNeice, Aoife. "'A Painful and Tender Sympathy Pervaded Every Class of Society': Consensus, Class, and Coercion in Global Giving during the Great Irish Famine." *Radical History Review* 2022, no. 143 (May 1, 2022): 165–76.

O'Loughlin, Ed, and Mihir Zaveri. "Irish Return an Old Favor, Helping Native Americans Battling the Virus." *The New York Times*, May 5, 2020. www.nytimes.com.

O'Neill, T. P. "The Scientific Investigation of the Failure of the Potato Crop in Ireland, 1845–46." *Irish Historical Studies* 5, no. 18 (1946): 123–38.

———. "The Society of Friends and the Great Famine." *Studies: An Irish Quarterly Review* 39, no. 154 (June 1950): 203–13.

Oram, Hugh. *The Newspaper Book: A History of Newspapers in Ireland, 1649–1983.* Dublin: MO Books, 1983.

Osthaus, Carl R. *Partisans of the Southern Press: Editorial Spokesmen of the Nineteenth Century.* Lexington: University Press of Kentucky, 1994.

Ó Tuathaigh, Gearóid. "O'Connell, Daniel." In *Dictionary of Irish Biography*, edited by James Quinn. Dublin: Royal Irish Academy, 2009.

Owen, David. *English Philanthropy, 1660–1960.* Cambridge, MA: Harvard University Press, 1965.

Owens, Gary. "Popular Mobilisation and the Rising of 1848: The Clubs of the Irish Confederation." In *Rebellion and Remembrance in Modern Ireland*, edited by Laurence Geary, 51–63. Dublin: Four Courts, 2001.

Owsley, Frank Lawrence. *Plain Folk of the Old South.* Baton Rouge: Louisiana State University Press, 2008.

Parcell, Lisa Mullikin. "Early American Newswriting Style: Who, What, When, Where, Why, and How." *Journalism History* 37, no. 1 (2011): 2–11.

Parmar, Inderjeet. *Foundations of the American Century: The Ford, Carnegie, and Rockefeller Foundations in the Rise of American Power.* New York: Columbia University Press, 2012.

Pasley, Jeffrey L., Andrew W. Robertson, and David Waldstreicher. *Beyond the Founders: New Approaches to the Political History of the Early American Republic.* Chapel Hill: University of North Carolina Press, 2004.

Penningroth, Dylan C. *The Claims of Kinfolk African American Property and Community in the Nineteenth-Century South.* Chapel Hill: University of North Carolina Press, 2003.

Perdue, Theda. "The Conflict Within: The Cherokee Power Structure and Removal." *The Georgia Historical Quarterly* 73, no. 3 (1989): 467–91.

———. "Race and Culture: Writing the Ethnohistory of the Early South." *Ethnohistory* 51, no. 4 (2004): 701–23.

Phillips, John A., and Charles Wetherell. "The Great Reform Act of 1832 and the Political Modernization of England." *American Historical Review* 100, no. 2 (1995): 411–36.

Pickering, Paul A., and Alex Tyrell. *The People's Bread: A History of the Anti-Corn Law League.* London: Leicester University Press, 2000.

Pletcher, David M. *The Diplomacy of Annexation: Texas, Oregon, and the Mexican War.* , Columbia: University of Missouri Press, 1973.

Pope, William F., and Dunbar H. Pope. *Early Days in Arkansas: Being for the Most Part the Personal Recollections of an Old Settler.* Little Rock, Ark: F. W. Allsopp, 1895.

Porter, Andrew. "Introduction: Britain and the Empire in the Nineteenth Century." In *The Oxford History of the British Empire, Volume III: The Nineteenth Century*, edited by Andrew Porter and Wm. Roger Louis, 1–46. Oxford: Oxford University Press, 1999.

Porter, Bernard. *The Lion's Share.* London: Longman, 2004.

———. *The Absent-Minded Imperialists: Empire, Society, and Culture in Britain.* Oxford: Oxford University Press, 2004.

Post, John D. *The Last Great Subsistence Crisis in the Western World.* Baltimore, MD: Johns Hopkins University Press, 1977.

Prentice, Archibald. *A History of the Anti-Corn Law League.* London: W. & F. G. Cash, 1852.

Prucha, Francis Paul. *American Indian Treaties: The History of a Political Anomaly.* Berkeley: University of California Press, 1994.

Quigley, Paul. *Shifting Grounds: Nationalism and the American South, 1848–1865.* New York: Oxford University Press, 2012.

Quinn, James. *Young Ireland and the Writing of Irish History.* Dublin: University College Dublin Press, 2015.

Raboteau, Albert J. *Slave Religion: The "Invisible Institution" in the Antebellum South.* New York: Oxford University Press, 1978.

Rand, Jacki Thompson. "Reconciliation." In *Famine Pots: The Choctaw-Irish Gift Exchange, 1847–Present*, edited by Padraig Kirwan and LeAnne Howe, 165–78. East Lansing: Michigan State University Press, 2020.

Reed, Julie L. *Serving the Nation: Cherokee Sovereignty and Social Welfare, 1800–1907.* Norman: University of Oklahoma Press, 2016.

Report of the British Association for the Relief of the Extreme Distress in Ireland and Scotland; with Correspondence of the Agents, Tables &c. and a List of Subscribers. London: Richard Clay, Bread Street Hill, 1849.

Reynolds, Emily Bellinger and Joan Reynolds Faunt. *Biographical Directory of the Senate of the State of South Carolina, 1776–1964.* Columbia: South Carolina Archives Department, 1964.

Robbins, Roy Marvin. "Horace Greeley: Land Reform and Unemployment, 1837–1862." *Agricultural History* 7, no. 1 (1933): 18–41.

Roberts, David. "Charles Dickens and the *Daily News*: Editorials and Editorial Writers." *Victorian Periodicals Review* 22, no. 2 (1989): 51–63.

Roeckell, Lelia M. "Bonds over Bondage: British Opposition to the Annexation of Texas." *Journal of the Early Republic* 19, no. 2 (1999): 257–78.

Roszman, Jay R. "The Curious History of Irish 'Outrages': Irish Agrarian Violence and Collective Insecurity, 1761–1852." *Historical Research* 91, no. 253 (August 1, 2018): 481–504.

Roy, Michaël. "Cheap Editions, Little Books, and Handsome Duodecimos: A Book History Approach to Antebellum Slave Narratives." *melus* 40, no. 3 (September 1, 2015): 69–93.

Ryder, Sean. "Reading Lessons: Famine and the Nation, 1846–1849." In *"Fearful Realities": New Perspectives on the Famine*, edited by Chris Morash and Richard Hayes, 151–63. Blackrock, Co.: Irish Academic Press, 1996.

Ryland, Robert. "The Origin and History of the First African Church." In *The First Century of the First Baptist Church of Richmond, Virginia, 1780–1880*, 247–72. Richmond, VA: Carlton McCarthy, 1880.

———. "Reminiscences of the First African Baptist Church." *American Baptist Memorial* 14 (1855): 262–65.

Salaman, Redcliffe N. *The History and Social Influence of the Potato*. Cambridge: Cambridge University Press, 1985.

Saltzman, Rachelle H. "Calico Indians and Pistol Pills: Traditional Drama, Historical Symbols, and Political Actions in Upstate New York." *New York Folklore* 20, no. 3 (January 1, 1994): 1–17.

Samuels, Shirley, ed. *The Culture of Sentiment: Race, Gender, and Sentimentality in Nineteenth-Century America*. Oxford: Oxford University Press, 1992.

Scally, Robert. *The End of Hidden Ireland: Rebellion, Famine, and Emigration*. Oxford: Oxford University Press, 1995.

Scheufele, Dietram A. "Framing as a Theory of Media Effects." *Journal of Communication* 49, no. 1 (1999): 103–22.

Scholnick, Robert J. "'The Fiery Cross of Knowledge': Chambers's Edinburgh Journal, 1832–1844." *Victorian Periodicals Review* 32, no. 4 (1999): 324–58.

Schonhardt-Bailey, Cheryl. "Ideology, Paty and Interests in the British Parliament." *British Journal of Political Science* 33, no. 4 (2003): 581–605.

Schroeder, John H. "Annexation or Independence: The Texas Issue in American Politics, 1836–1845." *Southwestern Historical Quarterly* 89, no. 2 (1985): 137–64.

Schudson, Michael. *Discovering the News: A Social History of American Newspapers*. New York: Basic Books, 1978.

Scott, A. B. "Latin Learning and Literature in Ireland, 1169–1500." In *A New History of Ireland, Volume I: Prehistoric and Early Ireland*, edited by Dáibhí Ó Cróinín, 934–95. Oxford: Oxford University Press, 2005.

Scott, James C. *Domination and the Arts of Resistance: Hidden Transcripts*. New Haven, CT: Yale University Press, 1990.

Scrope, George Poulett. *How Is Ireland to Be Governed? A Question Addressed to the New Administration of Lord Melbourne in 1834, Etc.* London: J. Ridgway, 1846.

"Sculpture in Ireland Honors Choctaw Nation | Choctaw Nation." Choctaw Nation of Oklahoma, July 5, 2017. www.choctawnation.com.

Sealander, Judith. "Curing Evils at Their Source: The Arrival of Scientific Giving." In *Charity, Philanthropy, and Civility in American History*, edited by Lawrence Jacob Friedman and Mark D. McGarvie, 217–39. Cambridge: Cambridge University Press, 2003.

Semmel, Bernard. *The Rise of Free Trade Imperialism; Classical Political Economy, the Empire of Free Trade, and Imperialism, 1750–1850*. Cambridge: Cambridge University Press, 1970.

Sen, Amartya Kumar. *Poverty and Famines: An Essay on Entitlement and Deprivation*. Oxford: Oxford University Press, 1981.

Shao, Stella. "Asian American Giving: Issues and Challenges (A Practitioner's Perspective)." *New Directions for Philanthropic Fundraising* 1995, no. 8 (1995): 53–64.

Shrout, Anelise. "The Famine and New York City." In *Atlas of the Great Irish Famine, 1845–52*, edited by John Crowley, William J. Smyth, and Mike Murphy, 536–46. Cork: Cork University Press, 2012.

Sidbury, James. *Ploughshares into Swords: Race, Rebellion, and Identity in Gabriel's Virginia, 1730–1810*. Cambridge: Cambridge University Press, 1997.

Sim, David. *A Union Forever: The Irish Question and U.S. Foreign Relations in the Victorian Age*. Ithaca, NY: Cornell University Press, 2013.

Simmons, Charles A. *The African American Press: A History of News Coverage during National Crises, with Special Reference to Four Black Newspapers, 1827–1965*. Jefferson, NC: McFarland, 2006.

Sinclair, Georgina. "The 'Irish' Policeman and the Empire: Influencing the Policing of the British Empire–Commonwealth." *Irish Historical Studies* 36, no. 142 (2008): 173–87.

Sinnema, Peter W. "Reading Nation and Class in the First Decade of the *Illustrated London News*." *Victorian Periodicals Review* 28, no. 2 (1995): 136–52.

Smith, Frank J. "Petition to the Hon. P. H. Cook Judge of Probate for Lowndes County," November 15, 1860. Records of the Probate Court, Minutes, 1859–1860, Vol. 9, 722–24. Lowndes County Courthouse, Hayneville, Alabama.

Sturm, Circe. *Blood Politics: Race, Culture, and Identity in the Cherokee Nation of Oklahoma*. Berkeley: University of California Press, 2002.

Summerhill, Thomas. *Harvest of Dissent: Agrarianism in Nineteenth-Century New York*. Champaign: University of Illinois Press, 2005.

Sznaider, Natan. "The Sociology of Compassion: A Study in the Sociology of Morals." *Journal for Cultural Research* 2, no. 1 (1998): 117–39.

Takagi, Midori. *Rearing Wolves to Our Own Destruction: Slavery in Richmond, Virginia, 1782–1865*. Charlottesville: University of Virginia Press, 1999.

Taylor, George Rogers. *The Transportation Revolution, 1815–1860*. New York: Rinehart, 1951.

Taylor, Miles. "The 1848 Revolutions and the British Empire." *Past & Present*, no. 166 (2000): 146–80.

———. "Cobden, Richard." In *Oxford Dictionary of National Biography*, 2009. www.oxforddnb.com.

Thornton, Russell. *The Cherokees: A Population History*. Lincoln: University of Nebraska Press, 1992.

Trevelyan, C. E. *The Irish Crisis*. London: Longman, Brown, Green & Longmans, 1848.

Tuchinsky, Adam-Max. "'The Bourgeoisie Will Fall and Fall Forever': The *New-York Tribune*, the 1848 French Revolution, and American Social Democratic Discourse." *Journal of American History* 92, no. 2 (2005): 470–97.

Turner, Michael J. "Before the Manchester School: Economic Theory in Early Nineteenth-Century Manchester." *History* 79, no. 256 (1994): 216–41.

U.S. Department of the Army, Office of the Surgeon General, and Thomas Lawson. *Army Meteorological Register, for Twelve Years, from 1843 to 1854, Inclusive: Compiled from Observations Made by the Officers of the Medical Department of the Army at the Military Posts of the United States*. Washington, DC: A. O. P. Nicholson, 1855.

Vaughan, W. E. *Landlords and Tenants in Mid-Victorian Ireland*. Oxford: Oxford University Press, 1994.

Wade, Richard C. *Slavery in the Cities: The South, 1820–1860*. Oxford: Oxford University Press, 1967.

Wakelyn, Jon L. *Biographical Dictionary of the Confederacy*. Westport, CT: Greenwood, 1977.

Waldstreicher, David. *In the Midst of Perpetual Fetes: The Making of American Nationalism, 1776–1820*. Williamsburg, VA: Omohundro Institute of Early American History and Culture, 1997.

Walker, Andrew. "The Development of the Provincial Press in England c. 1780-1914." *Journalism Studies* 7, no. 3 (2006): 373–86.

Wallace, Anthony F. C. *Jefferson and the Indians: The Tragic Fate of the First Americans*. Cambridge, MA: Belknap Press of Harvard University Press, 1999.

Walsh, Oonagh. *Anglican Women in Dublin: Philanthropy, Politics, and Education in the Early Twentieth Century*. Dublin: University College Dublin Press, 2005.

Washington, Booker T. Up from Slavery: An Autobiography. New York: Doubleday, Page, 1901.

Wasson, Ellis Archer. "The House of Commons, 1660–1945: Parliamentary Families and the Political Elite." *English Historical Review* 106, no. 420 (1991): 635–51.

Waters, Hazel. "The Great Famine and the Rise of Anti-Irish Racism." *Race & Class* 37, no. 1 (July 1, 1995): 95–108.

Watt, J. A. "The Anglo-Irish Colony under Strain, 1327–99." In *A New History of Ireland, Volume II: Medieval Ireland, 1169–1534*, 352–96. Oxford: Oxford University Press, 2008.

Weisbrod, Burton A. "Towards a Theory of the Voluntary Non-Profit Sector in a Three-Sector Economy." In *Altruism, Morality, and Economic Theory*, edited by Edmund S. Phelps, 171–96. New York: Russell Sage Foundation, 1975.

Wells, Ronald Austin. *The Honor of Giving: Philanthropy in Native America*. Indianapolis: Indiana University Center on Philanthropy, 1998.

Whelan, Kevin. "Settlement and Society in Eighteenth-Century Ireland." In *A History of Settlement in Ireland*, edited by Terence B. Barry, 203–21. New York: Routledge, 2000.

Whelan, Y. "The Construction and Destruction of a Colonial Landscape: Monuments to British Monarchs in Dublin before and after Independence." *Journal of Historical Geography* 28, no. 4 (October 1, 2002): 508–33.

Whitman, T. Stephen. *The Price of Freedom: Slavery and Manumission in Baltimore and Early National Maryland.* Lexington: University Press of Kentucky, 1997.

Wilentz, Sean. *Chants Democratic: New York City and the Rise of the American Working Class, 1788–1850.* Oxford: Oxford University Press, 2004.

———. "On Class and Politics in Jacksonian America." *Reviews in American History* 10, no. 4 (1982): 45–63.

———. *The Rise of American Democracy: Jefferson to Lincoln.* New York: W.W. Norton, 2006.

Williams, Heather Andrea. *Self-Taught: African American Education in Slavery and Freedom.* Chapel Hill: University of North Carolina Press, 2005.

Williams, Leslie. "Bad Press: Thomas Campbell Foster and British Reportage on the Irish Famine, 1845–1849." In *Nineteenth-Century Media and the Construction of Identities,* edited by Laurel Brake, B. Bell, D. Finkelstein, and Brake Laurel, 295–309. London: Palgrave Macmillan, 2016.

Wilson, Kathleen. *The Sense of the People: Politics, Culture, and Imperialism in England, 1715–1785.* Cambridge: Cambridge University Press, 1998.

Winstanley, Michael J. *Ireland and the Land Question, 1800–1922.* London: Taylor & Francis, 1994.

Winters, Donald L. *Farmers without Farms: Agricultural Tenancy in Nineteenth-Century Iowa.* Westport, CT: Greenwood, 1978.

Wirzbicki, Peter. *Fighting for the Higher Law: Black and White Transcendentalists against Slavery.* Philadelphia: University of Pennsylvania Press, 2021.

Wittstock, Laura W. *American Indian Giving and Philanthropy: The Overlaid Relationship.* Hubert H. Humphrey Institute of Public Affairs: University of Minnesota, 2010

Wolfe, Patrick. "After the Frontier: Separation and Absorption in US Indian Policy." *Settler Colonial Studies* 1, no. 1 (2011): 13–51.

Woodham Smith, Cecil Blanche. *The Great Hunger: Ireland, 1845–1849.* New York: Harper & Row, 1962.

Wordie, J. R. "The Chronology of English Enclosure, 1500–1914." *Economic History Review* 36, no. 4 (1983): 483–505.

Wright, Muriel H. "Organization of Counties in the Choctaw and Chickasaw Nations." *Chronicles of Oklahoma* 8, no. 3 (1930): 315–44.

Wynne, Deborah. *The Sensation Novel and the Victorian Family Magazine.* New York: Palgrave Macmillan, 2001.

Wyss, Hilary E. *English Letters and Indian Literacies: Reading, Writing, and New England Missionary Schools,* 1750-1830. Philadelphia: University of Pennsylvania Press, 2012.

Zaborney, John J. *Slaves for Hire: Renting Enslaved Laborers in Antebellum Virginia.* Baton Rouge: Louisana State University Press, 2012.

Zunz, Olivier. *Philanthropy in America: A History.* Princeton, NJ: Princeton University Press, 2012.

INDEX

ABOUT THE AUTHOR

ANELISE HANSON SHROUT is an Assistant Professor at Bates College, where she teaches in the History Department and the programs in American Studies and Digital and Computational Studies. She received her BA in history from the University of Chicago and her PhD in history from New York University. Her research explores the experiences of everyday people as they navigated spaces and bureaucracies in the nineteenth-century Atlantic world.